Sunshine and Storm in
Rhodesia

Frederick Courteney Selous

Sunshine and Storm in Rhodesia

The present edition is a reproduction of previous publication of this classic work. Minor typographical errors may have been corrected without note; however, for an authentic reading experience the spelling, punctuation, and capitalization have been retained from the original text.

ISBN: 978-1-64439-618-6

TO MY WIFE

WHO DURING THE LAST FEW MONTHS
HAS AT ONCE BEEN
MY GREATEST ANXIETY AND MY GREATEST COMFORT
I DEDICATE THIS BOOK

CONTENTS

PREFACE

It was during the early days of the recent insurrection that I first thought of utilising my spare time by writing some account of what was taking place around me, and these rough notes, written at odd moments during the campaign, I intended to have sent to the *Field* for publication in that journal, in the form of a series of articles dealing entirely with my own personal experiences. After the disbandment of the Bulawayo Field Force, however, and my own resignation as an officer in that corps, finding that I had leisure to do so, I determined to amplify these notes, and give some account of every skirmish which had taken place between the Colonists and the natives in Matabeleland up to the date of the disbandment of the above-mentioned Force. To this I add a short account of my personal experiences in the country during the months immediately preceding the outbreak of the insurrection, and finding that I had then sufficient material to fill the covers of a small book, I abandoned my original idea of getting what I had written published in weekly numbers, and determined for the third time to launch a book—always about Africa—on the long-suffering British public.

What I have written as it were historically regarding the events which have lately taken place in Matabeleland may, I think, be received as a simple and unadorned statement of fact, for where I have had to go outside my own personal experiences, my information has always been obtained at first hand and checked by the corroborating accounts of others who were also eye-witnesses of the events described. As to any conclusions I may have arrived at from given facts, they may be right or they may be wrong, but at any rate I claim the right to express my opinions frankly and fearlessly as long as they are my honest convictions. It may be said that, as I am a friend of Mr. Cecil Rhodes and of Dr. Jameson, I ought not to have expressed the opinion that it was the removal of the police force from Matabeleland to the Transvaal which gave the natives their opportunity to revolt, since the expression of such an opinion may be held to reflect upon the administration of the Chartered Company. My reply is, that I have written a history, which, to have any value, must be truthful, and that as Dr. Jameson cannot lay claim to infallibility, he was, like other mortals, liable to err. When he left Matabeleland he never dreamt that the removal of the police force would have any more effect upon the Matabele than the disbandment of the police in Mashunaland in 1891 had had upon the natives in that country. This opinion, moreover, must have been shared by the great majority of the inhabitants of Matabeleland, since no remonstrance was made by any public man at the time that the police left Bulawayo. We now know that the removal of the white police force was a mistake; but it is easy to criticise after the event, and as at the time the mistake was made no one in Rhodesia was wise or prescient enough to foresee the possible effect it might have on the natives of Matabeleland, it would be the height of meanness and injustice to hold Dr. Jameson morally responsible for the present insurrection.

Judging from the knowledge which we now possess of the secret history of the rebellion, it appears that the leaders of the movement must long ago have determined to revolt whenever a favourable opportunity occurred, and a rebellion would therefore in all probability have taken place sooner or later; so perhaps it is as well to have had it and got over it at the same time as the rinderpest. The latter plague will have far more lasting effects than the native rising; but when the railway from the south reaches Bulawayo, the country will once again be able to make a fair start, for with the greater knowledge now possessed by the authorities of the native character, the outcome of which will be a complete reorganisation of the native administration, no farther insurrection ought to be possible. For the rest, it is very evident that the Matabele broke out in rebellion because they disliked their position as a conquered people, and imagined that they were strong enough to throw off the yoke of their conquerors. But I fail to see that the fact that they have rebelled is any more an indictment against the general principles of the government of the Chartered Company, than were the numerous rebellions which have taken place from time to time in the Cape Colony an indictment against the wisdom and justice of the Imperial Government.

Now that the rebellion has occurred, it will very possibly be said that it was brought about by systematic brutality to the natives on the part of the white men in the country. Such an allegation, however, cannot be supported by facts, for, as the records of the magistrates' court will prove, the present Government has done all that any other civilised Government could have done to protect the natives from ill-treatment at the hands of irresponsible individuals; and as a native commissioner thoroughly conversant with the Matabele language, and well in touch with the people, was stationed in each of the districts into which the country has been divided, it cannot be urged that the natives had no opportunity of making their grievances known. Grievances of course they had, the chief of which, doubtless, was the loss of their independence as a nation, and the fact that they found themselves treated as a conquered people lately engaged in hostilities, who had only been permitted to return to the country from which they had been driven at the time of the first war under certain conditions, one of which was that the indunas should, through the medium of the native commissioners, supply miners and farmers with native labour—all the able-bodied young men in the country being required to work for a certain number of months per annum at a fixed rate of pay. This rate of pay was fixed at 10s. a month with food; but as a matter of fact mining work was almost always paid much more highly, as much as 30s. a month with food being often given for unskilled labour, whilst the managers of mines made it their business to see that the boys in their Company's employ were well treated, and cruel treatment by individuals was, I do not hesitate to say, the exception to the rule. Owing to the excessive indolence of the people, however, there can be no doubt that the labour regulations were most irksome to them. The indunas grew more and more disinclined to exert their authority in the matter of inducing their people to work when applications were made to them, with the result that native policemen were sent to their kraals to insist on the labour regulations being carried out, and these policemen, I fear, sometimes exceeded their duties, and used their position to tyrannise over the people.

I remember well that when Umlugulu [1] visited me for the first time, after I had taken up my residence on Essexvale,[2] he complained bitterly of the high-handed manner in which the "Ama Policey Minyama," the "Black Police," behaved to him and his people. "I have no complaints to make," he said, "against the white policemen; but the black police, wa duba, wa duba sebele—they give me trouble; they really give me trouble." I myself complained to the acting Administrator, Mr. Duncan, concerning the inconsiderate manner in which it appeared to me that the labour regulations were sometimes carried out, and I was led to believe that the whole question of native administration would shortly be gone into by the Government, and all grievances remedied.

The cattle question I have dealt with in the course of my story. It was never sagaciously handled, and its mismanagement probably caused more discontent against the Chartered Company's rule amongst the pure-blooded Matabele, or Abenzantsi, than anything

---

[1] One of the most influential men in Matabeleland in the time of Lo Bengula.

[2] The name of my Company's estate on which I was living before the rebellion.

else, whilst the irritation excited by the regulation exacting a certain amount of paid labour yearly from every able-bodied man produced a feeling of bitterness and discontent throughout the other classes of the community, which made them ripe for rebellion when they were called to arms by the leaders of the insurrection. However, although no impartial critic can deny that the confiscation of so large a number of their cattle, and more especially the manner in which that confiscation was carried out, was impolitic if not ungenerous; whilst the manner in which the labour regulations were enforced was sometimes calculated to provoke serious discontent; yet neither of these causes, nor both combined, would, in my opinion, have been sufficient to induce the mass of the population to break out in rebellion had there not been amongst them many men who, having once belonged to the ruling class in the country, were so dissatisfied at their loss of position and power under the white man's rule, that they had determined to regain their independence as a nation, or to attempt to do so, on the first favourable opportunity which offered. The rebellion was not the spontaneous act of the mass of the people goaded to desperation by an insupportable tyranny. It was a drama into which they were surprised, and in many cases dragged against their better judgment, by a few leading spirits, who planned and carried out the first murders and utilised the Makalaka Umlimo,[3] as a prophet.

To show that neither the cattle nor the labour questions were the only causes of the rebellion, I may mention that on Mr. Arthur Rhodes' block of farms on the Impembisi river, extending to some 50,000 acres, there was a considerable native population which had been altogether exempted from the general labour regulations—although required to supply Mr. Arthur Rhodes himself with any labour necessary on the farm for agricultural purposes; whilst there had been distributed amongst them 1600 head of cattle, which they held, in addition to their own, on exactly the same terms on which they had been formerly accustomed to tend cattle for Lo Bengula. Now here was a population living, one would have thought, in a state of the most absolute contentment—for they were receiving the full benefit of the milk from a far larger number of cattle than they had ever had to look after in Lo Bengula's time; had been allowed to build their kraals wherever they thought fit, make use of whatever land they desired for cultivation, and in fact to lead their own life in their own way undisturbed by any one, for the number of boys who came voluntarily to ask for employment was far in excess of what was required for agricultural work on the estate. And yet, when the

---

[3] God. See Chapter xxvi.

rebellion broke out, these people to a man (always excepting Captain Fynn's Delagoa Bay boy) joined the insurgents, and not only burnt down Mr. Arthur Rhodes' homestead and swept off all his cattle, but murdered Mr. Edwards the surveyor, who happened to be working in the neighbourhood; against whom they could have had no personal animus, as he was a complete stranger to them. Then, again, if any one had heard the natives living in the villages close round my homestead on Essexvale singing and dancing as they were wont to do on every moonlight night, he could not have maintained that they appeared to be weighed down by a sense of injustice and oppression, or, in fact, that they were anything but joyous and happy. It is very difficult to understand the workings of a Kafir's mind, as any one must admit who has lived long amongst natives, but the fact that the Matabele broke out into rebellion against the Government of the Chartered Company, appears to me to be no proof of any special iniquity *per se* on the part of that Government, since history has shown us, that wherever a savage race, entirely unaccustomed to order and restraint, has been conquered by a highly civilised people, who have forthwith essayed to govern that savage race as humanely as possible, but after all in their own interests rather than in the interests of the conquered people, a rebellion against the more intelligent ruling class has been the result; for the ways of the civilised man are not the ways of the savage, who, there can be no doubt, would rather put up with all the ills from which we consider we have freed him, than be subject to the restraints of a settled form of Government. Practically, he says "hang your *Pax Britanica*"; give me the good old times of superstition and bloodshed; then, even if I did not know the day nor the hour when I might be "smelt out" as a witch, and forthwith knocked on the head, at any rate I could have basked in the sun until my time came; and then, too, when the "impi" went forth, what glorious times I had, and how I revelled in blood and loot!

As to any general charges of systematic injustice and cruelty towards the natives, which may and will now be made by the personal enemies of Mr. Rhodes, against the Chartered Company, with the object of providing a justification for the brutal murders of European women and children which have been committed during the present rebellion, I would point out that such charges come rather late in the day, for the natives of Matabeleland had lived for over two years in an apparently fairly contented condition under the Government of the Company before the rebellion broke out, and during the whole of that time there were four missionaries belonging to the London Missionary Society, besides some people called "seventh-day adventists"—whatever that may mean, for I have not the least idea myself—all of whom were working amongst, and avowedly for the benefit of, the natives. Now, if systematic cruelty, injustice, and oppression of the Matabele by the Government of the Chartered Company had been going on constantly for over two years, it must have been very well known to all these men, and it was their duty not only to have protested against such gross misgovernment to the Company's Administrator in Bulawayo, but also to have reported such abuses to their Directors in England. No such allegations, however, were ever made prior to the rebellion, and should any be now brought forward they ought to be received with the very gravest suspicion. The fact, too, remains that although individual acts of brutality have occurred in Matabeleland—as they have done in every other country in the world—during the last two years, and although mistakes have been made, especially in dealing with the cattle and labour questions, yet, on the whole, the conditions under which the natives in that territory were living, were such that no one resident in the country, whether missionary or miner, imagined before the rebellion broke out that there could be any deep-seated discontent amongst them. That the government of the natives has been all that was desirable from their point of view I do not say, as it is my opinion that, when a black man's country has been conquered by Europeans, the laws by which that country will be subsequently governed will be made in the interests of the whites, and some of them will be very unpalatable to the conquered race, however just and equitable they may seem to their rulers. We Europeans make the mistake of thinking that, when we free a tribe of savages from what we consider a most oppressive and tyrannical form of government, substituting in its place an orderly rule, under which every man's life and property is protected and witch-doctors are not recognised, we ought to earn their gratitude; but the fact is we invariably fail to do so, as the present insurrection, as well as all the many rebellions by the natives of the Cape Colony against the rule of the Imperial Government has shown. Yet, as in the Cape Colony, so also will it be in Matabeleland. The savages will discover the uselessness of rebelling against the white man, and as time goes on will become more reconciled to the ways of their conquerors; that is, if their grievances are inquired into and as far as possible remedied, as I have every hope and belief that they will be as soon as the present rebellion has come to an end; for not until mutual confidence has again been restored between the whites and the blacks can Rhodesia prosper. From the black man's point of view the white man is probably not necessary as a factor in the prosperity of the country. He could get along very well without him. Unfortunately we cannot manage without the black man; he is absolutely necessary for the development of the country on the white man's lines. But a sulky, rebellious black man, only held in subjection by fear, is both a useless and dangerous personality, and, therefore, the dictates of policy will be at one with the promptings of humanity, in demanding that the natives of Matabeleland shall be governed both kindly and justly as well as firmly.

One word more. In the following pages I have given descriptions of many barbarous deeds which have lately been committed in Matabeleland. I have hidden nothing, but have told the naked truth, and related not only how white men, women, and children were lately murdered, and their senseless bodies afterwards cruelly mutilated by black men, but also how, subsequently, black men were shot down pitilessly by the whites, no mercy being shown or quarter given them by the outraged colonists. By those who seek it, matter will doubtless be found in some of my stories on which to found imputations against the colonists of Rhodesia, who will be held up to execration for the "slaughter" of "poor natives"; the insinuation being that the "poor natives" were ruthlessly killed, with little or no provocation, in order to gratify the lust for blood, which certain people in England appear to think takes possession of their countrymen whenever they set foot on African soil. But by the great mass of the English-speaking race I feel sure that the conduct of their kith and kin in Matabeleland during the late rebellion will not be too harshly judged. It will be remembered that they were the avengers of the women and children of their own colour, who had but lately been so mercilessly slain, and that, fighting as they were against hordes of savages eager to spill the life-blood of every white man in Rhodesia, savages in whose vocabulary no such words as pity or mercy are to be found, nothing else could be expected than that in the hour of victory no quarter should be given to the murderous foe. It is as unfair as it is ridiculous to talk of the "slaughter" of natives who, having come with arms in their hands, not only to kill you, but your wife and child also, find they have reckoned without their host, and are themselves discomfited and shot down by their would-be victims. Now, possibly, there might be found in England a philanthropist so meek and good that, were he suddenly confronted by a burglar who told him plainly that he meant to kill him and walk into his house, he would reply, although he carried a loaded revolver in his hand, "Kill me and walk on, for it would be against my creed and conscience to sully my hands with the slaughter of so fine a specimen of the human race as yourself." I do not say that so noble a character really exists within the four seas of Britain, but if he does,

I suppose he ought to be looked for amongst the ranks of those who have been loudest in their condemnation of the British settlers in Rhodesia, and who thereby arrogate to themselves the possession of a nobility of nature to which ordinary mortals cannot hope to attain. For the sake of example, therefore, let us say that such a man does exist, and that he is none other than the editor of *Truth*, Mr. Henry Labouchere. Well, granted then that Mr. Labouchere—the man whom, for the sake of example, I have endowed with such a noble nature—would be prompted to sacrifice his own life rather than sully his soul with the killing of a burglar, would he go yet farther and still spare the robber's life if he knew that, after he himself had been killed, his wife and child would also be put to death? I cannot believe that he would, but imagine rather that he would shoot as straight as possible to prevent such a catastrophe, and I for one would wish that in such a special case his practice might be better than his usual preaching.

Now the settlers in Rhodesia, on those occasions when they have been accused of slaughtering the natives, have only taken the same course as I think would have been adopted by the great-souled philanthropist, whom I hope I am not wronging by imagining that he would steel his heart to take the life of a burglar, if for no other reason than to save the lives of those dear to him; and therefore I would ask my readers not to judge too harshly of the deeds of the colonists which I have recounted in the following pages, but to remember, when judging of their actions, the terrible provocation which they had received. It may be that I have here and there shown a very strong racial feeling against the black man; but it must be remembered that my story has been written in the midst of all the horrors of a native rebellion, that I have seen many gruesome sights, and have with my own hands collected together the broken skulls of murdered women and children—Dutch and English—in order to give them Christian burial. Thus I have sometimes written under the influence of strong emotions, making too little allowance possibly for the black man smarting under what he perhaps had some reason to consider the arrogance and injustice of his white conquerors. However, my opinions after all are of little value, being those of a single individual; but I trust that whoever may take the trouble to read my narrative will accept my facts, and believe that the account I have written of events which have lately occurred in Matabeleland is a true and unvarnished one.

THE AUTHOR

Bulawayo, *21st August 1896*

CHAPTER I

I return to Matabeleland—Game plentiful near the Sewhoi-whoi river—An adventure with a leopard—Bulawayo reached—Prosperous outlook—We leave for Essexvale—Cattle-confiscation question—Its final settlement.

When, in the end of December 1893, immediately after the close of the first Matabele War, I rode away from Bulawayo and set out on my journey to England, I thought it more than probable that I should never again revisit the land over which Lo Bengula had so lately held sway. Destiny, however, willed it otherwise. Perhaps I found that the definition of "enough" as "a little more than you've got," when applied to income, was a true one; or perhaps I thought the ways of civilisation somewhat irksome, and at times pined for "a breath of the veld" and one more look at the wild game in the wild country where I had already passed so many years of my life. At any rate, when I was asked by my old friend, Mr. Maurice Heany, to go out once more to Matabeleland to assist him in the management of a land and gold-mining company which he had recently floated, I gave the proposal my very serious consideration, and when I found that my wife was quite willing to face all the troubles and difficulties incidental to a life in a new country, I agreed to undertake the duties required of me for a period of two years.

We—my wife and I—left England for South Africa on 30th March 1895, but we did not reach Bulawayo until the end of the following August; as, after landing at Cape Town, we spent two months in the Cape Colony and the Orange Free State, and then taking ship round the coast to Beira, proceeded by river steamer to Fontesvilla, and thence by rail to Chimoio. Here my waggon was awaiting us, and in it we travelled slowly and comfortably for two months, keeping the main transport road—which I had myself laid out four years before—to Salisbury, but from there going across country to my old hunting camp on the Hanyani river; thence to Hartley Hills on the Umfuli, and from there along the old hunters' road to Bulawayo. On this portion of our route I found game very plentiful, especially sable antelopes, large herds of which beautiful animals I saw almost daily. Near the river Sewhoi-whoi I was able to take my wife quite close up to the largest herd of these antelopes that I have ever seen. As they cantered past us within a hundred yards I counted them roughly and made their number between seventy-five and eighty. Having plenty of meat at the waggon I had

1

no need to shoot; so we just sat on our horses and admired them, though there was one cow with a beautiful curved pair of horns that tempted me sorely. On several occasions we saw the fresh spoor of lions, but we never either got a sight of the animals themselves or even heard one roar. At the Sebakwe river I saw the tracks of a herd of elephants that had passed only a few days before; and on this same day I met with rather a curious experience, which, although I am not writing an article on shooting incidents, I will take the liberty to relate.

Early on the morning of the day in question I had left the waggon and ridden down to the river—the Sebakwe—intending to follow its course to the point at which the road crossed it. Having plenty of meat, I took no native attendants with me, and resolved not to shoot at anything but a small antelope, a wild pig, or some animal the greater part of which I could have carried behind my saddle. However, I saw no game at all, large or small, with the exception of one reed buck ram bounding through the long grass, and was approaching the ford across the river without having fired a shot, when I noticed what I took to be a jackal sitting on its haunches in the grass about a hundred and fifty yards to my right. The grass being rather long I could not make out very well what it was even from my horse's back, and when I had dismounted I could barely see that there was anything there at all. However, aiming rather low in the grass, I fired, and distinctly heard the bullet strike something with a loud thud. Remounting my horse, and marking by a small bush the spot near which the now invisible animal had been before I fired, I rode leisurely up to see what I had shot. I was carrying my rifle across the saddle in front of me, without having reloaded it, and on nearing the bush I had marked pulled up my horse and was looking about for a jackal lying dead on the ground. However I could not see one, and was wondering how such a small animal could have moved away after being hit by an expanding bullet, when a loud grunting noise made me look up, and I saw a leopard rushing towards me through the grass. As it only charged from a distance of fifteen yards, it was close to me before I could even swing my rifle over the horse's neck, and I made sure that it would spring upon him and bite and claw him badly before I could load and shoot. However, strange to say, it simply galloped past, almost, if not quite, brushing against my horse's fore-leg, and passing beneath my right stirrup. After going about thirty yards it stopped and sat down on its haunches. By this time I had another cartridge in my rifle; so I hastily dismounted and gave the leopard a shot behind the shoulder, killing it instantly. It proved to be a large female in good condition, with a beautifully-marked skin. The first

2

bullet had struck it in the middle of the body, and going right through, had made a large hole on the further side, out of which a portion of the liver was protruding. This was of course sufficient to account for the animal's display of bad temper; but why it simply rushed past me without springing on to the horse, I don't quite know. Had my horse turned, possibly it would have done so; but being an animal of a very imperturbable temper he never moved, and his immobility may have disconcerted the leopard, and caused it not to act quite up to its original intention. After disembowelling it, I lifted it on to my horse, and carried it behind the saddle to the ford across the Sebakwe, where I found my waggon outspanned. This very mild adventure is the only incident of interest which I have to record as having occurred on our journey to Bulawayo, which we finally reached on 20th August.

When just twenty months previously I had left Matabeleland, there was no other Bulawayo save a ruined kraal, but lately wrecked and destroyed by the order of the unhappy Lo Bengula, who in despair at the defeat of his bravest regiments, had blown up his European house, burnt his chief town to ashes, and abandoning the land won by his father's assegais to the victorious troopers of the Chartered Company, fled away to die heart-broken in the forests to the north. Just across the stream which runs below the kraal stood the camp of the white invaders, a rough, hardy lot of men, whom some have called heroes and others filibusters; a confusion of titles equally applicable, I fancy, to the followers of Drake or Clive or any other body of men who have helped to make the British Empire what it is. The site of the new township had indeed been marked out, but not a house of any kind stood upon it. In the short interval, however, a European town had sprung up, containing many good, substantial buildings, whilst the bustle and movement in the dusty streets gave an air of life and vigour to the new Bulawayo, which is very commonly absent from the frontier towns of South Africa. In short, at this time—the autumn of 1895—everything was apparently *couleur de rose* in Matabeleland. Properties, whether farm lands, building sites in town, or mining claims, went up to very high values, whilst almost every one believed that within a year Bulawayo would contain a population of 5000 souls, and that the town itself would receive a plentiful supply of water from the reservoirs already in course of construction, and be lighted by the electric light. In fact, all was mirth and joy and hope in the future; for what was to hinder the ever-increasing prosperity of the country? Much good work had already been done on many of the reefs, and on the whole the promise was distinctly good. Then again, after a probation of eighteen months, the country had been pronounced favourably

3

upon by Dutch and Colonial farmers, especially for cattle-ranching, whilst many predicted that much of the high veld would carry sheep.

Apparently no difficulties with the natives were to be apprehended, and certainly were not foreseen, as no one could have recognised the identity in the quiet submissive native carrying nothing but a stick, to the arrogant savage of old times who was seldom seen without his shield and assegais, and who was usually insolent and brutal in his manner to the white man. No one dreamt that within a very few months the country would be well-nigh overwhelmed in calamity; that that terrible scourge the rinderpest, which has swept like a destroying angel from Masailand through Central and Eastern Africa, almost annihilating in its course all bovine animals as well as all the various and beautiful species of antelopes, was creeping ever nearer to the Zambesi river, and was destined ere long to cross that boundary, and travelling ever southwards destroy tens of thousands of cattle in Matabeleland, thereby paralysing its transport service, and rendering the cost of living almost prohibitive in a country separated by 600 miles of wilderness from the nearest railway station. Still less, looking at the submissive behaviour of the natives, did any one picture to himself in the furthest recesses of his mind, the vision of homesteads burned to ashes throughout Matabeleland, and around them the corpses of their owners, among them many women and tender children, all brutally murdered, lying unburied in their blood. Yet were these dire disasters, with partial drought and plague of locusts superadded, soon to crush all joy out of Matabeleland.

In spite of its air of prosperity and the light-heartedness of its inhabitants, Bulawayo with its constant dust-storms, scarcity of water, and general burnt-up appearance, had but few attractions either for my wife or myself, and we made our arrangements to get away to our Company's property of Essexvale as soon as possible. On this property a rough two-roomed house of poles, plastered with mud and thatched with grass, had been got ready for us temporarily, pending the arrival of a wire-wove bungalow that had been sent out from England in sections, and which was to be erected on a site chosen by myself. On our way to Essexvale we spent a night with my old friends the missionaries at Hope Fountain, and I had a long talk over old times, and the present condition of the natives in Matabeleland. Mr. Helm told me that although doubtless the members of the royal family, and the men of position under the old regime, regretted the downfall of their king and the conquest of the country by the white man, yet the great mass of the people acknowledged that they were better off under the rule of the

4

Chartered Company than they had been in Lo Bengula's time; for although individual white men were sometimes guilty of injustice and brutality towards individual natives, yet, speaking generally, the lives and property of the latter were now secure, and whatever they earned was their own, all of which blessings were unknown to them before the conquest of Matabeleland by the white man.

There was, however, one matter, Mr. Helm informed me, that was causing a great deal of discontent throughout the country. This was the periodical taking away of the cattle in small numbers by the Chartered Company, subsequent to the first confiscation immediately after the war. Probably if, after the subjugation of the country, the Chartered Company had at once taken all the cattle they ever intended to take, and given the natives the balance for their very own to do with as they liked, there never would have been any heart-burning over the cattle question at all. However, after the first confiscation, all the remaining cattle in the country—about 90,000—were branded with the Company's brand and left with the natives to look after. They were told that the Company would take more from time to time as they required them, but at the same time they were given to understand that only cattle which had belonged to the king would be confiscated, and none belonging to private owners interfered with. This promise was made under the belief that nearly all the cattle in Matabeleland had belonged to the king, and that the private owners had been but few in number. That this was a mistake I think there can be little doubt, as almost every man of any standing in Matabeleland had been a cattle-owner, some of the chief Indunas possessing large herds of private cattle. But when a native commissioner received an order from the Government to send to Bulawayo without delay a certain number of cattle from his district, he never could have done so had he listened to all the claims made to private ownership previous to the war, some of which were true, but others false; and he therefore had to use his own discretion in selecting the cattle necessary to make up the total required. In this way certain natives suffered wrong, more especially owners of perhaps only three or four cows, who in some cases lost their all, both in cattle and faith in the honesty and justice of the Government of the Chartered Company, which they deemed had broken the promise given to them, as indeed was the case, though the mistake was made inadvertently and through not considering the investigation of the whole question of sufficient importance to take any great trouble about.

"If," said Mr. Helm, "the Company would take, once for all, all the cattle they intend taking, and give the natives the remainder, it would restore their confidence, as they now believe that the cattle

5

will be constantly taken away from them in small lots until there are none left to them. However," he continued, "the Company can do what it likes with them, and treat them generously or otherwise as it pleases, for they acknowledge themselves to be a conquered people, and will submit to any terms imposed upon them." This remark was made by a man who had lived in close intimacy with the natives of Matabeleland for twenty years, but as subsequent events show, it was far from the truth. Shortly after this conversation, the Government of the Chartered Company, acting on the advice I believe of the chief native commissioner, Mr. Herbert Taylor, decided to finally settle the cattle question. There were at this time about 70,000 head of cattle in the hands of the natives, and of this number the Government determined to take two-fifths, leaving the remaining three-fifths as the absolute property of the Matabele. A meeting was called at Bulawayo, at which all the chief Indunas in the country were present, and when the proposition was laid before them, they expressed themselves as thoroughly satisfied, and assured Mr. Taylor that their people would also be satisfied; and from my own subsequent observation, I believe that this final distribution of the cattle caused a general feeling of relief throughout the country, and, in the district in which I was living at any rate, the people seemed well contented with this settlement of the question, which left them for the most part fairly well off.

CHAPTER II

Our life at Essexvale—Tree-planting and farming—Friendly disposition of the natives—Umlugulu visits us—His anxiety to know the truth about Jameson's surrender—Rumours of coming disaster—The Umlimo's prophecy—Appearance of the rinderpest in Matabeleland—Mr. Jackson's distrust of the native police— Superstitions regarding the Umlimo—I am appointed cattle inspector—Spread of the rinderpest—Apprehensions of famine— Rumours of a disturbance with the natives—Murder of a native policeman by the Matabele.

Of our life on Essexvale I have but little of interest to relate. In September and October the weather became intensely hot, but our well-thatched house we found to be much cooler than any building in Bulawayo, to which seat of light and learning we paid but occasional visits. Our wire-wove house did not arrive in Matabeleland until late in November, just as the rainy season was setting in, and it was not until towards the end of the year that it was put together and stood ready to receive us, on the site I had chosen for it. This was a very picturesque position on the top of a cliff about eighty feet above the Ingnaima river. Here we lived happily and contentedly for three months, and were apparently on the most friendly terms with all the natives living near us. Our Company bought about 1200 head of cattle, and these I distributed amongst the natives living on Essexvale—an estate of nearly 200,000 acres—to herd for us in lots of from ten to thirty in number, which they were very glad to do for the sake of the milk. To all the headmen living immediately round the homestead I gave a larger proportion of milk cows, on the condition that they brought me daily half the milk.

I was assisted in the management of the estate by a young German, Herr Blöcker, who had taken his diplomas in a German School of Forestry, as it was part of our Company's scheme to start a plantation of gum trees, the timber of which is valuable for mining purposes. We therefore cleared and ploughed up about forty acres of land, and planted out over 5000 trees raised from seed on a strip of eight acres near the house. The rest of the ploughed land we sowed with maize, reserving about an acre near the river for a vegetable garden. The ground round the house my wife laid out in flower-beds, and I had also beds prepared for the planting of orange and other fruit trees, which I had ordered from the Cape Colony; whilst several banana and grenadilla plants, which had been given us by the Rev. Mr. Helm, were already growing well. Altogether, in spite of the most unseasonable drought which prevailed during January, February, and March, our homestead commenced to look quite pretty, and another year's work would have made a nice place of it; whilst the view from our front door up the river, with our cattle and horses grazing on the banks, and ducks and geese swimming in the pools or sunning themselves on the sand, was always singularly homelike.

As I have said above, up to the day of the native insurrection, which broke out towards the end of March, all the natives on Essexvale appeared to be on the most friendly terms with us, and were always most civil and polite to my wife, who had grown to like them very much. We had done them many good turns, and I believe they liked us as individuals. Umlugulu, a relation of Lo Bengula's,

7

and one of the principal men in that king's time, as well as a high priest of the ceremonies at the annual religious dance of the Inxwala, was living about fifteen miles away, and often came to see us. He was a very gentle-mannered savage, and always most courteous and polite in his bearing, and by us he was always treated with the consideration due to one who had held a high position and been a man of importance in Lo Bengula's time. It is now supposed, and I think with justice, that this man was one of the chief instigators of the rebellion; but if this is so, I have strong reasons for believing that he only finally made up his mind that the time had come for the attempt to be made to drive the white men out of the country when he learnt that the whole of the police force of Matabeleland, together with the artillery, munitions of war, etc., which had been taken down to the Transvaal by Dr. Jameson, had been captured by the Boers. My reason for thinking so is, that before he heard this news he asked me several times to take some unbranded cattle from him, and have them herded amongst my own, or bought from him at my own price. This request I could not grant, but advised him to go and tell Dr. Jameson the story he had told me, as to how these cattle came to be in his possession without the Company's brand on them. After he heard the news of Dr. Jameson's surrender, Umlugulu never said anything more about these cattle, but he often came to see me, and always questioned me very closely as to what had actually happened in the Transvaal. Although at that time I had no idea as to the lines on which I now think his mind was working, I gave him little or no information, the more so that I could see he was very anxious to get at the truth.

Towards the end of February, Mr. Jackson, the native commissioner in my district, who was living with a sub-inspector and a force of native police at a spot on one of the roads through Essexvale about twelve miles distant from our house, informed me that rumours of coming disaster to the white man, purporting to emanate from the "Umlimo" or god of the Makalakas, who dwells in a cave of the Matopo Hills, were being spread abroad amongst the people of Matabeleland. Shortly before this there had been a total eclipse of the moon. This the Umlimo told the natives meant that white man's blood was about to be spilt. Further than this, they were informed that Lo Bengula was not dead, but was now on his way back to Matabeleland with a large army from the north, whilst two other armies were coming to help him against the white man from the west and east. "Watch the coming moon," said the Umlimo, "and be ready." He also claimed to have sent the rinderpest, which had just reached the cattle in the north of

Matabeleland—though of what advantage that scourge was to the natives I don't quite see—and promised that he would soon afflict the white men themselves with some equally terrible disease.

Now, although these rumours of a native rising were current in Matabeleland some time before the insurrection actually broke out, and were reported to the then acting chief native commissioner, Mr. Thomas, and to the heads of the Government, I do not think that they would have been warranted in taking any steps of a suppressive nature at this juncture; for there was absolutely nothing tangible to go upon, nor could any commission of inquiry have come to any other conclusion than that the natives had no intention of rebelling; for they were as quiet and submissive in their demeanour towards Europeans as they ever had been since the war, and there was absolutely no evidence of any secret arming amongst them; and the fact remains that, with one exception, all those Europeans in Matabeleland who had had a long experience of natives—that is, the native commissioners, missionaries, and a few old traders and hunters, amongst whom I must include myself—were unanimous in the opinion that no rebellion on the part of the Matabele was to be apprehended. I say there was one exception, as I have been told that Mr. Usher, an old trader long resident in Matabeleland, and who since the first war has been living altogether amongst the natives, has always maintained that the Matabele would one day rise against the white man.

For myself, I had many conversations with Mr. Jackson on the subject, and we came to the conclusion, after talking with several intelligent natives regarding the rumours going about, that the Matabele were not likely to rebel until Lo Bengula appeared with his army. "However," said Mr. Jackson one evening, "it is very difficult to worm a secret out of a native, and if there should be an insurrection those are the devils we have to fear," pointing to his squad of native Matabele policemen, sitting about round their huts all armed with repeating Winchester rifles. At that time no one would have imagined that these native policemen—all fine, active-looking young fellows, and very smart at their drill—would have been likely to mutiny, since they were not only very well disciplined but most civil and obedient to their white officers; whilst, on the other hand, they were constantly at loggerheads with their compatriots, whom they had to bring to book for any transgression of the Chartered Company's laws, and more particularly for evasion of the regulations exacting a certain amount of labour annually at a fixed rate of pay from every able-bodied young man. However, as subsequent events have shown, Mr. Jackson was right in his prognostication, for when the rebellion did break out, about half the native police at once turned their rifles against their employers. The remainder were true to their salt, but had to be disarmed as a precautionary measure.

I will now before going further say a word concerning the "Umlimo" or god of the Makalakas, who has apparently played such an important part in the present rebellion, but who, I think, has in reality only been the instrument employed by the actual leaders of the insurrection to work upon the superstitions of the people, and mould them to their will. To the best of my belief, there exists amongst the Makalakas, as amongst all the tribes of allied race throughout South-Eastern Africa, an hereditary priesthood, confined to one family, though from time to time certain other young men are adopted by the high priest and initiated into the mysteries of his profession. These men in common with the actual sons of the high priest are known henceforth as children of the god. The head of the family lives in the Matopo Hills, and is known as the Umlimo, but as far as one can understand from the rather conflicting statements made concerning him by the natives, he is not actually the Umlimo, but a being possessed of all the ordinary attributes of man,—in fact a human being, with a spiritual nature superadded which enables him to commune with the unseen Deity that pervades space, and communicate the wishes or commands of the invisible spirit to the people. The temple of the Umlimo is a cave in the Matopo Hills, whither the people repair to consult him; and I believe that the voice which is heard in answer to their questions from the depths of the cave is supposed to emanate not from the human Umlimo or priest, but to be the actual utterance of the invisible god. The human Umlimo is kept wonderfully well posted up concerning everything that happens in Matabeleland, probably by the various members of his family, who live in different parts of the country, and who often visit him. He is thus often enabled to make very shrewd answers to the questions asked him, and to show himself conversant with matters which his interlocutors thought were known only to themselves; and in this way he has gained a great ascendency over the minds of the people.

If one asks who the Umlimo is, the answer is that he is a spirit or supernatural being of infinite wisdom, known to man only as a voice speaking from the depths of a cave. He is said to be able to speak all languages, as well as to be possessed of the faculty of roaring like a lion, crowing like a cock, barking like a dog, etc. On the other hand, the human Umlimo accepts or rather demands presents from those who visit his cave for the purpose of consulting the Deity, and possesses not only cattle, sheep, and goats, but also a large number of wives. The great mass of the Matabele people seem

10

to me to have very vague ideas concerning the Umlimo; and sometimes I think that besides the priest in the Matopos through whom the voice of God is supposed to be heard, there are other priests,[4] or so-called Umlimos, in other parts of the country through whom they believe that the commands of the Almighty can be conveyed to them. At any rate, both prior to and during the present rebellion, utterances purporting to emanate from the "Umlimo" have been implicitly believed in, and the commands attributed to him obeyed with a blind fanaticism, that one would not have looked for in a people who always seem to be extremely matter of fact and practical in everyday life. It may seem strange that this "Umlimo," or god of the despised Makalakas, should be accepted as an oracle by the Matabele, but I know that Lo Bengula professed a strong belief in his magical powers, and from time to time consulted him. I believe, however, that the Umlimo was made use of for the purposes of the present rebellion by Umlugulu, and other members of the late king's family.

These men were naturally not content with their position under the white man's rule, and as ever since the war they had probably been rebels at heart, they only wanted an opportunity to call the people to arms. This opportunity they thought had come when they heard that the entire police force of Matabeleland, together with most of the big guns and munitions of war up till then stored in Bulawayo, had been captured by the Boers. For to them the police represented the fighting or military element amongst the white men, and they more or less despised all other classes, whom they usually saw going about altogether unarmed and defenceless. When the police were gone, therefore, they at once probably set about stirring up a rebellion, and got the Umlimo to play their game and work upon the superstitions of the people. This at any rate is my own opinion of the origin of the insurrection.

About the middle of March I was appointed cattle inspector for the district between the Umzingwani and Insiza rivers, and had to do a lot of riding about in my endeavours to assist the Government to arrest the spread of the rinderpest. However, one might as well have tried to stop a rising tide on the sea-shore, as prevent this dreadful disease from travelling steadily down the main roads, leaving nothing but rotting carcasses and ruined men behind it. Therefore, while still strictly prohibiting all movement of cattle from infected districts to parts of the country yet free from the

---

4 There can be no doubt as to this, as there is now an Umlimo or prophet with the insurgents in the north-east of Matabeleland, who has apparently no connection with the Umlimo in the Matopo Hills.

terrible scourge, the Government declared the main roads open for traffic on Tuesday, 24th March, in order that as many waggon-loads of provisions as possible might be brought into Bulawayo, whilst any oxen were still left alive to pull them; for at this time the only calamities apprehended in Matabeleland were famine, and the complete dislocation of transport throughout the country owing to the terrible mortality amongst the cattle from rinderpest. These dangers indeed seemed so pressing that the Government was called upon by a deputation from the Chamber of Commerce to at once purchase 2000 mules, to be used for the importation of food-stuffs into Bulawayo, and their distribution from that centre to the various mining districts.

On Sunday, 22nd March, I reached Bulawayo late in the evening, after a very long day's ride inspecting cattle, and I then heard rumours of a disturbance having taken place between some of Mr. Jackson's native police and the inhabitants of a Matabele kraal near the north-western boundary of our Company's property of Essexvale. On the following day I got a fresh horse and rode twenty-five miles down the Tuli road to Dawson's store on the Umzingwani river—the limit of my beat in this direction—issuing passes to all the waggons I met with to proceed on their way up or down the road on the following morning. Arrived at the store, I there met my friend Mr. Jackson, the native commissioner, and Mr. Cooke, and learned from them that a native policeman had been murdered by the Matabele on the previous Friday night, and that the murderers had fled into the Matopo Hills, taking all their women and children as well as their cattle with them. My friends were only waiting for a detachment of native police, under two white inspectors, to follow up the murderers and endeavour to bring them to justice.

CHAPTER III

First overt act of rebellion—Natives borrow axes from Mrs. Selous—Where are the white police?—Native woman gives information of the murder of whites—Natives run off with the cattle—Murder of three miners—Inscrutability of the Kafir mind—Matabele raid on cattle.

Now this murder of a native policeman on the night of Friday,

20th March, was the first overt act of rebellion on the part of the Matabele against the Government of the British South Africa Company, and I will therefore relate exactly what occurred. On the evening of the aforementioned day, eight native policemen, acting on instructions of Mr. Jackson, arrived at the town of Umgorshlwini, situated in the hills near the Umzingwani river. Being accompanied by several boys carrying their blankets, etc., they formed quite a little party, and so camped outside the native town. They were sitting talking over their fires after the evening meal, when a number of Matabele came up, and ranging themselves in a line in front of them, commenced to dance. These men all carried knob-kerries, and were led by a man named Umzobo,[5] who had held a post of importance at Bulawayo in Lo Bengula's time. The so-called dancing of all Kafirs of Zulu race is not dancing in the European sense, but consists for the most part in stamping on the ground, swaying the body and gesticulating with sticks. The stamping is usually accompanied by a chant, the words of which are often improvised for the occasion, and the effect of the whole dance is decidedly stimulating, as I have often watched a stolid, stupid-looking Kafir work himself up to a state of high excitability by this means. On the present occasion Umzobo and his men very soon showed that they had come to dance before the representatives of the law with a purpose, that purpose being to pick a quarrel with them. They soon commenced to "jia," or point with their sticks; then one of them ran out of the line, and coming close up to the police, stooped forward, and drawing his left hand rapidly backwards and forwards across his throat, said: "You are killing us, you are killing us; why don't you cut our throats, and make an end of it?" Then another ran out, and repeating the formula, "you are killing us," pressed his finger on his temple, and said: "Why don't you shoot us? why don't you put the bullet in just here?" The expression, "you're killing us," so frequently used by Umzobo's men, meant "you're making life unpleasant to us by enforcing the Company's laws."

When these hostile demonstrations had gone on for some time, the sergeant in charge of the police told Umzobo that he had better take his men away, and tell them to go to sleep, as nobody wanted to fight with them; but his words were without effect, and the dancing was still going on, when one of the policemen saw a man creeping stealthily towards them round the back of the cattle kraal. At once suspecting mischief, he jumped up, and calling to his comrades "Look out, we're amongst enemies," rushed upon the crouching figure that at once stood up and revealed a Kafir armed

5 His title was "Umlisa go Bulawayo," or Lieutenant of Bulawayo.

13

with an assegai. Before he could make use of his weapon, however, the policeman caught him by the wrist, whilst another guardian of the law who had followed close behind seized his other arm. They at once disarmed the man, and were putting the handcuffs on him, when a shot was fired out of the cattle kraal, aimed of course at the police, but so badly aimed that instead of hitting one of them, it struck their prisoner in the back, killing him almost instantly. Indeed, he fell dead with the handcuff on one wrist. Immediately the shot was fired some of the police rushed into the kraal and almost succeeded in capturing the man who had fired, so nearly in fact that he dropped his rifle in his hurry to escape.

Umzobo and his men had now disappeared, and the police having collected together, were standing in the light of their camp fires uncertain what to do, when a volley was fired amongst them from the bush outside the kraal. None of the police were hit, but one of their blanket-carriers was shot through the head and killed on the spot. Not knowing the number of their unseen enemies, the representatives of the law then thought it advisable to beat a retreat. They reached Mr. Jackson's camp at 1 A.M. on Saturday, handing him the captured rifle, and reporting the loss of two of their boys; for besides the one whom they knew to be dead, another small boy some ten or twelve years of age was missing. This boy Mr. Jackson found lying dead half under the kraal fence, when he visited Umgorshlwini with all the police he could muster on the morning after the disturbance. The town was then deserted, and Mr. Jackson thinks that this small boy must have been discovered trying to hide under the fence after the police had left. He had been murdered in a most brutal way, his skull having been smashed to atoms with knob-kerries.

But the murder of these two police boys and the accidental killing of one of Umzobo's men was not the only deed of blood which occurred on this Friday night. Amongst Umzobo's men was one Ganyana. After the retreat of the police this man went alone to the kraal of a nephew of Lo Bengula—Umfondisi, the son of Lo Magazi—and waking him up, told him what had happened. According to the report of a stranger who was sleeping in Umfondisi's kraal that night, Ganyana was very much excited and called out, "Come, Umfondisi; why are you sleeping? don't you know we're fighting? we've killed some policemen, come; blood is running and men are lying dead; come with me and let us do some more killing." Umfondisi was nothing loth, and arming himself with an assegai went off with Ganyana to a neighbouring kraal, the headman of which they at once awakened in order to tell him the news. At this kraal there happened to be one of Mr. Jackson's native

14

policemen. He was asleep in a hut when Ganyana and Umfondisi arrived, but the loud and excited conversation that was being carried on awoke him, and he got up and came out of the hut, asking as he did so what all the noise was about. "Who are you?" said Ganyana. "I am so and so, one of Mr. Jackson's policemen," was the answer. "What!" responded Ganyana; "do you tell me that you are one of the witches who are always troubling us?" and running up to him he shot him, and as he fell down mortally wounded, Umfondisi, the king's nephew, plunged his assegai into him.

When on Monday evening, 23rd March, I heard from Mr. Jackson what had happened on the previous Friday night, I imagined that the disturbance was merely the outcome of local discontent, and little thought that this attack on native policemen was but the prelude to the most terrible massacre of Europeans that has ever yet taken place in a native rising in South Africa; and more than this, that even whilst I listened to the story, white men, women, and children lay freshly murdered not many miles away. On the following morning, Tuesday, 24th March, I rode through the hills to my own place, passing Umgorshlwini on the way. Riding round the kraal I found bloodstains where the three men had been killed, but the bodies had been taken away and buried by the order of Mr. Jackson. The kraal itself, together with many smaller ones in its vicinity, was absolutely deserted, and a splendid crop of corn left standing in the valley below.

Having been absent since the previous Sunday morning, I was still all unsuspicious of danger, but knowing now all that actually happened during that time within a short distance of my house, I shudder to think of what might have occurred there during my absence; for my wife had been quite alone in the house with two little native girls; Mr. Blöcker, my German assistant, and a young Scotchman, Mr. Notman, occupying huts some distance away.

I reached home about mid-day, and found everything going on as usual. My wife told me that during the morning several men— all of whom I knew well—had come over to see her from the chief village of the district—Intuntini—which had been a big military kraal before the war. These men were all true-blooded Matabele, and several of them were in charge of cattle belonging to my Company. They all wished to borrow axes from her, to be used for the purpose of strengthening their cattle kraals, they said, but I know now that they wanted them as weapons of offence, as many of the murders were committed with axes. As we were accustomed to assist the natives in any small matter of this kind, she let them have all the axes that could be spared, and allowed them to sharpen them on the grindstone. About sundown some of these same men brought

15

the usual evening's milk, and my wife and I chatted with them for some time. We spoke about the recent murders on the Umzingwani, and the conduct of Umzobo and Umfondisi, and my wife asked me to say that she thought they had acted very foolishly, as the white men would punish them. At this they laughed, and one of them said significantly, "How can the white men punish them? where are the white police? there are none left in the country."

Soon after these men had left us, George, a colonial Kafir in my employ, came and said he wished to speak to me, and on my going aside with him informed me that his wife—a Matabele woman—had just heard from another native woman that white men had been murdered on the previous day by the Matabele, on the further side of the Malungwani range, amongst them a native commissioner, who, it was said, had had his throat cut by his own black police. On hearing this disagreeable news, which I did not doubt was substantially true, I began to think that we were going to have a native rising after all. However, I did not consider that we were in any danger, except from natives coming from a distance, as I could not believe that any of the people living close round us would be keen to murder either my wife or myself or any one living with us, as we had benefited them in many ways, and had certainly never given them any cause to dislike our presence amongst them. I, of course, said nothing to my wife as to what I had heard, but I told Mr. Blöcker and the young Scotchman to keep their rifles handy in case of accidents. I had, too, some very good watch-dogs that I knew would give me warning if any Kafirs came near the house, and I kept awake all night with my rifle and a belt full of cartridges alongside of me. But the night passed off quite quietly.

Why no attempt was made to murder us on that Tuesday night will always remain a mystery to me. I should like to think that because we had always treated them kindly and considerately, our immediate neighbours shrank from killing us; but after all that has happened I find it very difficult to believe this. They may have come with the intention of killing us on the Tuesday morning, but finding me absent, and Mr. Blöcker with a rifle in his hands—for when they arrived at the homestead he was just going off to shoot a cow whose hip had been dislocated in branding—may not have thought the opportunity, a good one. My wife noticed that they seemed very excited, and they also seemed very anxious to know when I would return.

All things considered, I am afraid we owe them little, as if they did not attempt to murder us they at any rate gave us no warning, and went off on the Tuesday night with all the cattle I had entrusted to their care, and in all likelihood assisted in the murder of Messrs.

16

Foster, Eagleson, and Anderson, all three of whom were carrying on mining work on Essexvale; Foster's camp being within four miles of my home.

The events of the last three months have taught me at least this, that it is impossible for a European to understand the workings of a native's mind; and, speaking personally, after having spent over twenty years of my life amongst the Kafirs, I now see that I know nothing about them, and recognise that I am quite incompetent to express an opinion as to the line of conduct they would be likely to adopt under any given circumstances.

On the following morning I got up early, and after seeing the Kafirs make a start on the work on which I was then engaged—which was the preparation of a piece of ground round the house for a plantation of fruit trees—I went up to George's hut and told him to try and get some farther particulars, through his wife, as to the murders said to have been committed on the previous Monday. Then I strolled back to the house and worked at one thing and another till breakfast time, and was just going indoors to sit down to that meal, when I saw George running down from his hut to our house, followed by a Kafir boy. As he came near he shouted out to the horse-herd who was standing by the stable, "Bring the horses, bring the horses; make haste!"

I knew then there was something wrong, and half thought that an attack was imminent, and having my wife's safety to provide for, was much relieved when George told me that no pressing danger threatened, but that armed Kafirs had driven off some of my Company's cattle. The boy who accompanied George belonged to a small kraal, to the members of which I had given some twenty or thirty head of cattle to look after for our Company, they getting full benefit of all the milk, a great boon to them, as they possessed no cattle of their own. He had been sent by the headman to inform me that just at daylight a number of Matabele from the kraal of Gwibu, a nephew of Lo Bengula, had opened the cattle kraal and driven off all the cattle, threatening the life of any one who interfered with them. These men, he said, were all armed either with guns or shields and assegais, and wore white ox-tails round their left arms and necks. Whilst I was still speaking, another messenger arrived to tell me that all the Intuntini people had left in the night, taking all their cattle with them, the greater part of which belonged to my Company. I now knew that we were face to face with a native rising, but I thought—what was indeed the fact—that this rising had been fomented by members of the late king's family, and was confined so far to the Abenzantsi, or Matabele of pure Zulu descent, and I cherished the hope that if energetic measures were at once adopted

17

by the Government, the more numerous and useful section of the nation, of Makalaka and Mashuna descent, might be kept quiet and the rebellion speedily suppressed.

CHAPTER IV

Precautions against native attack—Conference with the neighbouring headmen—I take my wife into Bulawayo—Insurrection reported general—Armed forces sent to disturbed districts—Return to Essexvale with small mounted force—Short supply of horses and rifles—My views of the Kafir rising—The progress of the insurrection at Essexvale and the neighbourhood—Wholesale murders.

The first thing to be done was to take my wife into Bulawayo, and then return at once with a body of armed men to Essexvale, in order to make a display of force which might deter those natives, who were still sitting quiet watching events, from joining the rebels; for I knew that the general idea was, that there being now no longer any police force in the country, the Government was practically powerless to cope with an organised rebellion. I therefore had all our horses saddled up immediately to be ready for emergencies, and in order to guard against surprise placed George as a vidette on the top of a rise behind the house, from which a good view of the surrounding country was obtainable. Then, whilst we were having breakfast, I sent messengers to summon all the headmen of the kraals in the immediate vicinity of the homestead. These men, I may say, were all in possession of cattle belonging to my Company, and as none of them were pure-blooded Matabele, I imagined they would have no sympathy with the insurgents.

They all answered my summons, accompanied by many of their people, and before leaving I spoke to them, and did my best to impress upon them the folly of rebelling against the white man. They professed themselves in perfect accord with all I said; averred that they were quite content to live with me as their "inkosi,"[6] and protested that they had nothing to hope for from the overthrow of

---

[6] Literally king; but the word is commonly used in addressing a European, as a complimentary title, conveying the idea of dependence on the part of the speaker.

18

the white man by the Matabele. In conclusion, I told them that I was going into Bulawayo to place my wife in a position of safety, but that I would return immediately with an armed force and endeavour to recover some of the cattle stolen by Gwibu and the rest of the Matabele. Mr. Blöcker wished to remain at the homestead until my return, but this I would not allow, as I did not care to leave a white man all by himself; and besides I required him to help me in getting some men together. George—the colonial Kafir—however, stopped behind, as he considered himself quite safe with Umsetchi's people,—Umsetchi being the headman of several little kraals close to the house, with the inhabitants of which we had always been on the most friendly terms.

Our ride into Bulawayo was altogether uneventful, as our road lay almost entirely through uninhabited country, and did not cross the line that the rebel natives of the district would have been likely to take on their way to the fastnesses of the Malungwani Hills. As, however, it was a scorching hot day it was a very trying experience for my wife.

Just before reaching town we met Mr. Claude Grenfell, who, with Messrs. Norton and Edmonds, was on his way out to Essexvale with a cart and horses to bring in my wife, and from them we learned that the insurrection was becoming general all over the country, and that forces had already been raised and sent out to relieve miners and settlers in the outlying districts. The Hon. Maurice Gifford had left the previous day for the Insiza, whilst Messrs. Napier and Spreckley were just on the point of starting for other disturbed parts of the country.

After handing over my wife to the kind care of her good friend Mrs. Spreckley, I at once set to work to get together a mounted force with which to return immediately to Essexvale, and thanks to the energetic assistance of Mr. Blöcker and Mr. Norton I was able to leave Bulawayo again at eight o'clock the same evening with thirty-six mounted men. I had wished to raise a force of 100 men, but found it impossible to do so, nearly all the horses and rifles in the possession of the Government having been given out to equip the forces already sent out before my arrival in town. There were men enough left, and good men too, ready to go with me anywhere, but the Government could only supply six horses—and not good ones at that—and twenty rifles. However, I managed to raise thirty private horses, and some private rifles, and got away about two hours after sundown with a compact little force of thirty-six mounted men.

The moon was now getting near the full, and by its light we pushed on, and at 2 A.M. on Thursday, 26th March, were back at my homestead, which is just twenty-three miles distant from

19

Bulawayo. Here I found everything as I had left it, George having installed himself with some of Umsetchi's men in the stable, which being built very solidly of stone, they might easily have held against any ordinary attack.

I had left Essexvale a few hours before, without any very bitter feeling against the Kafirs, for after all, looking at things from their point of view, if they thought they could succeed in shaking off the white man's rule, and retaking all the cattle that once were theirs or their king's, and all those brought into the country since the war as well, why shouldn't they try the chances of rebellion? I knew they would have to fight to accomplish their ends, and it was for them to consider whether the game was worth the candle or not. At that time, however, I was far from realising what had happened, and was inclined to judge the Kafirs very leniently. But my visit to Bulawayo had changed my sentiments entirely, and the accounts which I had there heard of the cruel and treacherous murders that had been perpetrated on defenceless women and children, besides at once destroying whatever sympathy I may have at first felt for the rebels, had not only filled me with indignation, but had excited a desire for vengeance, which could only be satisfied by a personal and active participation in the killing of the murderers. I don't defend such feelings, nor deny that they are vile and brutal when viewed from a high moral standpoint; only I would say to the highly moral critic, Be charitable if you have not yourself lived through similar experiences; be not too harsh in your judgment of your fellow-man, for you probably know not your own nature, nor are you capable of analysing passions which can only be understood by those Europeans who have lived through a native rising, in which women and children of their race have been barbarously murdered by savages; by beings whom, in their hearts, they despise; as rightly or wrongly they consider that they belong to a lower type of the human family than themselves.

I offer no opinion upon this sentiment, but I say that it undoubtedly exists, and must always aggravate the savagery of a conflict between the two races; whilst the murder of white women and children, by natives, seems to the colonist not merely a crime, but a sacrilege, and calls forth all the latent ferocity of the more civilised race. For, kind and considerate though any European may be under ordinary circumstances to the savages amongst whom he happens to be living, yet deep down in his heart, whether he be a miner or a missionary, is the conviction that the black man belongs to a lower type of humanity than the white; and if this is a mistaken conviction, ask the negrophilist who professes to think so, whether he would give his daughter in marriage to a negro, and if not, why not?

At any rate the lovers and admirers of the Matabele would do well to caution their protégés not to commence another insurrection by the murder of white women and children, for should they do so, they will once more have cause to rue a war of retaliation, that will be waged with all the merciless ferocity which must inevitably follow upon such a course; as, although the murder of Europeans by savages may commend itself to certain arm-chair philosophers in England, who can see no good in a colonist, nor any harm in a savage, yet the colonists themselves cannot look upon such matters from the same point of view, and will take such steps to prevent the recurrence of any farther ebullitions of temper, as were taken by the United States troops after the massacres of Minnesota, or by the British troops at Secunderabad and other places in suppressing the Indian Mutiny.

Before resuming my personal narrative, I will give a short account of what had already taken place in the progress of the insurrection on Essexvale itself, and in those parts of the Insiza and Filibusi districts which border upon Essexvale.

There is reason to believe that the outbreak of the rebellion, commencing as it did with the murder of a native policeman on Friday, 20th March, was somewhat premature, and thus there was an interval of nearly three days between the date of this murder and the day when the first white men were killed by the natives. From the Umzingwani, the flame of rebellion spread through the Filibusi and Insiza districts, to the Tchangani and Inyati, and thence to the mining camps in the neighbourhood of the Gwelo and Ingwenia rivers, and indeed throughout the country wherever white men, women, and children could be taken by surprise and murdered either singly or in small parties; and so quickly was this cruel work accomplished, that although it was only on 23rd March that the first Europeans were murdered, there is reason to believe that by the evening of the 30th not a white man was left alive in the outlying districts of Matabeleland. Between these two dates many people escaped or were brought in to Bulawayo by relief parties, but a large number were cruelly and treacherously murdered.

21

CHAPTER V

Massacre of the whites near Edkins' store—Evidence of a survivor—Mutilation and attempt to destroy identity—Murder of the Cunningham family—Herbert Pomeroy Fynn's sworn statement—Murder of Mr. Maddocks—Laager formed at Cumming's store—Hon. Maurice Gifford proceeds to the relief of the whites at Cumming's store—Derelict waggon—Murder of Dr. and Mrs. Langford—Relief of laager at Cumming's store—Repulse of Matabele attack—Retreat to Bulawayo—Hon. Maurice Gifford's letters.

Not far from the once large military kraal of Gorshlwayo, near the southern border of Essexvale, was a trading station known as Edkins' store. In the neighbourhood were several mining camps and the residence of a native commissioner, and it is here probably that the first murders of Europeans were committed during the present native rising.

At any rate some time on Monday, 23rd March,[7] seven white men, two colonial boys and a coolie cook were murdered there. Among the murdered men was Mr. Bentley, the native commissioner, who was shot or stabbed from behind, whilst sitting in his hut writing—the date above the last words he ever wrote being 23rd March. Mr. Edkins and three other white men, together with their two colonial servants and the coolie cook, were killed in and round the store, whilst Messrs. Ivers and Ottens were killed, the former near the Celtic mining camp, and the latter about half-way between the camp and the store, from which it was distant about a mile and a half. The corpses of these poor fellows were found by Colonel Spreckley's relief party four days subsequent to the massacre. A colonial native was also discovered still living, though terribly injured. He had evidently been left for dead by the Matabele, and besides the wounds which they had inflicted on him in order to kill him, they had slit his mouth open from ear to ear. It was not thought that this man could possibly live, but his wounds were dressed, and food given him, and, wonderful to relate, he eventually made his way to Bulawayo, where, thanks to the skilful

---

[7] There is some doubt as to whether these murders were committed on the Monday or the Tuesday; Colonel Spreckley thinks on the Monday, whilst Mr. O'Connor says it was Tuesday. It is possible that the latter may have been a day wrong in his reckoning, whilst the entry in Mr. Bentley's books seems to favour the earlier date.

treatment and kind nursing he received in the hospital there, he in time recovered from his injuries.

He was able to give evidence concerning the murders, which he said were committed suddenly and without warning by native policemen, aided by natives from the surrounding kraals under two brothers of Lo Bengula, Maschlaschlin and Umfaizella, who, with Umlugulu, Gwibu, Umfondisi, and other members of the king's family, were the chief instigators of the rebellion; and this being so, no peace can be made that will satisfy the colonists until all the members of the late king's family, as well as every Induna and every native policeman who it can be proved took part in the murders which marked the outbreak of the rebellion, have been either hanged or shot.

This may seem a big order to some people—who, however, do not probably contemplate residing on a lonely farm in Rhodesia— but it is necessary for the future safety of the country.

The bodies of Ottens and Bentley had been mutilated, and dry grass had been heaped up and burnt over the faces of all the dead, possibly with the idea of destroying their identity.

Almost simultaneously with the murders at Edkins' store, or at any rate on the same day, the massacre of the whites was commenced in the Insiza district, the first sufferers being probably the Cunningham family, who were living on a farm near the Insiza river. These poor people seem to have been attacked early in the afternoon, as when their homestead was visited on the following day by Messrs. Liebert and Fynn, the remains of the mid-day meal were still on the table, whilst old Mr. Cunningham seemed to have been murdered whilst reclining on a couch reading a newspaper. Here is the sworn deposition of Mr. Fynn, the assistant native commissioner for the Insiza district, as to the finding of the bodies.

Herbert Pomeroy Fynn's sworn statement:—

"I am an assistant native commissioner for the Insiza district. I accompanied last witness—Mr. Liebert—and Orpen to Cunningham's farm on Tuesday morning, 24th March. On arrival there I saw eight dead bodies lying on the ground about twenty yards from the homestead. We made a cursory examination and saw that the deceased persons had been murdered by means of knob-kerries and battle-axes, or similar weapons. The ground was covered with native footprints, and there were broken knob-kerries lying about. I identified among the dead bodies those of Mr. Cunningham senior, Mrs. Cunningham, two Miss Cunninghams, Master Cunningham, and three children whom I identified as the grandchildren of Mr. Cunningham senior. The deceased persons appeared to have been killed inside the house and afterwards

23

dragged out and thrown outside in the position in which we found them. From the fact that all the native kraals in the vicinity were quite deserted, I have absolutely no doubt that the persons who killed the deceased were Matabele natives. Young Cunningham, aged about fourteen years, was still alive when we arrived, but unconscious, and died immediately after our arrival."

Such is the bald account of the discovery of the battered and bloody remains of this unfortunate family, which, alas! was not the only one suddenly blotted out of existence, root and branch, during the first terrible days of the Matabele rebellion. The hideous barbarity of these murders, and the feeling of intense exasperation they would be likely to excite amongst the surviving settlers, seem to have been somewhat underrated in England; whilst for obvious reasons they have been carefully kept out of sight by those dishonest speakers who recently endeavoured to excite public opinion against the white population of Rhodesia. You can respect an honest enemy even if you can't like him; but when a fanatic endeavours to support either his or her theories by the suppression of truth, he or she becomes contemptible.

But we are thankful for the sympathy of that most determined enemy of everything Rhodesian—except the noble savages who therein dwell—Mr. Labouchere, who has professed himself "sorry for the women and children who have been killed." Sorry—only sorry! Wonderful indeed is the calm serenity of soul that enables that noble nature to view all mundane affairs from the same cold, passionless plane, whether it be the cruel murder of an English settler's wife and family in Rhodesia, or an accident to the wheel of a friend's bicycle in Hyde Park! But the men who have looked upon the corpses of the murdered ones, who have seen the shattered skulls of their countrywomen, the long grey locks of the aged and the sunny curls of the girls and little children all alike dabbled in their blood, are something more than sorry; indignation mingles with their sorrow, and they are determined to exact such punishment for the crimes committed, as shall preclude as far as possible their recurrence in the future.

At a distance of a few miles from the Cunninghams' farm was a mining property belonging to the Nellie Reef Development Company, where work was being carried on under the superintendence of Mr. Thomas Maddocks, the manager of the Nellie Reef Mine. At about a quarter to six on the evening of Monday, 23rd March, that is probably some four hours after the murder of the Cunningham family, Mr. Maddocks and two miners, Messrs. Hocking and Hosking, were sitting smoking outside their huts just before dinner, when some fifteen natives came up armed

24

with knob-kerries and battle-axes. The man who appeared to be their leader spoke to Mr. Maddocks and said that he and his companions had been sent by Mr. Fynn, the native commissioner, to work, and on being asked if he had a letter from that gentleman, called to some more natives who were standing not far off. What followed I will tell in the words of Mr. John Hosking, who, in his sworn statement regarding the death of Mr. Maddocks, deposes as follows:—

"The call was answered by a shout of 'Tchaia,' 'strike.' A number of natives joined those who were with us, and the leader then struck deceased on the head with a knob-kerry. I immediately retired into my hut for my revolver. When I came back three natives were hitting Hocking with kerries and axes. I fired a shot and dropped one man, and just as I had fired my second shot, I received a blow on the head causing the mark I now show. Hocking then managed to get into the hut, whereupon the natives cleared off; Hocking and I then went to Maddocks, but found him dead. We retired into an iron store, at which the natives fired a shot. The bullet passed inside through the iron, which caused us to retire again to the hut." By this time it was growing dusk, so the two wounded miners, fearing that the natives would soon return and fire the hut, crept out, and getting into the long grass, made their escape to Cumming's store, three miles from Maddocks' camp, where about twenty men had already collected, many of whom, however, were unarmed. A laager was at once formed, and Mr. Cumming and another rode into Bulawayo for assistance. They first, however, warned several miners and farmers living in the neighbourhood, that the natives had risen, thus saving the lives of these people, as they all got safely to the laager and ultimately escaped to Bulawayo, whereas but for this timely warning they would most certainly have been murdered.

Mr. Cumming and his companion reached Bulawayo on Tuesday morning, and at once reported themselves to Mr. Duncan, the Administrator.

At this time no organised force existed in the country, with the exception of the few men of the Matabele Mounted Police under Captain Southey; and there were only some 370 rifles in the Government stores. However, no difficulty was experienced in getting men together who were ready to proceed at once to the relief of their countrymen and countrywomen; and, as I have already narrated, three small corps under experienced leaders were despatched to various outlying districts within a few hours of the time when the first alarm was given. The Hon. Maurice Gifford, as energetic as he is brave, got off that same evening with about forty

25

men, including Captain Southey and twelve of his Mounted Police; his object being the relief of the men who had laagered up at Cumming's store. The first sign of the rising seen by this party was near Woodford's store, about fourteen miles beyond Thaba Induna, or twenty-six from Bulawayo. Here an abandoned waggon was found standing in the road, the sixteen donkeys that had been harnessed to it lying all of a heap dead. They had for the most part been stabbed to death with assegais, but some had been shot. Nothing on the waggon had been touched, though it was loaded with flour, whisky, etc. No trace of those who had been in charge of the waggon could be discovered, but it has been subsequently ascertained that they were murdered in the bush some little distance away. They were colonial boys taking down a load of stores to the Insiza district. Soon after this derelict waggon had been passed, three colonial boys were met making their way to Bulawayo, one armed with a rifle and another with a revolver. They reported to Mr. Gifford that the rising was general in the Insiza district, and said that a Dr. and Mrs. Langford had been killed on the previous day—Wednesday, 25th March—near Rixon's farm; but that Mr. Rixon, the Blicks, and others in the district had escaped to the laager at Cumming's store. They also told Mr. Gifford that they had seen several troops of cattle being driven by armed Matabele towards the Malungwani and Matopo Hills. On meeting Mr. Gifford these "boys" turned back and accompanied him to the Insiza, and did good service in the subsequent fight, in which one of them was wounded.

On Thursday night the relief party reached Cumming's store, where they found about thirty men in laager. Of these, however, a large proportion were unarmed, so that Mr. Gifford had only about fifty rifles at his command altogether. The night passed off quietly, but at about 5 A.M., just before daylight on Friday morning, a most determined attack was made on the position by a large party of Matabele, who did not finally retreat until they had suffered heavy loss from the steady fire of the white men. The natives came on with the utmost fearlessness, as may be inferred from the fact that one was killed with his hands on the window-sill of the store, whilst six others lay dead close round; and it was afterwards ascertained that their total loss was twenty-five.

On the side of the whites, Sergt.-Major O'Leary of the Matabele Mounted Police was killed, as well as an educated American negro, a servant of Mr. Wrey's, whilst six white men were wounded. As soon as the attack had been completely beaten off, the waggons were inspanned, and the beleaguered white men broke up their laager and commenced their retreat to Bulawayo.

26

The first portion of the road to be travelled led amongst broken wooded hills, through which it was expected they would have to fight their way; but although the Matabele once gathered on the top of a neighbouring hill, and seemed about to attack, they did not do so, and thus allowed the whites to get out into the open country, where they were comparatively safe, without further molestation.

I think it will not be out of place to here reproduce, with the kind permission of Mr. Maurice Gifford, two letters written by him on the night after the fight, of which I happen to have copies, as they cannot fail, I think, to interest my readers.

To A. H. F. Duncan, Esq.,
Bulawayo.

14 miles from Lee's Store,
10.5 P.M.

Dear Sir—We have relieved Insiza, and brought away thirty-six men and one woman. At 5 A.M. this morning were attacked and enemy repulsed. Details of same will be given you by bearer. We have at present six wounded, and the woman with a child. One of the wounded is a serious case. Suggest the following for your consideration and for our assistance. Send out two large American spiders with mules to bring them in. Leave it to your judgment to say whether you consider escort necessary. Suggest fifteen men. We can then bring in the remainder of the party. I am sending two men who have brought me dispatches this morning from Napier to advise him of the serious nature of this rising; but again leave it to your judgment whether you consider it advisable to send him advice from your end, taking into consideration the possibility of these two men not being able to reach him. If a doctor can come with the spiders, so much the better; also suggest making arrangements for beds for wounded. Advise me as to your knowledge of any possible attacks from natives *en route* from here to Bulawayo. Written by moonlight. We are all well and cheery, and hope to have a drink with you to-morrow night at 9 P.M.—Yours faithfully,

Maurice R. Gifford.

Written at the Camp where Thackeray and friend left you,
10.30 P.M.

Dear Napier—Your dispatch duly received. Just a line from

27

me to let you know that the Kafirs mean business this time. We were attacked this morning at one hour before sunrise by about three hundred natives, who came on in the most fanatical and plucky style—the old Zulu rush. Three natives were shot alongside the walls of our barricade. I mention this to you to put you on your guard, as you must have many new chums with you, and to advise great caution to prevent night surprises. We never thought an attack probable, but fortunately were well prepared. This, in my opinion, will prove a more serious business than the old war, and I am sure that prompt action is necessary.—Yours,

M. R. Gifford.

CHAPTER VI

Difficulties of the colonists much underrated—The Matabele campaign of 1893—Military spirit scotched, not killed—Estimated native losses—Disarmament of Matabele incomplete—Natives well supplied with arms and ammunition—Defections amongst the native police.

As will be seen from the last sentence of Mr. Gifford's letter to Colonel Napier, even at this early stage of the insurrection he predicted that it would prove a more serious business than the first war, and that this prediction has been fully justified will never I think be gainsaid by any man who has taken part in both campaigns. As, however, the difficulties experienced by the colonists in coping with the present rebellion have been very much underrated in certain quarters, and invidious comparisons instituted between Dr. Jameson's victorious march on Bulawayo in 1893 and the conduct of the present campaign, I will take the liberty of giving my own opinion on the subject; which is that the essential differences in the circumstances under which the two campaigns were conducted render it impossible to institute any comparison between them. In 1893 Dr. Jameson marched from Mashunaland to Bulawayo with a compact force of 670 white men, 400 of whom were mounted, a small number of native allies, and a strong party of artillery consisting of 5 Maxim guns, 2 seven-pounders, 1 Gardner gun, and 1 Hotchkiss. Choosing its own line, and under the guidance of Nyenyezi —a Matabele of high position, whose whole family to the number of seventy had lately been put to death by the order of Lo Bengula, and who was himself a proscribed fugitive—this force kept in the open country as much as possible, but were obliged to pass through some broken wooded country in the neighbourhood of the Tchangani river. Here, at 4 A.M. on the morning of the 25th of October, it was attacked for the first time by the eastern division of the Matabele army, computed at some 5000 strong, though it is improbable that all the regiments composing this division were actually engaged, as all the fighting seems to have been done by the the Insukamini regiment, aided by small detachments of the Inhlati and Umquicho.

The attack failed, the Matabele being beaten off from the laager with heavy loss, whilst the column marched on towards Bulawayo, and was not again attacked until after the Impembisi had been crossed.

At a point a few miles beyond this river the laager was again attacked on 1st November, this time in perfectly open ground, and in the middle of the day. The attack was made by the Imbezu and Ingubu regiments, computed by Sir John Willoughby to number together about 1700 men; some 5000 more of other regiments who were hanging round never having come into action at all. In this engagement these two regiments suffered very heavily from the fire of the Maxim guns, although, as they have both reformed and taken a prominent part in the present rebellion, they were certainly not annihilated. On hearing of the defeat of the Imbezu and Ingubu, one or other of which regiments he usually kept near him as a sort of bodyguard, Lo Bengula fled from Bulawayo, after first burning the kraal and blowing up his European house; but before doing so he recalled his son-in-law, Gambo, from the Mangwe Pass, thus leaving it open for the unopposed advance of the southern column under Colonel Gould Adams, who with the 400 men under his command was thus enabled to effect a junction with Dr. Jameson on 15th November. Gambo had been in command of all the regiments composing the Eegapa and the Umschlopay, the two largest military divisions of the four into which the country was divided, numbering together at least 8000 men. Excepting, however, a small detachment which attacked Colonel Gould Adams at the Singuesi river, none of the men composing this force took any part in the first Matabele war, although it numbered in its ranks some of the king's best regiments, such as the Inyama Nghlovu and M'schlaschlanglela. Neither were the men under Sikombo, Umlugulu, and many other influential Indunas living to the southeast of Bulawayo, ever engaged in the first war, as although they

29

were all mustered and were close to Bulawayo at the time of the defeat of their compatriots at the Impembisi, they seem to have lost heart when they heard of the disastrous result of that fight, immediately followed as it was by the flight of their king, and so retired to the Matopo Hills, and subsequently surrendered without fighting.

The death of Lo Bengula probably closed the campaign, for but for this event his pursuit to the lower Tchangani, resulting as it did in the death of Major Wilson and all his brave companions, would scarcely have had any other effect than to show the Matabele that although white men were invincible when defending a laager with Maxim guns, they were by no means so when only armed with rifles, if they could be outnumbered and surrounded in difficult country.

But the death of their king left them like a swarm of bees bereft of their queen. Their councils were divided; their military arrogance crushed out of them by the heavy defeats their best regiments had sustained at the Tchangani, the Impembisi, and in a minor degree at the Singuesi. Short of food, and living like wild beasts in the rocks and forests, with all the bitter discomfort which such a life entails even on savages during the rainy season in a sub-tropical country, they saw their women and children sicken and die day by day, until their only hope of life seemed to lie in a speedy return to the high and healthy plateau from which they had fled. But there lay the laagers of the white men strongly defended with cannon and Maxim guns. From such positions they could not hope to drive them, nor without a leader or any cohesion between the numberless little parties into which they were divided did they dare to try conclusions with the mounted patrols which scoured the open country. What wonder then that when liberal terms of peace were offered them, first one Induna with all his people, and then another and another, surrendered, until in a short time the whole nation had freely and frankly submitted itself to the white man's rule? Such is a brief account of the conquest of Matabeleland in 1893, which was practically settled by two battles, in which the Matabele attacked the white men in laager and were in each case driven off with heavy loss by the fire of the Maxim guns.

The brilliancy of the exploit, resulting as it did in the overthrow of one of the most cruel and barbarous despotisms that has ever existed even in barbarous Africa, and in the throwing open to European enterprise of a rich and fertile territory, blessed with a climate in which white men can live and thrive, will ever be remembered as one of the most brilliant episodes in the history of British colonisation in South Africa; and no one, in this country at any rate, would wish to detract one iota from the honour due to all those who took part in Dr. Jameson's historic march to Bulawayo in 1893. It was admirable both in the boldness of its conception and the steady and unflinching resolution with which it was carried out.

All I wish to point out is that in 1893 the fighting power and the military spirit of the Matabele nation was only scotched, not killed; for more than half the regiments which had formed the king's army at the time of the war did not lose a single man during the hostilities, never having been engaged in any of the fights; whilst the only regiments which lost really heavily were the Insukamini, the Imbezu, and the Ingubu. It is difficult to state with any degree of exactitude the number of men lost by the Matabele in 1893, but personally I find it difficult to believe that their loss in men killed or who died from wounds can have exceeded 1000—that is, 200 at the Tchangani, 500 at the Impembisi, 100 at the Inguesi, and 200 killed during the fighting on the lower Tchangani. Be it remembered by those who consider this too low an estimate, that if more than 500 Matabele were killed at the Impembisi fight, it would mean over 30 per cent of the entire force engaged, as the strength of the Imbezu and Ingubu together did not exceed 1700, whilst the number of the survivors who have been and still are taking part in the present rebellion is by no means inconsiderable. As regards the loss inflicted on the Matabele by Major Wilson and his brave companions during their last desperate stand on the lower Tchangani, we have nothing to go upon, except what natives who were there can tell us, and I think there is reason to believe that their loss there was not actually so heavy as at one time it was supposed to be, as they were always able to fire on the whites from behind the shelter of trees. Apart, however, from the direct loss sustained in the various fights, the Matabele must have suffered heavily from the ravages of sickness caused by exposure and want of food after the fighting had ceased. The greatest sufferers were naturally the women and children, the able-bodied men having been better able to withstand the unaccustomed hardships. Altogether, I think that if to the 1000, which is my estimate of those killed in battle, or who died from the effects of their wounds, another 1000 is added for the able-bodied men who died of sickness afterwards, the aggregate will be a very liberal allowance for the total losses sustained by the Matabele in fighting men during, and in consequence of, the war of 1893.

However, to avoid all cavilling let us add another 1000 to this number, making 3000 altogether. Subtract these 3000 from the entire fighting strength of the nation before the war, which has never been estimated at less than 20,000, and it leaves a residue of 17,000 able-bodied men. This total may be a thousand or two out

31

one way or the other; but, whatever the fighting strength of the nation may be, every man composing it throughout the length and breadth of the land is now in arms against the white men, with the exception of some of Gambo's people and a few others, numbering in all under 1000 men, about whom I shall say a few words later on.

But, it has been said, however many Matabele may have rebelled against the Government, they cannot be very dangerous foes, since the whole nation was disarmed after the first war. This is an error. After the war of 1893 a considerable number of guns were certainly given up, but that the total handed in and destroyed was but a small proportion of what they had possessed before the war no one who knew anything about the matter ever doubted. Besides muzzle-loading guns of every description, the Matabele were formerly in possession of at least 2000 breech-loading rifles, principally Martini-Henrys, a certain number of which were captured from them during the war or surrendered after hostilities were over. As no count seems ever to have been kept of the number of these rifles captured or handed in, no exact figure can be given. General report says 150 to 300, whilst the highest number I have ever heard ventured was "between 400 and 500."

Even taking the highest number to be correct, considering that a considerable number of Martini-Henry rifles have been illicitly sold to the Matabele during the last two years, that nearly 100 breech-loading rifles were taken over to the enemy by the rebel police, whilst many more were captured from murdered men during the first days of the rebellion, it cannot be denied that they have regained more than they lost, so that in the matter of breech-loading arms they entered upon the present insurrection with a larger supply than they possessed in 1893, whilst, as I have said before, however many muzzle-loading guns they may have surrendered, they kept back a great many which they are now using. As regards ammunition, I, for one, certainly thought when the present rebellion broke out that their supply would soon run short, but it has not yet done so, and, moreover, it seems to be fairly distributed through the whole nation, as every impi with which we have yet been engaged has shown itself to be well supplied, especially with Martini-Henry cartridges.

Thus we now see that after the first conquest of Matabeleland a very large proportion of the former military strength of the country was still available, and that although this large number of able-bodied savages were apparently without arms, their weapons were only hidden for the time being. Where the large supply of ammunition which they have proved themselves to be possessed of came from, I cannot say. Probably large quantities were buried with the rifles after the first war, and this store has been constantly added to by theft and illicit purchase ever since.

However, over two years of most submissive behaviour, unbroken by any attempt whatever to rebel against the authority of the Chartered Company, lulled every white man in the country into a feeling of security which events have not justified.

A native police force was raised, which was apparently working admirably up to the time of the rebellion; and even then, it is but fair to say, almost all the police who had been first enrolled, and who had done more than a year's service, held themselves aloof from the rebels, the great majority of defections occurring amongst those who had been but lately enrolled and amongst whom there was therefore little or no *esprit de corps*.

CHAPTER VII

Effect of removing the police force—Witch-doctors' influence—Originators of the insurrection—Gambo detained at Bulawayo—The Imbezu regiment—Unpreparedness of the Colonists at the outbreak—The Rhodesia Horse—Horses in possession of the Government—Rifles, guns, and ammunition in Government stores—Want of community of action of the Matabele—The Umlimo's mistake—Critical position at Bulawayo— Neglect of the Matabele to block the roads—Force in Bulawayo at the outbreak—The Africander Corps.

In spite of their submissive behaviour, it seems probable that all the members of the late king's family and many of the chief Indunas were only biding their time, and waiting for an opportunity to try the chances of a rebellion against the white man.

This opportunity did not present itself as long as there was a strong police force in the country, but once that police force was removed, I think the malcontents began to act.

That the plague of locusts with which Matabeleland has been afflicted ever since 1890, the first year of the occupation of Mashunaland by Europeans; the partial drought of the last two years; and, finally, the outbreak of the rinderpest, would all be ascribed to the evil influence of the white man, and made use of by the witch-doctors to incite the mass of the people to join the insurgents, is doubtless true; but that the insurrection can be fairly ascribed to the bitterness caused by these visitations alone, I very much doubt, for it is remarkable that throughout the Umzingwani, Filibusi, and Insiza districts, where all the first murders of white men were committed, the rainfall had been plentiful, and the locusts had done but little damage, so that, as I can personally bear witness, the crops throughout these portions of the country were exceptionally good, whilst as the rinderpest had not yet approached this part of Matabeleland, the people living in these districts could have known little or nothing about it. In its inception, the insurrection was, in my opinion, a rebellion against the white man's rule by the Matabele of Zulu origin alone, and I am convinced that, in the district where I was living at least, the other section of the tribe were at first not in the secret; however, the greater part of these soon joined, some unwillingly and under threats from their former masters, but most of them readily enough, believing, as they did, that with the assistance of the Umlimo they would be able to completely root out the white man, and revel once more in loot and wholesale murder. And a merry time they had of it, if it was but a short one, to be followed by a heavy retribution.

When the first news of the rising reached Bulawayo, Gambo was in the town on a visit to the chief native commissioner, by whom he was very wisely detained as a prisoner. Whether, if he had been at large, he would have joined the rebels or not, it is difficult to say. Since the war, he has lost control over the greater part of the people who formerly composed the Eegapa military division, and many of these have joined the ranks of the insurgents, but all Gambo's own people, under his head Induna, Marzwe, have remained loyal to the Government. Umjan, once the Induna of the Imbezu regiment, and now quite an old man, has also refrained from taking part in the present hostilities, although he is one of the few whose cattle were shot by order of the Government because they were infected with the rinderpest. He came in to Bulawayo soon after the outbreak of the rebellion with his wives and immediate attendants, and is now living quietly near the town. His sons, however, have joined the rebels, whilst the men whom he formerly commanded—the Imbezu—reformed themselves into a regiment, and have been fighting since the outbreak of the insurrection.

Besides Gambo's men, a few hundreds of Matabele Maholi (men of Makalaka and Mashuna descent) living on my Company's property of Essexvale, on Colonel Napier's land and round the Hope

34

Fountain mission station, have thought it advisable to stand by the Government, and have, therefore, come in to live near Bulawayo for protection. But putting aside these few hundreds of natives who have not joined in the rebellion, the fact remains that at least nine-tenths, I think I might safely say nineteen-twentieths, of the Matabele nation are now in arms against the whites.

And, now, let us see how the colonists were prepared to meet the onset of these hordes of savages. When the rising first broke out, with the exception of the native police, there was no organised force in Matabeleland worth speaking of; and as one-half of the native police at once went over to the enemy, and the remainder had to be disarmed, for fear lest they should follow suit, it may be said that there was no police force at all. Of the old Mounted Police there only remained forty-eight officers, non-commissioned officers, and men, in the whole of Matabeleland, under Inspector Southey. Of these, twenty-two were stationed in Bulawayo, and the rest distributed over the country at the police stations of Gwelo, Selukwe, Belingwe, Inyati, Mangwe, Tuli, Matopos, Umzingwani, and Iron Mine Hill. When the rebellion broke out only twelve of these men were available at Bulawayo for immediate service, and these, under Inspector Southey, accompanied Mr. Gifford to the Insiza. The Rhodesia Horse, a volunteer force which had been raised and equipped the previous year, had also practically ceased to exist as an effective force fit for use at a moment's notice, for although there were some six hundred men in Matabeleland who had enrolled themselves as members of this corps, they were scattered all over the country at the outbreak of the rebellion. Some of these were murdered, whilst others had to take refuge in the laagers of Belingwe and Gwelo. However, about five hundred were soon mustered in Bulawayo, but the services of the majority could not be utilised except to defend the town, owing to the want of horses, since, so great had been the ravages of the fatal horse-sickness during the rainy season then just coming to an end, that when Colonel Napier, the senior officer of the Rhodesia Horse, called on the Government for seventy horses for immediate use on 23rd March, he could only be supplied with sixty-two.

The actual number of horses in the possession of the Government throughout Matabeleland on the day when the first tidings of the outbreak of the insurrection reached Bulawayo is as follows:—

Horses in Government stables   77
Horses in possession of members of the Rhodesia Horse   117

Volunteers scattered over various parts of Matabeleland
In possession of cattle inspectors 28
Unfit for work 58

Of the 117 horses that had been issued to Volunteers, a good many never returned to Bulawayo, as they either died of horse-sickness or were taken to Gwelo or Belingwe, so that in the first days of the rebellion the Government could not command the services of more than 100 horses; but no expense was spared to procure more, and very soon all the private horses in Bulawayo were bought up, whilst others were sent up from the Transvaal, so that by the end of April there were nearly 450 horses in the Government stables, the large majority of which were fit for active service.

The number of rifles belonging to the Government throughout the country on 25th March was as follows:—

	Lee-Metford Rifles.	Lee-Metford Carbines.
At Gwanda	20	—
At Gwelo	40	—
With Colonel Napier's patrol	33	52
" " Spreckley's patrol	36	2
To guard coaches	7	—
In stores	295	70
Permanent staff	25	—
Total	456	124

Making a total of 580 rifles all told.

Besides these, however, there were about eighty old Martini-Henry rifles in the Government stores, but these were nearly all unserviceable at the outbreak of the rebellion, though the armourer has since been able to get most of them into working order. Of ammunition there was a good supply, viz. 1,500,000 rounds.

In the way of artillery there was in Bulawayo when the insurrection broke out one 303 Maxim gun in good order, and a second so much out of repair as to be useless; two 2.5 screw guns in good order, but with only seventeen rounds of ammunition for the two; one Hotchkiss gun and limber, one Gatling, one Gardner, one Nordenfeldt—all in good order—and one seven-pounder, useless except at Bulawayo owing to carriage having been destroyed by white ants. In addition to this ordnance there arrived in Bulawayo from Macloutsie, on the very day on which Mr. Maddocks was murdered, two old Maxims and two seven-pounders. These, however, were unserviceable at the time, one of the seven-pounders being without a carriage and the two Maxims being also out of repair. The armourer here has now, however, I believe, put them all in working order.

Taking these figures as correct—and they are absolutely beyond question—it cannot, I think, be said that the colonists in Matabeleland were very well prepared to cope with a sudden and unexpected rising of at least 10,000 natives, about one-fifth of whom were armed with breech-loading rifles and well supplied with ammunition, whilst many more were in possession of muzzle-loading guns; and when it is remembered that at the time of the outbreak the food supply was very low in Bulawayo, owing to the ravages of the rinderpest, it must be acknowledged that the position was at one time a very serious one, which a little more intelligence on the part of the Matabele might have rendered absolutely disastrous.

But all through they have behaved in an incomprehensible manner, their leaders apparently never having arranged any settled plan of campaign, the consequence being that there has never been any understanding or community of action between the various hordes into which the nation is now divided. All through there appears to have been a general belief amongst them that they would receive supernatural aid from the "Umlimo," or god, but this belief must be getting a little thin now, and they would have done far better had they worked together under one intelligent general.

Why, when the rebellion first broke out, they never attempted to block the main road to Mangwe will ever remain a mystery. No one doubts that they might have done so, nor that, if they had placed a couple of thousand men in the Shashani Pass, we could not have raised a sufficient force on this side to dislodge them and open the road; for it must be remembered that as there were over six hundred women and children in Bulawayo a large force was always necessary to protect them. Possibly there is some truth in the report that the road to Mangwe has been purposely left open by command of the Umlimo in order to give the white men the opportunity of escaping from the country. That this was an error of judgment, if it is a fact, is very clear, as in the critical time but few men left the country, and such as did could be well spared, as they were of no use as defenders of the women and children, and were only consuming valuable food. On the other hand, owing to the road having been left open, stores of arms and food and horses were constantly being brought in.

It certainly seems very strange that no attempt has ever been made to stop waggons and coaches on this road, when it is remembered that at one time Government House—which is less than three miles from the centre of Bulawayo—was practically in the hands of the rebels, sometimes in the daytime and always at nights for a period of about ten days, their impis during that time lying in a semicircle to the west and north of the town, and being sometimes within two miles of it.

Yet although two Dutchmen, living in their waggon standing near the boundary of the town commonage, about four and a half miles along the road from Bulawayo, were murdered, no waggon or coach moving along the road was ever interfered with, nor was the Government House burnt, the reason for this being, it is said, because the Umlimo told the people that when Bulawayo had been destroyed, and all the white men in the country killed, they would find Lo Bengula sitting there, ready to rule them once more; for, be it said, Government House has been built in the centre of the old kraal of Bulawayo, just where the king's house once stood.

For over a month, an impi, supposed to be at least a thousand strong, was camped just within the Matopo Hills, not ten miles from the nearest point on the road to Mangwe, and no one doubts that at any moment a portion of this impi might have moved over to the road by night, and, by shooting a mule or two, have had a coachload of white men at its mercy; and God help the unfortunate white man who has nothing else to trust to but the mercy of the Matabele!

Of course there were forts along the road, and patrols rode daily between the forts, but even so I maintain that much damage might have been done if the natives had determined at any moment to block the road. Now, however, that the impi of which I have been speaking has been driven from its position by the forces under Major-General Sir Frederick Carrington, it is not likely that the safety of the road will ever again be threatened.

And, now, let me hark back to the early days of the rebellion. I think I have shown by figures that on the outbreak of the insurrection the country was not over well supplied with either horses or arms, nor was there any superfluity of men, and the smallness of the number will, I think, astonish some critics of the present campaign in England. Turning to the *Matabele Times* of 6th April last, I find it stated under the heading "The Native Rising up to Date," "A census was taken of all those who had been in the

38

laager on Friday night as they made their exit on Saturday morning, or remained on the waggons. The count was carefully made, and showed that the refugees numbered 632 women and children, and 915 men, making a total of 1547"; and further on we read—"A general parade was held yesterday of the men now in town who have enrolled themselves in the Bulawayo Field Force. They fell in at ten o'clock, the scouts, under Captain Grey, in front making a splendid display of the class of men whom the hostile natives will not seek to tackle twice. The men on foot looked like business, and went through their movements with sufficient precision. The Africander Corps now consists of three companies, numbering 76, 64, and 73, with 6 on the staff. The total number on parade was over 500, of whom about 300 were fully armed, and about 100 were engineers and artillerymen. To this number have to be added the 169 out under the Hon. M. Gifford and Captain Dawson, and the 100 men gone down to Gwanda under Captain Brand and Captain Van Niekerk. The total efficient force now available for the reconquest of Matabeleland may be put down at 700, nearer 800."

From these figures it will be seen that at the outbreak of the rebellion there were under 1000 men in Bulawayo, some 200 of whom were unfit for active service. The remainder of the male population of the country were shut up in the laagers at Gwelo, Belingwe, and Mangwe, and therefore unavailable for offensive operations against the Matabele; whilst of the 800 fighting men in Bulawayo, it was necessary to have at least 400 always in town to protect the women and children, and 130 were drafted off to man the forts on the Mangwe road, leaving less than 300 available for active operations against the enemy. This force was, however, augmented by about 150 Cape boys, chiefly Amaxosa Kafirs and Zulus. These boys were got together and formed into a regiment by Mr. Johan Colenbrander, and they have done most excellent service during the present campaign, being man for man both braver and better armed than the Matabele.

Thus, all things considered, I do not think the colonists have done so badly. With small patrols they first succeeded in bringing in many scattered whites from the outlying districts, and then after a series of engagements, always fought on ground of the enemy's own choosing, succeeded in driving them from the immediate neighbourhood of Bulawayo, and forcing them to take refuge in the forests and hills, from which they will be finally driven by the forces now in the country under the command of Major-General Sir Frederick Carrington.

It is worthy of remark that whilst in the first war the Matabele attacked strong positions defended by artillery and Maxim guns, thereby suffering very heavy loss themselves but killing very few white men, in the present war all the fighting has been amongst broken ground, and in country more or less covered with bush, and all the killing has been done with rifles; for in the first war the natives learnt the futility of attacking fortified positions, and now only fight in the bush in skirmishing order, giving but little opportunity for the effective use of machine guns; so that, although a good many rounds have been fired from Maxims at long ranges, only a very small amount of execution has been done by them.

CHAPTER VIII

Cattle stolen by Matabele—I recover the cattle and burn down Matabele kraal—Start in pursuit of cattle-thieves—Surprise a raiding party and recover two bands of cattle—Reflections on the situation.

I will now again take up the thread of my own personal experiences. As will be remembered, I reached my homestead at 2 A.M. on Thursday, 26th March, and found everything as I had left it seventeen hours before. A mule cart carrying food supplies for my men was to have followed immediately behind us, but the men in charge lost the road, and the provisions did not turn up till late the next day.

On the following morning, just at daybreak, a native named Inshlupo, who had been in charge of a herd of over thirty head of cattle belonging to my Company, turned up and informed me that on the previous evening the headman of a small Matabele kraal, situated in the broken ground just below the Malungwani Hills, had paid him a visit, accompanied by several armed men, and taken off all the cattle.

On the receipt of this news I had the horses saddled up at once, as, it being still so early, I had little doubt that, if no time was lost, we should find the stolen cattle still in the kraal to which they had been taken the previous evening. Before moving, however, I said a few words to my men, telling them that my object in visiting Essexvale and other parts of the country with an armed force was twofold, namely, to endeavour by prompt action to strike terror into the hearts of some of the rebels before they had time to

40

concentrate, and at the same time to reassure those who were content with the white man's rule, but who, in the absence of any display of power on the part of the Government, might be led to believe that their only chance of safety from the vengeance of the Matabele lay in taking part with them in the rebellion. In conclusion, I told them that any Kafirs we might find with arms in their hands, who had left their kraals and gone off into the hills with stolen cattle, ought to be shot without question and without mercy, as they were every one of them more or less responsible for the cruel murders of white men that had already been committed.

Under the guidance of Inshlupo we reached the neighbourhood of the kraal where I hoped to find my Company's cattle before the sun was an hour higher. Here I halted my men, and sent half of them round under the shelter of the bush to a certain point where they were to show themselves, that being the signal for a simultaneous advance as rapidly as possible on the kraal from both sides. However, although we found all the cattle still in the kraal, there were no men there, and in fact no one but a Matabele woman, the wife of the headman, and several children. The woman would offer no explanation of the undeniable fact that my Company's cattle were in her husband's kraal, and would give no information concerning his whereabouts, so, after driving out the stolen cattle, I had the whole place burnt, first allowing the woman to remove all her private effects. When this had been done, I sent the recaptured cattle back to the homestead, in charge of two of Inshlupo's boys, and then proceeded straight into the Malungwani Hills, in the hope of coming across some of the rebels who had gone off with the first lot of my Company's cattle that had been stolen on the previous Tuesday night.

As we proceeded, the hills became thickly wooded, and in the valleys between them we found the spoor of a good many cattle that had passed during the last two days, although we saw no fresh tracks.

About nine o'clock I gave the order to off-saddle in a little grassy hollow, after first placing sentries all round to guard against any sudden attack, for we were now, of course, in the enemy's country. After an hour's rest the horses were just being caught when one of the sentries reported that a herd of cattle was being driven up a valley at the foot of a high ridge to our left. I at once went up to have a look myself, but by this time the cattle were out of sight. However, I carefully examined the ground, and saw that by following another valley running parallel to the one in which the cattle had been seen, and then ascending the steep ridge at its head, we should in all probability drop right on to the rebels in charge of them.

And this is exactly what happened, as upon cresting the ridge we found that both Kafirs and cattle were immediately below us. Some of the former were driving the cattle, but most of them were in the bush ahead. We at once opened fire on them, which they made no attempt to return. Indeed, taken by surprise as they were, and having so much the worse of the position, and, moreover, not being in any force, they could scarcely be expected to do anything else but run for it. And run they did, throwing down almost everything they were carrying, and abandoning the cattle. I saw one man throw a gun away, probably fearing lest he should be caught with it in his possession, but most of them were, I think, only armed with assegais. We chased them up and down several hills, and expended a lot of ammunition on them, but did them I am afraid very little damage, as the hills were all thickly wooded, and our horses were not able to climb up and down them any faster than the light-footed savages we were pursuing. In the second valley we found another herd of cattle, but could see no Kafirs near them, and I think they must have heard the firing, and run off before we came in sight. Altogether we captured over 150 head of cattle, every one of which had been taken from white men, a large number having Mr. Colenbrander's brand on them.

I have stated plainly that we fired on these Kafirs at sight, and that although they offered no resistance, but ran away as hard as they could, we chased them and kept on firing at them as long as we could see them, and this action may possibly be cited as an example of the brutality and inhumanity of the Englishmen in Rhodesia. The fact that the Kafirs whom we sought to destroy—with as little compunction as though they were a pack of wild dogs—were taking part in a rebellion which had just been inaugurated by a series of the foulest murders it is possible to conceive, and the ultimate object of which was evidently to stamp out the white man throughout the land, will, of course, be entirely lost sight of or quietly ignored. In fact, I should not be at all surprised to see it stated that the rebellion was caused by the inhuman behaviour of the white men in Rhodesia, who, it will be said, were in the habit of shooting down the poor, meek, inoffensive Matabele.

The Kafirs upon whom we fired were, of course, caught red-handed, driving off a herd of cattle, every animal in which had been taken from a white man, and we afterwards learnt that they were the very men who had stopped Mr. Meikle's waggon two days before on the Insiza road (some eight or ten miles distant), murdered the colonial boys in charge of it, and assegaied the sixteen donkeys harnessed to it.

For breaking out into rebellion against the white man's rule, and for taking all the cattle in the country, I should have borne them no great animosity, especially as the great majority of these cattle had once belonged to their king or to them personally. Being a representative of the race that had conquered them, I should, of course, have lent the services of my rifle to help to quell the rebellion no matter what form it had taken; but had it not been accompanied by the cruel murders of white women and children, I should not have been animated by the same vengeful feelings as now possessed me, as well as every other white man in Matabeleland.

"But," the kind-hearted, untravelled humanitarian may say, "such incidents are the necessary accompaniments of a native rebellion against Europeans, and ought not therefore to excite any greater surprise or indignation in your colonist than they do in myself; and, moreover, given that you admit that, looking at things from their point of view, the Matabele were justified in rebelling against the white man's rule, go further and acknowledge that the white men were wrong in ever attempting the colonisation of any of the territories between the Limpopo and the Zambesi, since it was the occupation of Mashunaland in 1890 that led to the various disagreements between Lo Bengula and the Chartered Company which culminated in the invasion and conquest of Matabeleland in 1893."

To this proposition I would answer that the whole question of the colonisation by Europeans of countries previously inhabited by savage tribes must be looked upon from a broad point of view, and be judged by its final results as compared with the primitive conditions it has superseded. Two hundred years ago, the Eastern States of North America were inhabited by savage tribes who, by incessant internecine war and the practice of many abominable customs, constantly deluged the whole land with blood. Now the noble red man has disappeared from those territories—has been exterminated by the more intelligent white man—and in place of a cruel, hopeless savagery there has arisen a civilisation whose ideals are surely higher than those of the displaced barbarism. In like manner, before Van Kiebek landed at the Cape of Good Hope, the whole of South Africa was in the hands of savages, a people, be it noted, who were not living in Arcadian simplicity, a peaceful happy race amongst whom crime and misery were unknown quantities, but on the contrary, who were a prey to cruel superstitions, involving a constant sacrifice of innocent life, and who were, moreover, continually exposed to all the horrors of intertribal wars. Now an orderly civilisation has been established over a large area of this once completely savage country, and no one but an ignorant fanatic would, I think, assert that its present condition is not preferable from a humanitarian point of view to its former barbarism. Well, the present state of Matabeleland is one of transition. Its past history—and this fact ought not to be ignored by the impartial critic of what is happening there to-day—has been one of ceaseless cruelty and bloodshed. But in time a civilisation will have been built up in that blood-stained land, as orderly and humane as that which has been established—in place of a parallel barbarism—in the older States of South Africa.

Yet, just as in the establishment of the white man's supremacy in the Cape Colony, the aboriginal black races have either been displaced or reduced to a state of submission to the white man's rule at the cost of much blood and injustice to the black man, so also will it be in Matabeleland, and so must it ever be in any country where the European comes into contact with native races, and where at the same time the climate is such that the more highly organised and intelligent race can live and thrive, as it can do in Matabeleland; whilst the presence of valuable minerals or anything else that excites the greed of the stronger race will naturally hasten the process. Therefore Matabeleland is doomed by what seems a law of nature to be ruled by the white man, and the black man must go, or conform to the white man's laws, or die in resisting them. It seems a hard and cruel fate for the black man, but it is a destiny which the broadest philanthropy cannot avert, whilst the British colonist is but the irresponsible atom employed in carrying out a preordained law—the law which has ruled upon this planet ever since, in the far-off misty depths of time, organic life was first evolved upon the earth—the inexorable law which Darwin has aptly termed the "Survival of the Fittest."

Now there may be those who maintain that the aboriginal savagery of the Red Indians in the Eastern States of North America, or of the Kafirs in the Cape Colony, was a preferable state of things to the imperfect civilisations which have superseded them. To such I have no reply. "Chacun à son goût." Only I would ask them to endeavour to make themselves as well acquainted as possible with the subject under discussion, either by actual travel or by reading, and I would beg them not to accept too readily the assertions constantly made without any regard to truth or honesty by the newspaper opponents of British colonisation, which are broadly to the effect that no savagery exists in Africa except that practised on the blacks by Europeans.

CHAPTER IX

Return to Essexvale—Cattle left at Essexvale in charge of the natives—Essexvale burnt down by Matabele and all the cattle carried off—Start for Jackson's station—Desertion of the native police—The Makalaka—False rumours—Start for Spiro's stores—Colonial boys report the district quiet—Decide to return to Bulawayo through the Matopo Hills.

When on the afternoon of Thursday, 26th March, we got back to my homestead with the recaptured cattle, both men and horses were tired out, as the heat had been intense, and the former had had no food since early dawn. However, the cart carrying provisions having arrived, the men were soon able to get a good meal, whilst the horses were turned into a twenty-five acre patch of maize, which, although it had been sadly destroyed as a crop by the locusts, still afforded an abundance of sweet succulent food for stock. In order to allow the horses time to recover from the effects of their hard day's work in the hills, I resolved to let them feed and rest until the cool of the afternoon of the following day, and then make a night march over to Mr. Jackson's police station at Makupikupeni, where I hoped to be able to get some news as to the whereabouts of Colonel Spreckley's patrol, with which I was anxious to effect a junction. I should have sent the recaptured cattle at once in to Bulawayo, had it not been for the rinderpest scourge which would have rendered such a course worse than useless, since every one of them would have died within a week. The only other plan open to me was to commit them to the care of the natives living immediately round my homestead, who, at this time at any rate, did not seem at all inclined to take part in the rebellion.

As there were now at least 500 head of cattle collected together in a small area, I fully recognised the danger there would be lest so rich a bait should attract a Matabele raiding party as soon as it became known that there was no one left to defend them. However, no other course was open to me, so the cattle were left on the off chance that they would not fall into the hands of the rebels.

Some ten days later the not unexpected came to pass. Inxnozan, an old Matabele warrior, whom I knew well, and whose manly independent bearing I had always admired, descended upon my homestead with a following of some 300 men, burnt down my house and stables and all adjoining storehouses and huts, and either carried off or destroyed everything they contained. Then they

45

collected all the cattle in the neighbourhood, all of which belonged to my Company by right of purchase or capture, and went off. All the Kafirs who up to this time had been living quietly in their kraals looking after my cattle went away into the hills after Inxnozan's visit, and as they have never sent me any message, I do not know whether they have joined the rebels or have only taken refuge in the hills until the war is over. At any rate I shall do all I can to protect them, as they must have been placed in a very difficult position— fearing the enmity of the rebels on the one hand, if they refused to join them, and the vengeance of the white man on the other for suspected complicity in some of the outrages that had taken place in the district if they remained at their kraals.

On the Friday afternoon we made a start for Mr. Jackson's police station, passing the remains of the once large military kraal of Intuntini, and still the largest in the district. Such as it was, we set it alight, and as it was situated on the shoulder of a hill the burning huts must have been plainly visible to the people who had so lately deserted it, from almost any point in the Malungwani range, to which they had probably retired.

Shortly after midnight we reached the police station, which we found entirely deserted, though all the huts were still standing. A closer inspection showed that these huts had been very hastily evacuated by the native police to whom they had belonged, as they were still full of their personal effects, such as coats, hats, blankets, etc. In one of the huts we found a broken Winchester rifle, and in one of the coats a purse containing a few shillings in silver, about the last thing a Kafir would willingly leave behind him. We afterwards learned that Colonel Spreckley's patrol had reached the police station—which was situated on the main road to the Filibusi district from Bulawayo—late at night on the previous Wednesday. At this time there were seven native policemen with a sergeant in the huts. These men, hearing the horsemen approaching, immediately fled, taking nothing with them but their arms and ammunition, and went over to the rebels. That they must have previously made up their minds to desert, is, I think, certain, otherwise there was no reason why they should have left the station of which they were in charge on the approach of the white men. In one of the huts we found several bags of maize, and so were able to give all our horses a good feed.

On the following morning I paid a visit to several kraals in the neighbourhood, the inhabitants of which were in charge of cattle belonging to my Company. These people I found in their villages. They were subsequently attacked by the rebels, who carried off a large proportion of the cattle in their charge. They however escaped with the remainder, which they brought in to Bulawayo, where they very soon all died of rinderpest. These Kafirs are amongst the few who out of the entire nation have stood by the Government and rendered active assistance to the white men during the present crisis. They are Matabele Maholi of Makalaka descent, as I think are all the "friendlies," with the exception of a small leavening amongst them of "Abenzantsi" or Matabele of pure Zulu blood, and I think I am correct in stating that there is not a single Maholi of any other descent who is not in arms with the pure-blooded Matabele against the Government.

The Makalaka proper, a numerous people living on the western border of Matabeleland, have—except possibly with some individual exceptions—held themselves resolutely aloof from any participation in the present rebellion, just as they took no part in the war of 1893. They are an industrious, peaceable people, and have found the rule of the Chartered Company if not perfect, at any rate a vast improvement on the oppressive tyranny under which they lived in the good old days of Lo Bengula.

At Makupikupeni we heard a rumour, which happily proved to be entirely false, though at the time it disturbed my peace of mind very much, to the effect that the ninety native police who had accompanied Mr. Jackson and his companions into the Matopo Hills, on the trail of Umzobo and Umfondisi, had mutinied and murdered their officers, Mr. Jackson having been bound to a tree, and then having had his throat cut. We also heard that Colonel Spreckley had buried the white men who were murdered at Edkins' store, and then crossed over to the Tuli road and returned to Bulawayo.

This being so, I determined to make for Spiro's store, situated just on the edge of the Matopo Hills on the main road from Bulawayo to the Transvaal, and about twelve miles distant from the Makupikupeni police station, as I was in hopes of there hearing something authentic concerning the fate of my friend Mr. Jackson and his companions. I knew the way across country to the store well enough myself, but had I not done so, I had a good guide with me in the person of one Mazhlabanyan, a Matabele—not of Zulu blood, but of Makalaka descent—who had joined me that morning. This man had known me in former years when he was an elephant-hunter in the employ of the late Mr. Thomas, and on hearing that I was residing on Essexvale, had come with his wives and family to live near me, and I had given him a nice little herd of cattle—amongst them some good milk cows—to look after for our Company, for which he was very grateful. He fought in the war of 1893 against the whites and was with the Imbezu at the battle of the

47

Impembisi, on which occasion he was the recipient of a bullet through the shoulder.

During the present troubles, however, he has stood by the Government, and joined the rest of the "friendlies." Shortly before sundown we reached Spiro's store, which we found had been deserted by its occupants not many hours prior to our arrival. The colonial boys in charge of the coach mules were still at their post, and reported everything quiet in the district as far as they knew, nor could they give any information concerning Mr. Jackson.

Since mid-day the weather, which had been intensely dry and hot for some time past, had changed suddenly, the sky became overcast and a light rain commenced to fall. Luckily, however, there proved to be sufficient accommodation in the out-buildings and beneath the broad verandah which surrounded the store for all my men, and we were thus spared the disagreeable necessity of sleeping out on the wet ground and beneath a rainy sky.

The next day—Sunday, 29th March—broke fine, but cool and cloudy, a very pleasant change after the excessive heat we had recently experienced. The question now arose as to whether any other course was open to me but to return at once to Bulawayo by the Tuli road. To my left lay the rugged mass of broken granite hills called the Matopos, within whose recesses it was believed by many people at Bulawayo that the Matabele had already massed in large numbers. Now I fully realised that had this been the case, it would have been madness to take so small a force as that at my disposal into so difficult a country. As, however, I had very good reasons for believing that as yet no large number of Matabele had assembled in this part of the country, I was anxious to make a reconnaissance through them in order to see what the difficulties of the country really were.

Before starting I paraded my men and told them what I wished to do, stating that in my opinion, although we should have some very rough country to get over, and should have to walk and lead our horses most of the way, we should not meet any large force of hostile Kafirs, or indeed be likely to fire a shot at all unless we met some of the revolted police who had murdered Jackson—for at this time I believed that he had really been murdered. However, I told them that I did not wish any one to go with me who did not care to do so, which was unnecessary, as no one was willing to be left behind.

48

CHAPTER X

Through the Matopo Hills—Skirmish with the rebels—A narrow escape—Capture a band of cattle—Retire with wounded— Fidelity of Mazhlabanyan—Reach Dawson's store—Arrive at Bulawayo.

It was about seven o'clock when we entered the first gorge leading in amongst the foothills, which were here well wooded. Mr. Blöcker, who is an excellent walker and a very good shot, I told off to scout on foot a short distance ahead of us, whilst Messrs. Simms and Fletcher, two Cape Colonists and both steady, reliable men, scouted on the left and right flanks respectively.

After we had proceeded for about an hour through very broken and, for the most part, thickly wooded country, we emerged upon a huge bare granite rock. Here Mr. Simms rejoined us and reported that as he was scouting on the left flank, upon emerging from a patch of bush, he had come suddenly upon four Kafirs, one carrying a gun whilst the rest were armed with assegais. These men quickly moved out of sight, fearing to attack Simms lest there should prove to be more white men behind him, whilst he on his side did not care to fire on them, as he did not know how many more natives there might be close at hand.

Beyond us there now lay a large open grassy valley enclosed on every side by rocky granite hills. In its broadest part this valley was over a mile in width, but at its top end it gradually narrowed into a rocky gorge, which apparently led on to some higher ground beyond the farthest hills we could see. Much of the valley was under cultivation, and a splendid crop of corn was standing, still unreaped, in the fields. Mazhlabanyan told me that these cornfields belonged to Banyubi, a tribe allied to the Makalakas, and who are the aboriginal inhabitants of the district. After carefully looking over the country on ahead, I decided to keep straight up the valley, and make my way to the higher ground by the gorge I have spoken of. When we were half-way through the open valley, Kafirs began to shout to one another amongst the hills to our left, and presently we saw some, but they were a long way off and we could not make out whether they were armed or not. I now gave orders that any Kafir who approached us must be fired on if he was armed, but not unless.

We had just entered the neck of the gorge and were finding a good deal of difficulty in getting our horses through a stream that

49

was too deep to ford and could only be crossed on flat slippery stones, when some shots were fired at us from a rocky kopje about 300 yards to our left rear. However, as the Kafirs who had fired were hidden behind rocks, we could see nothing of them, nor did we catch a glimpse of the enemy until we had all crossed the stream. We then saw a few natives amongst the wooded hills directly ahead of us, and at once commenced a skirmishing fight with them. They were in no great numbers, and they retired before us without firing many shots or giving us much of a chance at them. In this way we had advanced slowly but steadily in extended order for about 300 yards through rocks and bush when we suddenly came upon a kraal filled with cattle, at the foot of a mass of bare castellated rocks. From these rocks we drove the enemy, without any loss on our side, though many of us were fired at at very close quarters, but, as has so often been remarked, Kafirs always make wretched shooting if at all hustled. Personally I had one little piece of luck. A Kafir had fired either at me or Mr. Blöcker—we were close together—from behind a buttress of rock, and as I knew that his rifle was therefore empty, and hoped he had been alone, I ran up the flat slope of rock on which I was standing, thinking to get a good shot at him round the corner of the rock. When I got there, however, I did not see the man who had fired at me, but found another Kafir waiting for me with his rifle at his shoulder. He was on a lower level than the rock slab on which I was standing, and must have heard me approaching as he was evidently on the lookout for me to show myself. I was carrying my own rifle at the ready, but had to get it up to my shoulder before I could fire. There was no time to get a sight, so, looking at him, I raised my rifle as quickly as possible and fired, and at almost the same moment he fired at me. The result was mutually disappointing, as we both missed our mark. How I managed to make so bad a shot I don't know, as the Kafir was not more than fifteen yards from me. However, had I waited for the few seconds necessary to get the sight on him, he might very likely have shot me first, whilst my quick snap-shot very probably disconcerted him and made him miss. Immediately he had fired, he dodged behind a rock, and I did not get another chance at him.

We now took possession of the rocks above the cattle kraal, and got a few good shots at a lot of Kafirs running away amongst the trees to the left. Having placed several men as sentinels on the highest boulders, I went down to look at the cattle, considering it very bad luck having ever come across them, as I did not like to leave them and then continue my reconnaissance, nor did I think it would be possible to drive them out of the hills to the Tuli road without any Kafirs on foot to help. I first thought of shooting the lot, but as there were over a hundred, could not spare the ammunition that would have been required for the purpose. I therefore determined to try and drive them out of the hills and take them to Bulawayo.

With a great deal of trouble we got them down to the broken ground above the stream, but farther than this we could not drive them, as they scattered in all directions, but would not go down the rocks. Over and over again we rounded them up and tried to force them to go the way we wanted them to take, but without success, and I was once more thinking of shooting them all when some shots were fired at us from the broken ground to our left front. By a mistake the sentinels had left their posts on the top of the rocks and rejoined the rest of our party, and the Kafirs, now heavily reinforced, had got back to positions amongst the wooded cliffs above us without being observed. I at once sent Mr. Blöcker and a few men who were good shots to take up a position beyond the stream, from which they could check the enemy's fire, whilst the rest of the men were crossing. I myself with Mr. Claude Grenfell and a few more men protected the rear. However, before we got down into the open ground, we had four horses killed and two men wounded, Mr. Stracey and Mr. Munzberg. How it was that more men were not hit, I don't know, as the bullets were pinging about pretty freely. Everyone, I think, although I spread the men out as much as possible, had some narrow shaves, and my Sergeant-Major got two bullets through his gaiter, and one through his trousers between his legs, yet he was not touched.

Not knowing how many Kafirs we had to deal with, nor whether some of them would not try to get round in front of us, I now sent Mr. Blöcker on with half the troop and the wounded men to take up a position on ahead, on our line of retreat; whilst Mr. Grenfell and I with the rest of the men remained behind to keep the Kafirs from coming out of the broken ground behind us. However, having lost a few of their number, they showed no disposition to leave the shelter of the rocks, so we retired slowly and off-saddled on an open spot just beyond the hills.

The Kafirs with whom we had been engaged had been for the most part, I think, members of the native police force, as I had seen several myself who were wearing the white knickerbocker trousers of the police uniform. They all, too, seemed to be young men, and were shooting with Winchester rifles; and did not shoot badly either—that is for natives. It was most fortunate that neither of the two men hit was mortally wounded, as if they had been we should have found it very difficult to carry them. Mr. Stracey was shot through the knee, though fortunately the bone was not much shattered, so he not only did not lose his leg, but will eventually, the doctor promises, have as good a limb as ever. Mr. Munzberg, a young German, was hit in the small of the back, and had a wonderful escape, as the bullet struck a kind of chain belt he was wearing round his waist. It went through this, but being much flattened out lost its velocity, and only inflicted a deep flesh wound.

In some ways the Kafirs may be said to have had the best of this encounter, as we left them in possession of the field. However, whilst we lost no men, we left a few of our opponents ready for burial, and our retreat, although it was a retreat, was of the slowest and most orderly character. Our horses were simply a nuisance to us amongst the granite boulders, and we could have done much better without them. Indeed, I saw enough this day to assure me that all subsequent fighting in the Matopos would have to be done on foot.

During the firing old Mazhlabanyan had behaved with great coolness. At first, when we were driving the Kafirs from the rocks above the cattle kraal, he had remained below holding my horse, but after recrossing the stream, I told him to go on with Mr. Blöcker. Finding that I did not immediately follow, the old fellow seems to have got very nervous about my safety, as after asking Mr. Blöcker a great many times where his master was, he came back to look. However, old Jack will be comfortably settled on my Company's land when these troublous times are over, and when the rinderpest has died out, and fresh cattle can be brought into the country, his fidelity will not be forgotten. After an hour's rest we again saddled up, and made straight across country to Dawson's store, at the Umzingwani ford on the Tuli road, twenty-five miles from Bulawayo. Here we were able to obtain a stretcher on which to carry Mr. Stracey, Mr. Munzberg still being able to ride.

As there could now be no doubt that there were hostile Kafirs at no great distance, I advised Mr. Boyce, who was in charge of the store, to lock up everything and accompany us to Bulawayo, which he did.

We started at sundown, all of us taking it in turns to carry our wounded comrade, and reached the post station, twelve miles from Bulawayo, soon after midnight. Here we passed a wretched night in the mule stable, as we were all wet through, a soaking rain having come on about an hour previously, which lasted for the rest of the night.

I sent two men on at once to Bulawayo, asking that a cart and a doctor might be sent out for the wounded men in the morning. The cart was sent, but no doctor could be spared. However, by mid-day we reached Bulawayo, and the wounded men were soon made comfortable in the hospital.

CHAPTER XI

O'Connor's wonderful escape—The importance of the Native Question in Rhodesia.

In the course of conversation, during our journey to Bulawayo, Mr. Boyce, the manager of Mr. Dawson's store on the Umzingwani, told me that, on the night before our arrival there, a miner named O'Connor had reached the store in a dreadful condition, having been terribly beaten about the head by Kafirs, from whose tender mercies he had escaped on 24th March. This poor fellow had been sent in to the hospital on the morning of the day on which we readied the store, and as his escape was a most remarkable one, I will tell it as I heard it from the man's own lips.

O'Connor, it appears, was engaged in mining work together with two other miners named Ivers and Ottens, on a reef called the Celtic, situated some mile and a half from Edkins' store.

On the morning of Tuesday, 24th March, after their early cup of coffee, the three miners were discussing matters in general, and more particularly the fact that during the last few days thirteen of their boys had run away for no apparent reason, unless it were that they had gone off to take part in a beer drink at the neighbouring kraal of Gorshlwayo. About seven o'clock they had an early breakfast, and shortly afterwards Ottens went off to see the Native Commissioner, Mr. Bentley, who was living at the police camp not far from Edkins' store. Then Ivers went away to see how the work was progressing at one of the shafts on the Celtic reef, leaving O'Connor alone. He, after kneading a loaf of bread and placing it in the sun to rise, went into his hut, and sitting down on his bed, threw his hat on a chair beside him, and lit his pipe. He had been sitting smoking some few minutes, when he was suddenly startled by the loud and angry barking of Ottens' dogs, Captain and Snowball, just outside his hut. "The angry condition of the dogs was so unusual," said O'Connor, "that I give you my word I thought there was a lion in the camp." Jumping up, he ran to the door of the hut, only to find a Kafir standing just on one side of the entrance with a musket pointed towards him in his hands. "For an instant," said O'Connor, "I was paralysed, and retreated back into the hut, the door of which was immediately afterwards blocked by a crowd of Kafirs all armed with heavy knob-kerries. Then, seeing that they had come to murder me, I became mad, and rushed in amongst them. I succeeded in wresting two knob-kerries from them, and with these I fought desperately, always making my way towards the mouth of No. 1 shaft, which was something over 100 yards from my hut. I was repeatedly knocked down, and heavy blows were continually rained upon me, but, now on my knees, again on my feet, and sometimes rolling, I got to the mouth of the shaft with the remains of two broken sticks in my hands."

During this desperate struggle, O'Connor remembers hearing the Kafirs, who were attacking him with sticks, continually calling to the one with the gun, *u injani wena ai posa*—"why don't you shoot?"—and says that this man actually fired at him more than once, holding his gun at his hip, and always missing him. Just as he fell at the mouth of the shaft he was fired at for the last time. Then O'Connor rolled down the shaft "like a football," as he expressed it.

This was what is called an "incline shaft," going down for 136 feet at an angle of about 45 degrees. From the bottom of the incline shaft a tunnel had been driven into the reef 170 feet in length. Arrived at the bottom of the shaft, the hapless miner was at once attacked by his own boys—ten in number—who had been working in the tunnel. These devils fell upon him with hammers and drills, O'Connor defending himself as best he could with stones, and finally driving them all, as he thought, up the shaft.

After the terrible punishment he had received, which included thirteen scalp wounds—one of which had broken the outer table of the skull above the left temple—heavy blows with a hammer on each cheek-bone, and bruises and contusions all over the body, it may be wondered how O'Connor managed to retain his senses. But the fact remains that he did, and, thanks to a good old Irish head, still lives to tell the tale of the sufferings he endured, which, however, were not yet over by any means.

Believing that all his assailants had left the mine, he bethought him of a place of refuge, at a spot some half-way up the incline, where a vertical shaft had been cut into it. Here the shafts cut through some old workings, which formed a recess, into which O'Connor crept. Just as he was about to avail himself of this hiding-place, a Kafir, who, during the last fight, must have run back down the tunnel, rushed past him up the incline shaft. This man must have told the rest of the would-be murderers where the white man was hiding, and they did not leave him long in peace, for shortly afterwards several Kafirs came down the shaft, some with lighted candles, and four with guns. Two of these men carried muzzle-loaders, whilst the other two were armed with breech-loading rifles. The latter O'Connor recognised by the light of the candles as "boys" who had been working for himself and his companions. Their names were "Candle," and "Makupeni," and they had been in the employ of the miners for nearly eighteen months, and as they were both good shots they had often been sent out with the only two rifles in camp to shoot game for the sake of the meat. Latterly, so implicit was the trust reposed in them by their masters that the rifles had been left entirely in their possession, but now they were among the first to volunteer their services to put an end to their employer in his sore extremity.

When O'Connor recognised his own trusted servants amongst his assailants he spoke to them, asking what harm he had done them, and why they wished to kill him, to which they answered, "We're going to kill you and all the white men in the country." However, although their would-be victim could see them, they could not see him, and seemed afraid to advance their heads into the recess where he lay—as they would have had to do in order to shoot him—for fear probably of being hit with a lump of quartz, which, even though it had been gold-bearing, might have made a nasty mark on their skulls.

During this time the Kafirs at the top of the shaft kept continually calling out to those below with the guns, "What are you doing; why don't you shoot the white man?" but still the cowardly murderers lacked the courage to creep into the recess and finish their victim. Suddenly there was a commotion at the top of the mine, and shouts of "*Amakiwa, Amakiwa*"—"white men, white men,"—and the four men with guns, together with those who were holding the candles, ran up the shaft, leaving the white man once more alone.

This cry of "white men" must have been a false alarm, as all the Europeans at the neighbouring police station and at Edkins' store were murdered without offering any resistance, having been taken completely by surprise. However, it gave O'Connor a few minutes' respite and enabled him to gain the shelter of another hiding-place where he thought he would be more secure from the guns of his enemies. This was a spot about half-way down the tunnel, where some loose ground had fallen in and rendered a certain amount of timbering necessary. Here, behind some boulders, O'Connor took refuge, but his enemies having recovered from their alarm and again come down the mine with candles, soon found out, probably by his tracks, where he had hidden. And now the fruits of education were brought to the aid of native devilry to compass his destruction, for some of his own boys threw two charges of dynamite with short fuses into his hiding-place. Then the Kafirs all ran out of the mine, nor did they return, thinking probably that they had blown the white man to pieces. Having only seen the wonderful effects of dynamite when employed for blasting rocks and exploded at the bottom of a hole drilled deep into solid stone, they did not know that a loose charge exploded on the surface of the ground would have comparatively little effect. However O'Connor, except that he was nearly suffocated by the fumes of the dynamite, remained uninjured in the shelter of the boulder behind which he lay. Shortly after the explosions he thinks he must have become unconscious and remained so for many hours. When he came to himself, hearing no sound that betokened the proximity of his enemies, he crept from his hiding-place, and made his way to the mouth of the tunnel, and then ascended the incline shaft.

It was a bright moonlight night, and from the position of the moon he judged that it was about eight o'clock. A glance showed him that his camp had been destroyed and all the huts burnt down, but he could see no Kafirs about. He then made his way to an old mining camp about one and a half miles distant, called Nelson's Camp, from which he could look down on the police station, which he still hoped to find in the possession of white men. In the brilliant moonlight he saw the huts still standing; but there was no life or movement perceptible, and no lights or fires burning, and he therefore felt assured that the whites had either been murdered or left the camp. Then he went down to the stream which ran between the police camp and Edkins' store, and as he expressed it "wallowed in it like a pig."

After having quenched his thirst and washed the blood from his wounds he carefully approached Edkins' store, which he found had been burnt down, whilst the smell of murder was in the air, and the deathlike stillness was unbroken by even the bark of a dog. Then, indeed, the unfortunate man recognised to the full all the terrors of his dreadful position. All hope of succour from his immediate neighbours was gone; they had all been killed or forced to flee for their lives, whilst he stood alone amongst a nation of murderers. But his stout Irish heart never quailed, and weakened as he was by loss of blood he set out to the north-west, towards Bulawayo.

Leaving the Matabele kraal of Gorshlwayo as far as possible to his left, he at length reached the Insiza river some four miles from the camp he had left. By this time he was completely exhausted, and lay down in the reeds on the river's edge. Here he remained hidden all that night and the next day. On Wednesday night he again tried to get on towards Bulawayo, but by this time he was becoming more or less light headed, and unable to steer a good course, nor does he know exactly where he wandered. He lay hidden by day, and only moved at night, nor was it until Saturday night at about eleven o'clock, more than 110 hours after he had been attacked by the Kafirs, that he found his way to Mr. Dawson's store on the Umzingwani river.

All this time he had had no food. On approaching the store he found two men standing outside—Messrs. Schultz and Judge—whom he knew well, but who had looked upon him as dead. As he approached them in the moonlight, hatless, his face and head covered with wounds, he thinks they took him for an apparition come to call the white men to avenge his murder, for they fell back as if they had seen a ghost, and he said, "What, don't you know me—Joe O'Connor?" Then as they rushed up and seized him by the hands, he fell down senseless and they carried him to the store. Mr. Judge at once rode in to Bulawayo to try and get a doctor to come out and dress his wounds.

The following morning he was sent on by waggon from the Umzingwani store, and was met half-way by Mr. Lyons, the dispenser at the hospital, who, as no doctor could be spared, had volunteered to go to the wounded man's assistance. On Sunday afternoon he reached Bulawayo, where he lay a long time in hospital. All that medical skill and kindly nursing could do for him was done, and he eventually recovered from the dreadful injuries he had received; but the terrible experiences he has passed through have turned his hair partially grey, he being a young man of only twenty-six years of age. He has, too, to mourn the loss of his brother and cousin, both of whom were murdered by the Matabele.

I was present in Colonel Napier's office, when a Zambesi boy, who had been working for them, gave evidence as to the manner in which they had been killed. He said, "I saw them killed with my eyes; they were killed by their own boys. O'Connor's brother was drawn up from the bottom of the shaft in which he was working by two men, who held the windlass still when his head came above the level of the ground, whilst others beat his brains out with knob-kerries; the other man—O'Connor's cousin—was stabbed to death with assegais." I have made many inquiries concerning O'Connor, and find that he bears the character of being a hard-working man, whilst he was known to the Native Commissioner of his district as one who always got on well with the natives.

From some remarks which he made, however, subsequent to

57

the relation of his trying experiences, I judge that he has now abandoned any latent intention he may ever have had of becoming a member of the Aborigines Protection Society, nor do I think that the funds of that admirable institution are likely to be added to by any donation from Mr. O'Connor.

The worst feature in the foregoing history of the attempted murder of O'Connor and the actual murder and mutilation of his two companions, Messrs. Ivers and Ottens, is the participation in the crimes by two trusted servants who had been in the employ of the murdered men for so long a time as eighteen months, since the very fact that these boys had worked for so many months for the same white men shows conclusively that they must have been kindly treated by them, for no Kafir will remain long in the service of a master who ill-treats him.

Now I am not so unreasonable as to think that the natures of the Matabele natives ought to be judged of by the unamiable qualities shown by two individuals; indeed I know that as a set-off, even during the present rebellion, the lives of some few white men have been saved by the fidelity of natives in their employ. But unfortunately the evil deeds get more noised abroad, and they add to the bitterness of the exasperation felt by the whites against the blacks; for it seems inevitable that during an insurrection such as the present, the average nature of the native will be judged of by the average European on the spot, according to the worst atrocities that have been committed, and such an instance of treachery as I have related will harden the kindest heart and produce a feeling of distrust in the whole race that can never be eradicated from the mind. In many, too—and these by no means the most brutal or worst educated in the community—such acts, coupled with the indiscriminate murder of women and children, produce a conviction that beings who are capable of such deeds, who can lick your hand and fawn upon you for eighteen months and then one day turn and murder you, and afterwards perhaps mutilate your senseless corpse, are not men and brothers, but monsters in human shape, that ought to be shot down mercilessly like wild dogs or hyaenas, until they are reduced to a state of abject submission to the white man's rule.

In time, however, let us hope that the cruel deeds of the last few months will be forgotten, and the fierce passions they have evoked on both sides gradually smoulder out and die from the lack of fresh fuel. Henceforth it will, I trust, be recognised by the authorities that the native question in Rhodesia is one of the very first importance, and that it is also one which demands the most careful handling in order to ensure the future peace and prosperity of the country. When this rebellion is quelled and the natives have once more submitted themselves to the white man's rule, they must know exactly the terms on which their submission has been accepted; and they must also understand precisely what will be required of them in the shape of hut-tax, labour, etc. Then if they are treated kindly and justly, as well as firmly, they ought not to have any valid reason for again rebelling against the government of their white conquerors; but lest they should ever be inclined to make such an attempt without any valid reason, they must now be so thoroughly and completely disarmed as to render any such action futile.

CHAPTER XII

Laager formed at Bulawayo—Matabele scare—Colonel Spreckley's valuable services—Meet Mr. Jackson—Disarmament of native police—Account of the insurrection—Mr. Grey's narrow escape—Returns to Bulawayo to give warning of the rising— Fortunate escape of a hunting party—Wholesale murders—Grey's Scouts.

On our return to Bulawayo, we found that a very strong laager had been formed in the large square round the Market Buildings. Within this laager the whole population of the town, with few exceptions, slept every night; the women and children within the buildings, whilst the men manned the waggons in readiness to resist any sudden attack.

The Bulawayo laager was probably the strongest ever constructed in South Africa, and the whole Matabele nation, I think, would never have taken it by assault. But if 2000 of them, or even a smaller number, had made a night attack upon the town before the laager had been formed, I think it more than probable that the entire white population would have been massacred. It appears that there was a terrible scare on the very night on which I had left the town for Essexvale, viz. Wednesday, 25th March. This scare was absolutely groundless and seems to have been caused by a drunken man galloping about calling out "The Matabele are here; the Matabele are here."

My wife was resting in Mrs. Spreckley's house at the time, being much fatigued by her long ride in the hot sun from Essexvale. However, she and her kind hostess, as well as all the other ladies living on the suburban stands, were hurried over to the new Club-house, nearly a mile distant, in the centre of the town. Here the large number of women and children in Bulawayo, many of them hastily summoned from their beds, and most of them terribly frightened, passed a miserable night all huddled up together, but getting neither rest nor sleep, as they were constantly kept on the *qui vive* by fresh rumours, all equally groundless, as happily at this time there was no force of hostile natives within twenty miles of Bulawayo. On the following day the laager was formed, and by the time I got back to town Colonel Spreckley and Mr. Scott (the town major) had, after an immense amount of hard work, got everything into good order.

These two gentlemen deserve the utmost credit not only for getting the laager into good order, but also for keeping it in that condition for the next two months. Major Scott was indefatigable in looking after the sanitary arrangements, whilst Colonel Spreckley, by his genial good nature, backed by great common sense and strength of character, kept all the various human elements shut up in that confined space not only in good order but in good humour. Nobody in Bulawayo, I think, could have performed the very difficult duties required from the chief officer in charge of the laager so ably as Colonel Spreckley during the first two months of the insurrection, and his conduct was all the more admirable because he was carrying out a very arduous and harassing duty against his inclination, or rather burning desire, to be out of town at the head of a patrol doing active work against the insurgents.

Soon after my arrival in town, I was delighted to meet the Native Commissioner of my district, Mr. Jackson, whom I had never thought to see again. He and his white companions had received warning of the rising from his sub-inspector, and were also cautioned lest there should be a plot on foot for their murder by the native police. At this time, however, the ninety men they had with them, each of whom was armed with a Winchester rifle and seventy rounds of ammunition, did not know that the rebellion had commenced, and they managed to bring them all in to Bulawayo without any trouble, where they were at once disarmed.

Now by this time it had become evident that the insurrection had become general throughout the length and breadth of Matabeleland, and I will give a brief account of what had happened so far as is known.

I have already related that Mr. Cumming and another man

brought the first news of the murders of white men in the Insiza district to Bulawayo. On reaching Lee's store, twenty-four miles from the town, they found that their horses were completely knocked up, and they could thus only have proceeded on foot, had not Mr. Claude Grenfell just happened to be passing the store with a cart and horses on his way from Gwelo to Bulawayo.

On hearing the alarming news Mr. Grenfell took Mr. Cumming on with him at once to headquarters, his companion, Mr. Edmunds, giving up his seat to him, and walking. Before reaching Lee's store, Mr. Grenfell had met Mr. George Grey, travelling alone in a Cape cart with a coloured boy, on his way to inspect some of his mining properties near the Tchangani river, and when the news of the murders in the Insiza district became known, much anxiety was naturally felt concerning Mr. Grey's safety, as well as that of all other Europeans who were living at a distance from Bulawayo in mining camps or on lonely farms.

Early on Thursday morning, however, Mr. Grey returned to town, having escaped death by the merest chance, as he must only just have escaped falling into the hands of more than one party of murderers.

On reaching the Pongo store some twelve miles from the Tchangani river, Mr. Grey had found all the outhouses just burnt. The store itself seemed to have been looted, but was not at this time burnt down. No trace of the owners could be found, but the ground was thickly covered with the naked footprints of natives, and, more ominous still, a large pool of blood was seen in the road in front of the store. We now know that at this time the recently-murdered corpses of three white men were lying, two of them close to the store, and the third on the top of a rise a short distance away. I was present some six weeks later when the bodies were discovered and buried. The unfortunate men must have been suddenly attacked with knob-kerries and axes, as their skulls had all been smashed in. In this instance the clothes were not removed from the bodies.

This was the first intimation that Mr. Grey got that mischief was brewing in the country. Soon after passing the Pongo store, he turned off the main road and went down to the Eagle mine some four miles distant. This he found had been only recently deserted by the Europeans employed there, and with his suspicions now fully aroused he returned at once to the main road, and made for the Tchangani store. On his way there he came across a white man on the roadside, who had escaped from a party of Kafirs, after receiving two severe battle-axe wounds, one of which had cut his face open from nose to ear, whilst the second had cut his arm to the bone and severed all the tendons of the wrist. This man had been working

61

with two companions on a farm in the neighbourhood, when on the previous day—Tuesday, 24th March—they had been suddenly and without any warning attacked by a party of Kafirs armed with knob-kerries and battle-axes. Although two of them were wounded, they managed to retreat to their hut, on which the natives, probably thinking that they had firearms there, retired.

After sundown the three white men left their hut, intending to make for Stewart's store at the Tekwe. Unfortunately it was a bright moonlight night, and the Kafirs must have been watching them, as they immediately followed, and chased them into a maize field, through which they hunted them. During this pursuit the white men became separated. One of them reached Mr. Stewart's store in safety; the second, Mr. Scott by name, found his way to the road near the Pongo store and was picked up and taken to the Tchangani by Mr. Grey; but the third must have fallen into the hands of the Kafirs, and, of course, been murdered, as he has never again been heard of from that day to this. The man who made his way to the Tekwe had received a severe blow on the head with a knob-kerry.

Arrived at the Tchangani, Mr. Grey found seventeen Europeans in laager there, amongst them the men from the Eagle mine, who had been pursued on their way to the store. The natives, however, were afraid to come to close quarters with them as they were armed with rifles, and at this time the rebels in this district had not yet dug up the firearms which they had buried after the war of 1893, and were therefore only able to kill white men whom they could take by surprise with knob-kerries and axes.

Now fully realising the very serious aspect of affairs, Mr. Grey, instead of remaining in the shelter of the laager, most pluckily determined to return to Bulawayo at once, making use of the post mules along the road, in order to warn all people with as little delay as possible that the Kafirs had risen.

A few hours after he had left the Tchangani, the garrison of the laager was augmented by the arrival of Messrs. Farquhar, Weston Jarvis, Currie, and Mr. Egerton (M.P. for Knutsford) and his son. These gentlemen had been on a hunting trip to the Sebakwe river, and were returning to Bulawayo only just in time, as had they remained out in the veld any longer they would certainly have been murdered, for although they would doubtless have given a very good account of themselves, yet a few men cannot fight an army.

On the following day—Thursday, 26th March—two small patrols were organised and sent out from the Tchangani, one of which, consisting of Mr. Mowbray Farquhar and two companions, visited a mine where a white man was known to have been working a day or two previously, whilst the other, consisting of Mr. Robinson and two others, visited the Pongo store and the Eagle mine. A careful search was made by the latter all round the store, and the bodies of two out of the three men who had been murdered there two days previously were discovered and covered with blankets, which were still in their places when we buried the remains some six weeks later. The third corpse they did not find, as it was lying some distance from the store.

Mr. Farquhar and his two companions visited Comployer's camp, and found the unfortunate man lying murdered in front of the door of his hut. They tried to get on to Gracey's camp, but could not do so for fear of being surrounded and cut off by the Kafirs, who were all in their kraals watching them. It has since been ascertained that Gracey was murdered on the same day as Comployer.

On returning to the laager, they found that a mule-waggon had been sent from Gwelo, with orders from the officer commanding there that all Europeans should come in as quickly as possible to assist in the defence of the town against the Kafirs.

Leaving the Tchangani at 5 P.M. on Thursday evening, the whole party reached Gwelo in safety on Friday morning at half-past eight. In the meantime Mr. Grey, travelling at express speed with relays of coach mules, reached Bulawayo early on Thursday morning. On passing the Tekwe store, he found assembled there Mr. Stewart, five other white men, and two women, who were endeavouring to fortify a hut. Promising them speedy relief, Mr. Grey hurried on to warn others of their danger, but beyond the Tekwe he found that the occupants of the roadside hotels and post stations had already taken the alarm and made their way to Bulawayo.

On Thursday, 26th March, Mr. Grey got together twenty-three good men, and started back for the Tekwe that same evening. These men formed the nucleus of a force which has done splendid service in the suppression of the present rebellion, under the name of Grey's Scouts. They were a picked body of men, and neither their name nor their brave deeds will ever be forgotten in Rhodesia, whilst I think we all regard Captain Grey as one of the finest specimens of an Englishman in the country—quiet, self-contained and unassuming, but at the same time, brave, capable, and energetic.

CHAPTER XIII

Captain Grey's timely arrival at Tekwe store—Colonel Napier's column arrives at Tekwe—Murder of Wood—Salisbury coach chased by Kafirs—Forty-three persons rescued by patrols—Account of Captain Pittendrigh's rescue party—Severe fighting—Massacre of whites at Inyati—Escape of Madden—Defence of Campbell's store—Relief of Captain Pittendrigh's party—Fight their way back to Bulawayo—Courage and skill of the Africander Corps—Gallant conduct of Henderson in bringing in a wounded comrade.

Captain Grey and his men reached Tekwe store about 2 P.M. on Friday, 27th March, and were only just in time to save the beleaguered whites there; for shortly before their arrival a party of Kafirs had driven off all Mr. Stewart's cattle, and killed a horse belonging to him. At the same time they had been kind enough to send him a message by the boy who had been looking after his cattle, to the effect that they meant to return and kill all the white people that night. However, they made no attack when they found that Mr. Stewart's small party had been reinforced by some twenty well-armed men.

On the following day Colonel Napier's column, which had left Bulawayo on the previous Tuesday, and had been patrolling the country in the direction of the Insiza river, came across country to the Tekwe store. Besides saving the lives of Mr. Stewart and his party, the presence of Colonel Napier and Captain Grey with the men under their command on the Salisbury road at this juncture was the means of saving the lives of nine other white men and two coloured boys, the latter being the drivers, whilst the former were the guard, sent down with the last mail coach from Gwelo.

This coach left Gwelo on Saturday, 28th March, arriving at the Tchangani early the following morning. Here they found the body of a white man, just murdered and stripped stark naked, lying in the middle of the road in front of the store. This was the body of a prospector named Wood in the employ of Willoughby's Consolidated Company, who had come across country from the Selukwe district. Unfortunately he arrived at the Tchangani store on the day after it had been evacuated by the white men who had been in laager there, and he probably found it in possession of the Kafirs, who of course murdered him.

On seeing this ghastly sign of the times, the men in charge of the coach determined to drive on at once without outspanning, and soon observed Kafirs running in the bush and keeping pace with the coach on both sides of the road. These natives, however, seemed to have no guns, and by continually firing at them the white men kept them from coming to close quarters. After a time the Pongo store was reached, but no halt was possible owing to the threatening attitude of the Kafirs. The mules were now almost done up, and could only get the coach along at a walk, but still the Kafirs hung on either flank, as thirsty for blood as a pack of wild dogs awaiting the moment to rush in upon a wounded buffalo.

Some three miles farther on the poor mules came to a standstill, and the white men were forced to leave the coach, and keep on on foot along the road, the Kafirs ever keeping pace with them in the bush on either side, and doubtless only waiting for the darkness of night to enable them to rush in and kill them with as little loss to themselves as possible. But just at dusk they reached Colonel Napier's column in a very exhausted condition.

Some six weeks later, when we found the bodies of the men who had been murdered at the Pongo store, we also found some three miles on this side of the store the coach which had been captured by the Kafirs. A linch-pin had been removed, and one of the wheels taken off. The pole had also been sawn in two, and all the mail bags cut open, their contents being scattered all over the ground. The poor mules had all been stabbed to death with assegais, and lay in a heap together, still in their harness.

Altogether the combined patrols under Colonel Napier and Captain Grey collected and brought back with them to Bulawayo forty-three persons, including two women and a child, many, if not all of whom, had they not been thus timely rescued, would have fallen victims to the Kafirs. The names of the poor fellows murdered at the Pongo store are Frederick Hurlstone, J. Beddington, and H. Zeeburg. At midnight on the Saturday before my return to Bulawayo from the Matopo Hills, Captain Pittendrigh of the Africander Corps had left town with a small party only eleven strong, in order first of all to reinforce for the night a small party at Jenkins' store, and then push on some thirty miles farther, in order to relieve Mr. Graham, the native commissioner at Inyati, who with Sub-inspector Hanley and five other white men was believed to be in laager there. There were many volunteers for this expedition, but as the Government was unable to furnish them with horses or rifles, only those could go who were in a position to equip themselves.

Jenkins' store was reached at half-past two on Sunday morning. Here ten men were found in laager, including a younger brother of Mr. Graham the native commissioner. He, with an assistant native commissioner, Mr. Carter, a cart and four mules and two spare horses, had been on his way to Inyati to bring his brother, who was suffering from an attack of fever, into Bulawayo. As an attack had been expected on the store that night, the thatch had been removed from the roof, and a rough fence put up round the building. However, no attack was made, and at 5 A.M. the whole party, now consisting of nineteen men, with the two spare horses and the cart and mules driven by two colonial boys, set out for the Bembisi,[8] twenty-three miles distant.

For the subsequent experiences of this small rescue party, I am indebted to the kindness of Mr. Moodie Thomson, the able editor of the *Matabele Times*, who accompanied Captain Pittendrigh and wrote an account of the expedition. This he has kindly placed at my disposal, and I will take up his narrative at the point when the start was made from Jenkins' store early on Sunday morning. It proceeds as follows:—

"We were now in a very different country from the open veld of the earlier ride. Kopjes were close on either hand, the road was of the roughest, and progress with the mule cart consequently slow. The word was constantly given for a good look-out on either hand, but for over an hour not a man or a woman was seen, though tracks crossing the path were met with at frequent intervals. The kopjes in which we had expected to have trouble were passed, and the more open undulating ground at the Elibaini Hills reached. Progress was slow along this portion of the ascending road, and near the highest point skirting the base of the most prominent hill a strip of bush was entered. No sooner had we made our way into this cover than a shot was heard from the hill-slope. In a second it was seen to be occupied by half a dozen or so natives, who sent in another and another shot. It was impossible to make a sufficient reply from our position, and a dash was made from the road through the strip of bush to the open slope of the hill. One or more of the natives was shot as they retreated over the crest, and a hot pursuit was made.

"When those of our party who were foremost reached the top of the hill they found that affairs had assumed a different aspect from repulsing a handful of stray rebels. A glance was sufficient. The natives were there in a dense mass, throwing out skirmishers on either flank to surround us, one body proceeding rapidly around the lower slope to cut us off. Our advance men fell back, and the natives began to show themselves in the open. Firing became hot on both sides, but taking advantage of the strip of bush we were able at first to inflict considerable damage. The natives to the number of

_____

[8] Correct name "Impembisi."

66

about three hundred were soon in the bush also, advancing in excellent open order and becoming formidable. Several rushed in to close quarters, and Captain Pittendrigh, who had dismounted, lost his horse. Before he could get one of the spare horses, a native armed with an assegai grappled him, and a hand-to-hand struggle took place. The native, however, was thrown off and shot, and the captain escaped with some slits in his coat. At the same moment Thomas Haden, who had been fighting most determinedly in the front, received a shot on the upper part of his bandoleer, which exploded three of his cartridges, one bullet passing through his shoulder and with a ricochet entering his neck and passing through his cheek. Immediately after Mr. S. Carter received a bullet through his ankle. The natives began to approach closer in their attack despite our heavy fire, and as they were gradually surrounding us, it was found advisable, encumbered as we were with two wounded men, to retire to the road.

"With a rush through without further casualty on our side, we regained the road and found that one of our boys at the mule waggon had vanished, and the other was getting away on one of the spare horses. The mules and cart had therefore to be abandoned, and at a good pace we cut across through the lower bush over rough ground, avoiding the curve round the hills, to where the road bent round on the open.

"Here half-sections were again formed, the wounded in front, and a quick canter gave us a good start. Looking back, the natives could be seen in hot pursuit, and it was thought they might be able to reach one of the kopjes ahead whose base we must skirt. Suggestions as to taking up a position on a kopje were untenable on account of the wounded men, and there was nothing for it but to get over the seventeen miles to the Bembisi as rapidly as possible. Again and again the natives seemed to be closing up on us, and sundry indications were closely scrutinised as to the presence of hostile forces ahead. The ride was made heavier by two of the ponies becoming done up. It was an anxious time, as the road ran through the hollows, but the clearness of the day gave abundant scope for noting the absence of an enemy ahead and the black mass falling farther astern.

"About eleven o'clock Campbell's store came in sight, and we crossed the Bembisi with gladdened spirits. These, however, were immediately damped. The news was awaiting us that the party at Inyati, eight miles farther on, which we had been sent to relieve, had been massacred. The intelligence was given by Patrick Madden, miner, who, and a native in his employ, were the sole survivors. This man told with most circumstantial and convincing detail how

67

Native Commissioner Graham, Inspector Hanley, George Hurford, George Case, and S. H. Corke had fought against ever-increasing odds on the evening of the previous Friday—this was now Sunday— until they were killed. Madden, another miner named Tim Donovan, and a colonial native had made for the hills, and after two days' hiding Madden and the native had reached this store.

"The narrative, it may be said, has been fully corroborated since from other sources, with the addition that Donovan was also pursued and killed. Further, there was the news that an impi of from 1200 to 1500 lay at Inyati. It was hard to decide to abandon the projected relief, but the facts were obvious that with an impi ahead, and with a body of 300 at least following us, and very shortly seen to be in the bush across the river, there was nothing for it but to take up the strongest position possible.

"Across the river the natives could be seen in the bush, and were we even to venture with our wounded to go by the road, we were at their mercy. At the store we had found Mr. Campbell with a waggon and oxen, hourly expecting to be pounced upon, and it was resolved to set to work to fortify the store. The verandah thatch was cut away, passages were pierced so that there might be free communication through the large building, and loopholes were cut through the brick walls in every direction. In addition, a case of dynamite was found in the store which was utilised to lay mines with ingeniously-contrived short fuse, and to make a score or so hand grenades with a radius of about fifteen yards that could be thrown at assailants. The large stock of meal in sacks was put into service to block windows, and then we were certain that, having about 2000 rounds of ammunition, we could hold out well against a night attack.

"It was necessary, however, to send word to Bulawayo of our condition and the intelligence we had received, and to obtain reinforcements which we calculated could arrive in time to fall on the rear of the natives attacking us at daybreak. Messrs. Fincham and Mostert were mounted on the best horses as despatch-riders. A diversion was made by the whole party crossing the river as if returning by the road we had come, and as we saw the natives moving to meet us the despatch-riders went off at an angle by the Queen's Reef road, passing the Shiloh Hills. The rest of the day was spent in completing our fortifications. Strong guard was set at night, and we waited eagerly for the natives to come for the reception prepared for them. The wounded had been bandaged and made as comfortable as possible; the horses were stabled in the bar and store-room, and every man was at his post carefully looking out.

"About four on Monday morning the silence was broken by

the sound of firing, and speculation was rife as to its meaning. It came nearer and nearer, and it was soon decided that this was the reinforcing party fighting its way through the natives lying in wait for us. There was silence for a time, broken again by the cracking of shots, and with the dim dawn we could see a body of men emerging from the thick bush. As they came nearer it became plain that they were white men, and we left the store to send up a cheer to let them know we were still safe. As day came more brightly, in they rode across the open veld, and with answering cheers dashed up the river-bank to the store. They were thirty strong, fifteen from the Africander Corps under Commandant Van Rensburg and Captain Van Niekerk, and the remainder from various Rhodesia Horse Volunteers, troops or volunteers under Captain Macfarlane. They had ridden the whole night through, with only a brief halt at the Queen's Reef, and in our vicinity had been met in the black darkness of the bush with a volley fired not twenty yards off. They had replied, and a running fire had been kept up for about half an hour. No one in the party had been wounded, but two men in the advanced guard, Messrs. Celliers and Henderson, were missing. Several dead bodies of natives seen in the bush testified later to the effect of the replying fire.

"About nine o'clock it was decided that the whole party should return by the Queen's Reef road and ride straight for Bulawayo. A start was made with strong flanking parties, Captain Pittendrigh's men being placed in the rear-guard after the waggon containing our two wounded. Cautious progress was made through the bush where the natives had been assembled and where spoor was thick, but without a sign of life visible. The Queen's Reef was reached about eleven o'clock, and at noon the column got again into dangerous bush.

"Nothing occurred, however, until the Shiloh Hills were reached, when on the spur of a kopje and in the bush below natives were seen. They opened fire, but their aim was high. Those of them who were venturous enough to make the attack were summarily disposed of—nothing being more convincing of the perfection of the fire of our party than the manner in which seven, eight, or nine shots would simultaneously bowl over a native who exposed himself even for a moment. On our side a horse—one of Mr. Zeederberg's finest animals—was shot through the lower part of the stomach, and subsequently died from the effects of the wound. This was our only casualty, and on the other side there must have been a loss of a dozen men at least. The fire was fairly hot while it lasted, but a party of about fifty was too strong for the natives, even though they may

69

have been several hundred. They had to depend upon their firing, as close quarters against such marksmen was almost an impossibility.

"The Kotki river was reached after a heavy detour through the bush to avoid giving the natives around us too much opportunity at the kopjes, and a halt made for an hour. Just before reaching there a herd of native cattle had been met and seized, and heifer steaks cooked on ramrods proved refreshing after our twenty-mile ride at ox-waggon pace. Then on again, the remaining fifteen miles without further attack, until in the darkness a cheer from the pickets about ten o'clock announced that Bulawayo had been reached.

"The wounded were conveyed to the hospital, and tired horses and men had the satisfaction of seeking what comfort was available in a laagered town. The men in Captain Pittendrigh's party who had this experience of Matabele skirmishing, were, with one or two additional exceptions, members of the Africander Corps. It is useful to testify that their courage, their determination, their skill with the rifle, and their expert employment of every ruse in such fighting as we had at the Elibaini Hills, command the highest admiration. We were in a fairly tight place, as may be judged when hand-to-hand fighting was possible, and we were only nineteen against several hundreds; but the pluck and brilliant dash displayed, as well as the good comradeship throughout, are convincing that in a like or even a stiffer affray one could neither wish nor hope to have better men than these. It remains to be said that the two missing men came in to Bulawayo on Wednesday morning. Celliers had had his horse shot under him and was himself badly wounded in the knee. With that consideration which is akin to heroism Henderson placed him on his horse, and walking beside him for three days they had hidden amongst the hills, making their way through most dangerous country. Henderson tended his wounded comrade in every way possible, and succeeded in keeping clear of natives, though at times they passed in unpleasantly close proximity. Such conduct is something more than typical of the men who are bent upon holding Matabeleland."

The devoted courage shown by Mr. Henderson in giving up his own horse to his wounded comrade and sticking to him for three days, during the whole of which time they were surrounded by the enemy, and in continual danger of being discovered, appears to me to be as brave a deed as has yet been chronicled in the annals of Rhodesia. I commend it to the notice of Mr. Labouchere, as I feel sure that it will be quite a revelation to him to learn that there exists amongst the "Buccaneers"[9] at least one man who has shown himself

---

[9] "Buccaneers" is the term of endearment commonly bestowed upon the Englishmen in Rhodesia by the editor of Truth.

capable of a self-sacrificing and generous act. Yet all Mr. Henderson's gallantry could not save his comrade's life, as Mr. Celliers eventually died from the effects of the amputation of his leg, owing principally to the length of time which had elapsed between the time when he was wounded and the date when the operation was performed.

CHAPTER XIV

Mr. Dawson's patrol—The last coach on the Tuli road—I take a patrol down the Mangwe road—Interview at "Fig Tree" with Makalaka Induna—Proceed to Shashani—Meet a shooting party—Death of Captain Lumsden—I ride on by myself to Mangwe—Hearty reception—Ravages of the rinderpest—Extraordinary absence of vultures.

Besides the patrols of which I have already spoken that were sent out from Bulawayo during the first days of the insurrection, I must not forget that which was taken down to the Gwanda district by Mr. James Dawson. Mr. Dawson, who has lived amongst the natives of Matabeleland for many years, and both speaks their language and understands their character well, could not believe that a general rising throughout the country was possible, and even after hearing of the murders in the Insiza and Filibusi districts, and my own report as to what had taken place on Essexvale, imagined that the disturbance was only local. However, in order to assure himself of the true position of affairs, he got together some ten or twelve men, and leaving Bulawayo with them on Wednesday night, 25th March, proceeded down the Tuli road to his own store at "Amanzi minyama," situated in the Gwanda district, and distant about seventy-five miles from Bulawayo.

On his way there he found everything perfectly quiet along the road, all the wayside stores being still in the occupation of their owners, none of whom had heard anything about the native rising— a state of things which of course confirmed Mr. Dawson in his scepticism.

On the return journey, however, shortly before reaching Spiro's store, which is distant thirty-seven miles from Bulawayo, the fresh tracks of numbers of natives—men, women, and children—as

71

well as of cattle, goats, and sheep, were noticed crossing the road. These were doubtless the trails made by the Matabele from the Filibusi district, who were making their way to the Matopo Hills, and at once aroused suspicion.

Spiro's store was reached on Sunday, a few hours after I had left it the same morning on my way into the hills. Here Mr. Dawson found no one, for after my departure the boys who had been looking after the coach mules became frightened and took them in to Bulawayo, leaving the cattle behind; and these were still in the kraal, with no one to tend them, when Mr. Dawson passed. Not quite liking the look of things, the patrol went on beyond the store, and slept some four miles away from it.

On the following morning early they reached the wayside hotel at the Umzingwani river, which we had left at sundown on the evening before. Here in one of the huts were found the blood-stained shirt of Mr. Munzberg, and also a sock soaked with blood that had been taken from Mr. Stracey. During Monday Mr. Dawson and his men remained at the Umzingwani, but sent messengers to Bulawayo to obtain news as to what was going on.

Late that evening an answer was received requesting him to come on to town at once, as the Kafirs were reported to be massing in the neighbourhood. Before this there had been several alarms, and it was believed that natives were on the watch round about the store. Thus when the start was made for Bulawayo, the lights were left burning, in order to make the Kafirs believe that some of the party were still in the house. Arrived at the river some 600 yards distant from the store, Mr. Dawson rode back alone to reconnoitre, but hearing natives talking, retired and rejoined his men.

Early on Tuesday morning Inspector Southey was met with a small force at the head of the pass leading down to the Umzingwani. He had been sent out to escort the coach to Bulawayo, which was now some time overdue from Tuli. However, as Mr. Dawson had heard nothing of this coach, it was thought that it must have turned back; so Inspector Southey, who had been ordered not to descend the pass, returned to town, where shortly after his arrival the coach turned up too without an escort.

This was the last coach that ran on the Tuli road, and it seems to have been missed by the natives by a miracle, as they had broken into the Umzingwani store and gone away again in the interval between the time of its arrival there and Mr. Dawson's departure.

This coach reached Bulawayo on the morning of Tuesday, 31st March, and on the same day—the day after my own return from the Matopos—I was asked to take a patrol of twenty-five men down the Mangwe road, in order to ascertain if it was still clear, as a coach

72

loaded with rifles and ammunition and ten waggon-loads of provisions were on their way up.

We left town about 2 P.M., each man carrying three days' rations with him, and reaching Mabukitwani, twenty miles distant from Bulawayo, the same night, arrived at "Fig Tree" by noon the following day, where we found a store and mule stable in charge of Mr. Elliott.

The people living in the neighbourhood are nearly all of Makalaka descent, and have taken no part in the present insurrection. At the time of my visit they were in a great state of alarm, and the greater part of them had left their villages and fled into the hills, fearing lest the white men should visit the sins of the insurgents upon them. I therefore sent one of Mr. Elliott's boys to call the principal Induna to come and see me. With this man, an intelligent-looking Makalaka named Jackal, who bears a striking resemblance to the chief Khama, I had a long interview, and finally persuaded him to send messengers to the refugees ordering them to return to their kraals. Jackal assured me that the first news of the rebellion was brought to him by the son of Umfaizella (the brother of Lo Bengula, who with Umlugulu and others is responsible for the murders at Edkins' store), who was sent by his father to incite some of the Makalaka to revolt. When he found that Jackal's people did not seem very anxious to assist the Matabele in their attempt to regain their independence, he said to him, "You say that your people don't want to fight; that they wish to sit still. Don't you know that the white men are killing all the black men they can catch? Don't you know that they have shot Gambo through the head, and thrown his body to the birds? Have you not heard that every Kafir boy who was working in Bulawayo has had his throat cut?" "I did not believe him," said Jackal, "and soon afterwards one of my own men, who had been working in town, came home, and told me that the white men had killed no one in Bulawayo except a few Matabele spies. Then I knew that the son of Umfaizella had lied to me, but still the bad news frightened my people." I may here state that Jackal expressed the opinion that if they were unable to kill all the white men, a large section of the Matabele would probably leave the country with as many cattle as they could get together, and seek a new home beyond the Zambesi. What amount of truth there may be in this view, and how far the original plan may have been modified owing to the destruction of all the cattle by the rinderpest, remains to be seen. At present, however, no section of the tribe seems actually to have made a move beyond the outskirts of Matabeleland proper.

In the afternoon we proceeded to the Shashani. Before

reaching "Fig Tree," the coach, loaded with ammunition, had passed us on its way to Bulawayo in charge of the escort that had accompanied it from Mangwe. As, according to the information I had received before leaving town, the convoy of waggons ought now to have been close at hand, and I did not wish to tire all my horses by taking them any farther than necessary down the road, I left Lieutenant Grenfell in charge of the patrol at the deserted shanty, which had done duty as an hotel, near to which we had off-saddled, and rode on alone.

Shortly before reaching the Shashani hotel we had met a light waggonette drawn by a team of horses on its way to Bulawayo. In it were two gentlemen, Captain Lumsden (late of the 4th Battalion Scottish Rifles) and Mr. Frost, on their way to Matabeleland on a shooting expedition. We halted and gave one another the news from up and down country respectively, and had a laugh and a joke about the kind of shooting one was likely to get in Matabeleland at the present time. When Captain Lumsden got out of the waggonette I saw what a fine specimen of a man he was—tall and broad-shouldered, with a pleasant face and keen blue eye—and I little thought that when next I met him, only a week later, it would be in the Bulawayo hospital, where, poor fellow, he lay with a leg shattered by a Kafir's bullet, on what soon proved to be his deathbed, for he died from the effects of the subsequent amputation of the limb.

After leaving my men I rode quietly on, but only met the waggons I was looking out for when close to Mangwe. Having many friends in the laager there, I determined to ride a little farther and pay them a visit. First, however, I exhorted the man in charge of the waggons to push on at once, as I was anxious to return to Bulawayo as soon as possible, in the hope of getting something more exciting to do there than escorting waggons.

When still some three miles from Mangwe I met a party of horsemen riding towards me along the road. They proved to be old friends who had come out to meet me, as they had heard by telegraph that I was coming their way. Amongst them was one of my oldest and most esteemed friends, Cornelius Van Rooyen, with whom in the good old days I had wandered and hunted for months together over the then unknown wilds of Mashunaland.

Arrived at the laager, I received a very warm welcome from both Dutch and English. Major Armstrong was in command, whom, though a very young man, I thought both shrewd and capable, and the excellent service he has done for the Government during the present insurrection has, I think, been fully recognised.

Before leaving Bulawayo I had heard it said that in the Mangwe laager order and discipline were conspicuous by their absence; but this I did not find to be at all the case. On the contrary, it seemed to me that Major Armstrong and Commandant Van Rooyen, by the exercise of great tact, had between them got everything into excellent order; and this is no small praise, for it must be remembered that the occupants of the Mangwe laager belonged to two nationalities, Dutch and English, each of which has its own way of doing things, and the two can only be brought to work harmoniously together by the exercise of both forbearance and good sense on the part of the officer commanding the combined force.

All my Dutch friends at Mangwe had suffered terrible losses amongst their stock from the rinderpest; indeed, some who had been rich men a couple of months before, possessing several hundred head of stock, had now scarcely a beast left. All along the road, too, from Bulawayo to Mangwe the evidences of the ruthless severity of this plague were most lamentable. Hundreds of carcasses in every stage of putrefaction everywhere lined the track, whilst here and there were groups of empty waggons abandoned by their owners, who, having lost their means of livelihood through the death of their oxen, had left the rest of their property standing uncared for in the wilderness, and walked away ruined men.

At Wilson's farm, six miles from Bulawayo, where herds of infected cattle had been slaughtered in the hopeless endeavour to stamp out the disease, acres of carcasses were lying festering in the sun, and any one passing along the road did not require to look at them to know they were there. Strangely enough, in spite of the exceptional opportunities offering for free meals throughout Matabeleland at this time, not a vulture was to be seen. I have heard it said that too hearty an indulgence in rinderpest meat in the early days of the plague killed all the vultures, and whether this is so or not, certain it is that these useful birds are now as scarce as cows in Matabeleland.

CHAPTER XV

Escort a convoy of waggons to Bulawayo—Murder of a Greek trader—Mr. Gordon saved by native police—Mr. Reed warned of danger by Makalakas—Patrols sent to Gwanda and Shiloh districts—Proceedings of the Gwanda patrol—Scenes of pillage and desolation—Lieutenant Webb's narrative—Six hours' severe fighting—Narrow escape of patrol from annihilation—Captain Van Niekerk's cool judgment and bravery—Gallant conduct of the patrol.

Leaving Mangwe on 2nd April, I rejoined my men on the following day, and we then escorted the convoy of waggons to Bulawayo, where we arrived early on the morning of Saturday, 4th April.

Before reaching Bulawayo, I had heard that a Greek trader had been murdered in the Bulilima district, near the Maitengwe river, and this news was confirmed by the Rev. Mr. Reed and Assistant Native Commissioner Gordon, both of whom had been stationed in the same district, and both of whom owe their escape to the fact that they received notice from friendly natives that their lives were in danger. Mr. Gordon was informed by his own native police that a Matabele Induna, named Langabi, had given orders to his people to kill him, and they not only warned him of his danger, but escorted him by bypaths through the dangerous part of the country, and put him on to the main road to Bulawayo.

These police, thirty in number, have all remained loyal to the Government. One of them was murdered by the rebels, but the remainder all reported themselves to the Chief Native Commissioner, by whom they were disarmed, but they have since been employed on Government service.

Mr. Reed was saved by the Makalaka amongst whom he was working. They informed him that the Greek trader living near him had been murdered, and told him plainly that he too would be killed unless he got away to a place of safety. At the same time a horse was sent to him by the Rev. Mr. Carnegie from Hope Fountain, together with a letter containing information concerning the generally disturbed state of the country. This decided him to leave his station for the time being and retire on Bulawayo, which place he reached safely the day before the return of my patrol from Mangwe.

During my absence two patrols, somewhat stronger than those first sent out, had been despatched to the Gwanda and Shiloh districts. The first, under Captains Brand and Van Niekerk, had left town on the previous Thursday, in order to relieve a party of prospectors and families said to be in laager in the Gwanda district. This patrol consisted of one hundred mounted men—fifty of C troop and fifty of the Africander Corps—and was accompanied by a mule waggon and a Maxim gun. The second patrol, numbering one hundred and sixty-nine men all told, and accompanied by a Maxim gun, was commanded by the Hon. Maurice Gifford, and had started on the Friday night to dislodge an impi, which it was reported had gathered in the hills near Shiloh. I will first give a short account of the proceedings of the Gwanda patrol, for the most interesting portion of which, namely the account of the return journey to Bulawayo, I am indebted to Lieutenant Webb of the Africander Corps, who has most kindly placed the graphic description which he has himself written of this fateful march at my disposal.

Leaving Bulawayo at six o'clock on Thursday evening, 2nd April, the first halt was made at Spargot's store, some six miles from town. Here the horses were off-saddled for an hour. During the halt one of the sentries found a wounded Kafir lying in the grass, who, on examination, proved to be the colonial boy "Jim," who had been so terribly knocked about by the Matabele at Edkins' store, that when discovered there it was not thought he could possibly survive many hours; and yet, thanks to the food that had been left with him, he had not only been able to keep body and soul together, but had recovered in the course of a few days sufficiently to enable him to make his way slowly and by easy stages, travelling always by night, to Bulawayo. Fortunately he was never short of food, as the rainy season being not yet over, the young maize cobs—green mealies— were standing ready for plucking in all the native fields.

After leaving Spargot's the next halting-place was Dawson's store at the Umzingwani river, which was reached late at night. The store it was found had been burnt and destroyed by the Kafirs, but the mule stables were still standing, and in them a plentiful supply of maize was obtained for the horses. The latter were all placed inside the stable fence, whilst the men lay down behind their saddles on the rising ground outside. The pickets were fired on during the night, but a few volleys from a portion of the Africander Corps drove the Kafirs off, though they were afterwards heard calling to one another in the hills near the river.

"When day broke no natives were to be seen, and the horses were at once saddled up, and the march continued. Spiro's store, thirty-seven miles from Bulawayo, was found to have been totally destroyed by fire, but Grainger's hotel, twelve miles farther on, was still standing. The Kafirs had, however, apparently only just left it before the patrol arrived, as everything was in the utmost disorder, and water was discovered in a bucket which had evidently only just been brought up from the stream, as some of it had been spilt on the ground. A large supply of maize was again found in the mule stables, so the horses got another good feed.

In the evening the expedition moved on to Grainger's second store, which it was found had not been interfered with by the natives. Here Friday night was passed, the men again lying down behind their saddles. Early the following morning Dawson's store at "Amanzi minyama" was reached. It was found to have been very recently deserted by its European occupants, and since their departure had been partially looted by Kafirs. From here a move was made to Mr. Nicholson's camp, some four miles farther down the road, where it was thought that all the white men in the Gwanda district had probably collected. On arriving there a most excellent fort was discovered on the top of a kopje near the camp. Whilst the fort was being strengthened, Mr. Zeederberg, the well-known post contractor, and three more men rode down the Tuli road to discover how far ahead the Gwanda people were. Mr. Zeederberg and one of these men rode through to Tuli, in order to despatch telegrams to Bulawayo; but the other two returned the following day, after having caught up the waggon with the people from Dawson's store, who were retiring on Tuli, and who reported that the Gwanda party was thirteen hours ahead of them, making for the same destination. On Sunday, 5th April, two more despatch-riders were sent to Tuli with farther messages for Bulawayo, asking that reinforcements and a Hotchkiss gun should be sent down to meet the patrol on its return, as, from information received from a native scout, it was believed that the Kafirs would attack them in force at some point along the road. On Wednesday morning the despatch-riders returned, with a message informing Captain Brand that it was impossible to send the reinforcements asked for, and requesting him to return as soon as possible to Bulawayo. On Monday, the day after the despatch-riders had left, an escort which had been sent in charge of a waggon to Dawson's store to bring in some supplies was fired on by the Kafirs. Captain Van Niekerk with some men of the Africander Corps, and some of C troop under Mr. Holland, immediately went off in pursuit, but beyond a few stragglers saw nothing of them. On the following day Captain Van Niekerk and Mr. Purssell went out with a force to patrol round the store and bring in all the remaining stores left. They found the country strewn for several miles with blankets, boots, etc., left by the Kafirs in their hasty flight on the preceding day, but again no resistance was met with.

From this point I will proceed with the narrative in Lieutenant Webb's own words, as follows:—"We started early the next morning, 9th April, on our return journey. By lunch time we had marched fifteen miles, and reached Grainger's store No. 2. This place we found had been burnt to the ground by the Matabele during our stay at Gwanda, and judging by the spoor a large number of them had been at work. We decided to stay the rest of the day at this place, and were careful to take every necessary precaution in case of a night attack. Next morning we saddled up at daybreak, and covered twelve miles to Grainger's store No. 1, before halting. This store had in our absence shared the same fate as the other, and we recovered nothing from the ashes. As we were now entering a most dangerous section of the road, we were careful to use extra vigilance. At about ten o'clock we came up with some cattle at the foot of the range of hills on our left, but before capturing them, narrowly inspected the hills for natives, as we suspected a trap. Sure enough on a ridge about 1000 yards away we made out a body of men hiding under cover. We at once put the Maxim on them, and as they retreated in haste up the side of the hill, we found that several hundreds of them had been waiting in ambush. They only returned our fire with one or two shots. We were then going through thick bush, with hills a couple of hundred yards away towering on each side.

"Upon emerging from these, we came to the ruins of Spiro's store, and about a mile beyond we saw a column of smoke ascending, and rightly conjectured that this was the place where they meant to attack us. The situation was all in their favour. We had to pass through a narrow neck amongst the hills in order to emerge into comparatively open country, though even this latter afforded them ample cover from our fire. The first evidence we had of the ambuscade was a steady and prolonged fire directed at the head of the column (composed of our corps) from the kopjes on the left flank. We at once returned the fire; but so well was the enemy concealed amongst the rocks, that I may tell you—though you will hardly credit my statement—that I scarcely saw one of them for half an hour. As the column was pressing on to get out of the dangerous position we were in, a few of Captain Brand's men fired just in front of the faces of the mules drawing the provision waggon. The mules swerved round suddenly, and broke the disselboom. Whilst the damage was being repaired, Mr. Jobson, who was in command of the Maxim, brought his gun into action with the greatest coolness and promptitude; but this unfortunate accident delayed us for half

79

an hour, and was largely responsible for the wounds of many horses and men.

"When we at last emerged from the pass, the disorganised appearance of the column showed the severity of the enemy's fire, and I firmly believe it was due to the fact that there were a number of old campaigners in the Africander Corps, which was commanded by our cool and experienced chief Captain Van Niekerk, that we escaped annihilation. When we had got the men into skirmishing order, we were better able to cope with the enemy; and when I tell you that the latter were over 1000 strong and followed us for over five miles at a distance of little more than 200 yards, you will be better able to judge of the task we had in hand. Our route lay over successive ranges of ridges and valleys, and afforded plenty of cover for the enemy, as the grass was about three feet high, and the country thickly studded with bush and trees. They formed a half-moon round us and skirmished excellently, taking advantage of every bit of cover. They also fought with ferocious determination, and often showed pluck verging on lunacy. They were kept well in hand by their leaders, who constantly urged them to fire low. Our horses and men were now falling with deadly monotony, and we all saw the importance of getting into more open country. Our men were firing steadily and rapidly all this time, and the Maxim did good service; but being on the move and owing to the tactics of the enemy, did not do the execution we were accustomed to see in the first Matabele war.

"At last, after about three hours' fighting, we saw about a mile ahead of us a round stone kopje, for which we made in order to take a short halt. The enemy at once saw through our movement, and a number of them endeavoured to defeat our object by out-flanking our advance. Our horsemen, however, were too sharp for them, and by hard riding reached the kopje first, and held them in check until the main body arrived. The kopje we thus reached was nothing but a huge flat rock, showing out about twelve or fifteen feet above the surrounding country. It was almost surrounded by broken rocks and trees, and under this cover—in some instances only some thirty to forty yards from where we were standing—the Matabele concealed themselves, and continued their fire upon us. This alone will give you some idea of their astounding audacity and bravery. We had to charge them four times to make them at last give in and retire. It was now about sundown (5.30 P.M.), and we had actually been about six hours fighting over five miles of country.

"When at last we had time to look about us, we saw a scene that I for one shall never forget. The men still stood at their posts about the kopje keeping a good look-out. Across the plain through which we had come could be seen the carcasses of horses slain, and the bodies of men lying as they fell. On the kopje itself was the little ammunition waggonette, capable of holding two men comfortably, and now surrounded by the wounded and dying. We found that we had lost five men shot dead, and two more were dying, whilst over twenty others were wounded, and thirty-three horses had been killed. Of the enemy we estimated that we had killed and wounded between two and three hundred. I do not think that any one of us had reckoned upon having such a tough job in getting through the pass, and even now our position was very grave. Prompt action was needed to get us out of our difficulty, and after consultation amongst the officers, we decided at once to move on, so as to give the Matabele no time for united action to surround us during the night. Our greatest difficulty was the conveyance of our wounded, and how any of the poor fellows survived that night will always remain a mystery. In the little waggonette we had to place eight, and on the Maxim gun-carriage we carried several more. The remainder were fortunately able to ride.

"We left the kopje at dusk, and for the next sixteen miles had a most unpleasant section of the road to traverse, on any portion of which the Matabele had us at their mercy had they chosen to attack. Whether they had had enough fighting, or whether they did not suspect our departure, is not known, but we were all heartily glad to get through that section of the country unmolested. At half-past four on the morning of the 11th of April, we met the relief force sent to meet us, and two hours later we halted in front of the Government Offices in Bulawayo. That afternoon we buried one of my most intimate friends, poor Baker, who had been shot in the fight, and died on the homeward march."

From the foregoing narrative it is evident that this small patrol of 100 men narrowly escaped annihilation at the hands of the Matabele; and I should be doing an injustice if I did not state that, in the opinion of at any rate the majority of those who took part in the fight, they were only saved from destruction by the determined bravery combined with cool judgment—the result of long experience gained in many a previous fight with Kafirs in the Old Colony and the Transvaal—shown by Captain Van Niekerk, who took over the command during the action. Captain Brand, who was the senior officer, and who is as gallant a fellow as ever stepped, indeed brave to the point of foolhardiness, but who had had no previous experience of native warfare, showed both generosity of character and soundness of judgment in asking Van Niekerk to take over the command directly he saw that his men were in a tight place. Van Niekerk himself speaks enthusiastically of the cool bravery shown

81

throughout this trying time by all the men forming the patrol. They were all equally brave, he says. But amongst the Africanders there were many old Kafir fighters, such as old Mr. Steyn and Messrs. Loots and Ferreira, and these old campaigners were naturally more useful than inexperienced men. Lieutenants Webb and Holland, Purssell and Jobson—the latter in charge of the Maxim gun—did their duty throughout the engagement as coolly as if they were on parade. Five dead men had to be left on the field, viz. Messrs. Forbes, Pack, Greer, Hayland, and Green. Mr. Baker died on the Maxim carriage, and his body was laid on the roadside eight miles from Bulawayo.

On the following morning, Saturday, 11th April, a party was sent out to bring in the body, which they did, but they were fired on from a kopje near the road. No damage however was done, and poor Baker was buried the same afternoon.

About half-past eight on the previous evening, a messenger— Mr. White, attached to the Africander Corps—had reached town, with a despatch from Captain Brand, saying that he was in a tight place and feared that his ammunition might run short if the fight lasted much longer. Mr. White had left the patrol about four o'clock in the afternoon, and some two hours earlier had been struck on the head by a bullet, which luckily however only inflicted a scalp wound, stunning him for the moment.

On his arrival there was great excitement in Bulawayo, and a relief force was at once organised to go to Captain Brand's assistance. Being then in town, I and my men of course volunteered like every one else, and I well remember how bitterly disappointed we were that we could not go. As it happened, the relief force was not required to rescue the patrol, which had extricated itself from a very difficult position without assistance; but its appearance must have been most welcome to the jaded men, whose horses when they reached Bulawayo had been upwards of twenty-six hours under the saddle without food or rest. Thus ended one of the toughest fights of the present campaign, in which more than one-third of the men engaged were either killed or wounded, and more than one-third of the horses were likewise killed. Several men, whose wounds were slight, never reported themselves at all. Brave Captain Van Niekerk was twice hit, one bullet cutting his bandoleer-strap and bruising his shoulder, and the second smashing the stock of his revolver and bruising his side. The Kafirs, although they probably lost heavily, had the satisfaction of getting possession of the dead bodies of five white men to mutilate, together with the saddles and other accoutrements of the horses killed; whilst, worst of all from our

82

point of view, several Lee-Metford rifles and bandoleers full of cartridges fell into their hands.

CHAPTER XVI

Gifford's fight in the Shiloh Hills—Strength of the patrol—First skirmish with the Matabele—Form a laager—March resumed—Second skirmish—Patrol reach Fonseca's farm—Fight at Fonseca's farm—Death of a witch-doctor—Colonel Gifford wounded—Messengers sent to Bulawayo for assistance—Laager strengthened—Fighting renewed—Captain Lumsden wounded—Matabele retire—Relief column arrives—Return to Bulawayo—Death of Captain Lumsden—Colonel Gifford's arm amputated.

For the following narrative of what is now known as Gifford's fight in the Shiloh Hills, I am indebted to an officer in Gifford's Horse, who has done very good service throughout the campaign, but who however has modestly asked me not to mention his name.

"The patrol under Lieutenant-Colonel Gifford—now commonly known as the Shiloh Patrol—consisted of Gifford's Horse, with thirty-one men of F troop under Captain Dawson, and eleven men of Grey's Scouts under Lieutenant F. Crewe—one hundred and eighteen Europeans in all, with one Maxim gun and forty-nine Colonial Boys under Captain Bisset. Captain J. W. Lumsden accompanied the patrol as chief of the Staff and second in command.

"We left Bulawayo about one o'clock on Saturday morning, 4th April. It was bright moonlight, and we travelled on without any delay or anything exciting happening till the sun rose, when we outspanned at M'Kisa's kraal, about twelve miles from Bulawayo. I believe we had a sort of roving commission to go down to the Khami river, break up an impi or two there, then to go over to Inyati, do the same there, and finally to come out on the Salisbury road at the Bembisi.

"At our first outspan however Colonel Gifford obtained information that there was an impi encamped down the Umguza, on Holm's farm, about fourteen miles to the north of us, and he determined to have a go at them. We therefore broke camp about two o'clock and trekked on through very bad country, heavy sand and thick bush.

"We had just got into better and more open country when continuous firing was heard on our right, in which direction a few of our scouts were out, and shortly afterwards a party of two or three hundred Matabele were seen coming down from a ridge on our right, and the rear-guard—B troop, under Captain Fynn—were soon engaged with them. At this juncture Colonel Gifford sent back Captain Dawson's troop and the Colonial Boys to support Captain Fynn, and after about an hour's heavy firing the Matabele withdrew into the hills close by.

"In the meantime, the rest of the column had drawn out into an open space and laagered up. The scouts turned up just before the Matabele attacked, having narrowly escaped being cut off. We passed a quiet night as the enemy made no move, though we could see them in the hills, and they fired occasional shots at the laager before it got dark. Next morning we started again after breakfast, but had not gone more than a couple of miles, when the wily Matabele showed himself again, and in stronger force. Our advance guard, A troop, under Captain Meikle, were attacked, and at the same time a party of two or three hundred came down on our right and attacked the column. They did not come on very close—to do this they would have had to cross the Umguza river, and this they did not seem to care about doing, but kept on the other side of the river firing at the column and showing themselves in pretty strong force. Colonel Gifford then opened on them with the Maxim at about 600 yards, and this quite quenched their military ardour. It was funny to see the way in which they all immediately lay down in the grass and then spread out, and finally strutted off into the bush, bending down and hiding themselves as much as they could in the grass all the time.

"During this time A troop had beaten off the attack on the advance, and Captain Bisset's boys who were on the left advance fell on the already defeated party and did some damage, killing twenty or thirty of them. As the enemy appeared to be all round us, we outspanned again, and, the men remaining at their posts, a biscuit each was served out all round, and the horses were allowed to graze. No further attack was made, and we trekked on again to Fonseca's farm without any further hindrance from our enemy, though we could see an impi on our right keeping along with us all the way, though at a safe distance.

"We camped and laagered behind our saddles in an open glade. Behind us was a ridge of kopjes, on one of which was the homestead, on our left was thick bush, and on our right was a dry

84

river-bed. Just beyond, and parallel to it, ran a stream in which were some deep pools of water. These riverbeds afterwards proved to be our salvation, or at any rate of great assistance in our defence.

"We passed another quiet night, and next morning, Easter Monday, at daybreak, the men made the fires and were soon brewing their coffee, as it was bitterly cold. The usual patrol of five or six men was sent out to scout round, and the Colonial Boys were sent out to look for cattle, as we had so far only had "bully" to eat, and a change was desirable. They had not been out long when Lieutenant Rorke, who was in command of the morning patrol, came across the impi holding an "indaba" in a kraal. He and his patrol opened fire on them, to which they promptly replied by rushing our men. Lieutenant Rorke had a very narrow escape; his horse broke away from him, and he was compelled to retire as best he could on foot. The Colonial Boys, who were not far behind, and his own few men, however, checked the enemy, and saved his life.

"This opened the ball; as soon as the firing was heard in camp, Colonel Gifford ordered Dawson's troop out in support, and B troop under Captain Fynn were ordered up into the kopjes where Fonseca's homestead stood. The battle soon became general, and there was heavy firing through the bush on our left, which was occupied by the Colonial Boys, Captains Dawson's and Fynn's troops. Colonel Gifford then gave the order for the men in laager to take cover in the bed of the stream to which I have already referred. The two small waggons, one of which carried ammunition, and the other our provisions, and on which the Maxim was standing on its tripod, were quickly drawn up alongside of the gully, and the men took up their positions and manned the banks of both streams, which formed a natural laager. Colonel Gifford then sent out the gallopers to call the troops in to laager, not a minute too soon. Captain Fynn's troop, with whom was Captain Lumsden, were fairly rushed by the enemy, who poured a fire into them at close range. Here Trooper Kenneth M'Kenzie was shot through the head and dropped dead from his horse. Trooper Fielding was wounded in the leg, and his horse shot under him, and Captain Lumsden's horse also fell shot under him. Captain Fynn, however, brought his men into laager in good order, returning the enemy's fire. Captain Dawson and the Colonial Boys also retired in good order into laager.

"The Matabele came on close behind, and our men were hardly in laager when they rushed out into the open from the bush, with the evident intention of charging the laager. The steady fire from the men, however, soon checked them, and a few shots from the Maxim made them retire into the bush again. A few of their bravest, having taken cover behind some stumps and dead trees which were lying in the open, kept up a galling fire on the laager, but these were soon picked off by some of our good shots.

"One man, however, came on in the open and appeared to bear a charmed life, as no bullets touched him; he had no gun or assegai, but came on alone down the valley towards us. He must have got to within about 150 yards of the laager when he fell shot in the leg. He rose again, and only then turned to fly, but the charm seemed to be broken, and he fell dead, shot through with several bullets.

"In the afternoon, when we were able to go out to where he lay, we found he had in his hands a skin-bag full of fat, and some of the usual witch-doctor's throwing bones—no arms of any sort. Apparently he was a witch-doctor, or one of the priests of the much-talked-of 'Umlimo,' who thought he'd do for the white man by means of his bones and incantations and that the white man's bullets were to turn to water before him as had been predicted. The Matabele lined the bush all down our front and took to the kopjes, from where, at about 600 yards, they kept up a continuous fire.

"Colonel Gifford had all the time been standing on the waggon alongside of the Maxim directing the fire, and giving his orders to the men. The enemy on our front were not more than 200 yards away, and were making good shooting, aiming especially at the waggon and Maxim. Here poor Reynolds was mortally wounded, having been shot through the arm and lungs, and dying within a brief space. Soon afterwards Colonel Gifford was wounded in the shoulder. The men saw he had been hit; but he called out, "It's all right, boys, don't mind me—give it to them—give it to them." He had soon, however, to be lifted down from the waggon and carried into the bed of the stream, at the same time calling on Captain Lumsden to take command. Troopers J. Walker (Gifford's Horse) and Eatwell (Dawson's) were wounded shortly afterwards.

"The fire from the enemy slackened soon after this, but they kept up a desultory fire till about twelve o'clock, when they finally drew off and left us in peace, though we could see them every now and then in the bush.

"Shortly after Colonel Gifford was wounded Captain Lumsden, after consulting the officers, sent in to Bulawayo a despatch by two of Captain Bisset's boys on horseback, reporting that Colonel Gifford was wounded, and asking for assistance, as both ammunition and food were running short.

"As soon as the natives drew off the horses were let out to graze, and we spent the afternoon, as far as we could, strengthening our position. As the sun went down we could see smoke from what we judged to be the enemy's camp behind the kopjes, and on the top

86

of one of these, against the sky, we saw what was evidently their sentry carefully watching us. We passed a quiet night, and next day had a repetition of our Monday's experience.

"After an early breakfast of one biscuit per man all round, some of the Colonial Boys were sent up on to the kopjes to see where our enemy had got to. This was soon very evident, as the Matabele came up from beyond the kopjes and chased our boys down and back into camp. They came out into the open again exactly as on the previous day, but this time from the kopje side. The fire from our men soon checked them and drove them back into the bush, and they then spread right round us and opened fire from every side. Captain Lumsden was wounded in the leg while walking about the laager, giving orders and directing the Maxim, and immediately carried down into the donga, which was our place of safety. Captain Bisset then took command. Lieutenant Hulbert was soon afterwards wounded in the leg by a Lee-Metford bullet. After keeping up a desultory fire till about mid-day, the enemy again retired, as we afterwards found out having had quite enough of the white men in the dongas. In the afternoon some of B troop and the Colonial Boys went out and recovered poor M'Kenzic's body, which was lying where he fell. Both he and Corporal Reynolds were buried by their comrades in the centre of our laager, between the two dongas.

"At about two o'clock a despatch-rider arrived from Captain Macfarlane, who, with the relief column, was about five miles off.

"Captain Macfarlane's column arrived soon afterwards, and we were very glad to see them, as provisions were running short. We had about a biscuit per man and seven tins of bully beef left, and not too much ammunition for another fight. Our troubles were then over, except for our poor wounded.

"We broke laager next morning, and carried them off on the waggons as carefully as we could into town, arriving in Bulawayo that night (Wednesday), late. It was, however, a long weary journey for them, twenty-two miles over the stumps and stones of a South African road. Captain Lumsden died next day in hospital, to the universal regret of all who had met him and served under him. Our own brave Colonel had to lose his arm, so our leaders suffered severely. Certainly they by their coolness and daring behaviour inspired confidence in their men, and helped to keep the fire steady. That the firing of our men was exceptionally steady there is no doubt. After the first rush it was impossible for a Matabele to show himself without receiving three or four bullets most uncomfortably near him, if he did not receive his quietus. It was estimated that the patrol killed at lowest 200 of the enemy, and many more must have been wounded. The Maxim did not have much chance, as after the first rush the Matabele spread themselves out in the bush, and kept under very good cover, and it then became a matter of sharpshooting. On the Monday, and the last day's fight, the enemy must have been about 1500 strong. As we could see, they increased every day, and we afterwards heard from native reports that reinforcements were joining them all the time. We also heard that after the failure of the last attack the impi retired and sent round the country for still further reinforcements. When they arrived and the impis came back to the scene of their flight, they found the dongas empty—the white men had gone."

CHAPTER XVII

Despatch from Captain Laing—Laager formed at Belingwe—Strange conduct of a native policeman—Three Matabele caught looting and hanged—"Young Tradesman's" letter to the Daily Graphic—Matabele capture a herd of cattle and murder some Zambesi Kafirs near Bulawayo—Determination to build forts between Bulawayo and Mangwe—I am sent to establish forts and take command of all troops on the road—Fort Molyneux—I return to Bulawayo to report my views—Curious position of affairs in Matabeleland.

On the day before the return of Brand's patrol, the first news was received from Belingwe that had reached Bulawayo since the outbreak of the insurrection. The despatch was from Captain Laing, who was in command there, and was to the effect that all the whites in the district were in laager, and that they felt confident of being able to resist any attack made upon them by the natives.

This news gave great relief to many people who had friends in the Belingwe district, for it was not known whether they had been able to collect together and form a laager, or whether they had been surprised and murdered before they were aware that anything was amiss; as indeed they would have been, in all probability, had not Mr. H. P. Fynn, the native commissioner in the Insiza district, sent a message to Captain Laing to warn him that a native rising seemed imminent immediately after he was informed of the murder of Mr.

Maddocks. This message was faithfully carried by one of Mr. Fynn's native policemen, and Captain Laing, recognising the gravity of the situation, at once acted with the promptitude and decision which always distinguish him, and ordered all the whites in his district to immediately come in to laager at Belingwe.

They were only just in time, for the natives showed their teeth very soon afterwards, and although fearing to attack the laager, succeeded in driving off a considerable number of cattle. Captain Laing, accompanied by only nine men—all he was able to mount— then in his turn attacked the insurgents, and succeeded in recapturing some of the cattle, though these were of little value, as the rinderpest was amongst them. It is worthy of remark that the native policeman who took the message to Captain Laing, which probably saved many white men's lives in the Belingwe district, never returned to his duty, but as is now known, went over to the rebels with his rifle and bandoleer full of cartridges. This fact, taken in conjunction with many other circumstances, goes to prove that the secret of the actual date of the outbreak of the insurrection was not known to the mass of the people, though probably, owing to the prophetic utterances ascribed to the Umlimo, which had been diligently circulated amongst them, they were in a state of expectancy; but this policeman, for instance, must have been thoroughly taken by surprise, and after the first murders remained loyal to the Government until he was got at by some one capable of explaining to him the scope of the whole plot.

On 10th April, too, a further excitement was caused in Bulawayo by the arrest of three Matabele rebels. They were captured near Soluso's, some twenty miles west of Bulawayo, by Marzwe's Friendlies, and sent in to town by Josana, having been caught red-handed, looting and burning property belonging to white men. I was present when the evidence was taken, and it certainly seemed to me to be overwhelming, especially as one of them was known to Mr. Colenbrander, and they all three acknowledged themselves to be the subjects of a certain Induna named Maiyaisa, who with all his people has been amongst the rebels from the first outbreak of the insurrection. They were caught, too, with assegais in their hands, looting a white man's farm, so that it might very reasonably be asked "que diable allaient-ils faire dans cette galère?"

At any rate they were condemned to death, and hanged forthwith, all three on one tree on the outskirts of Bulawayo. Besides these three men who had been incontestably guilty of taking part in the rebellion, and who were hanged together, six others were hanged singly and at different times, all of whom, if they were tried in a somewhat rough-and-ready fashion, were undoubtedly spies and rebels.

These are the only Matabele who have been hanged during the present insurrection, and a letter therefore on the subject of hanging natives which appeared in the *Daily Graphic* of Saturday, 13th June, purporting to have been written by a young tradesman of Bulawayo, is a trifle incorrect, to say the least of it. A portion of the letter runs as follows: "My stand has one big tree on it, and it is often used as a gallows. Yesterday there was a goodly crop of seven Matabele hanging there; to-day there are eight, the eighth being a nigger who was heard boasting to a companion that he had helped to kill white men, and got back to town without being suspected."

This letter was reproduced by Mr. Labouchere in *Truth*, as well as another he got hold of at the same time, in which the writer expresses it as his opinion that "it is grand fun potting niggers off, and seeing them fall like nine-pins," while further on he speaks of it being "quite a nice sight" to see men shot as spies. I can quite believe that a man who can write in this strain would take pleasure in, or "would not object," as he puts it, to seeing Kafirs shot, but I doubt very much if such an one would ever risk his skin to enjoy "the grand fun" he speaks of.

It seems a pity that a writer who takes "Truth" as the motto of his paper, should seize upon every little scrap of published matter he can discover (apparently without inquiry as to its real value), and not only reproduce it as gospel in an ensuing number of his journal, but found a sermon upon it into the bargain on the iniquities of his fellow-countrymen in Rhodesia. However, we have the consolation of knowing that nothing has discredited the editor of *Truth* in the eyes of all fair-minded men so much as the hostile feeling he has ever shown against the British settlers in Rhodesia, whilst, happily for that colony, his rage is as impotent as that of "a viper gnawing at an old file."

During the week in which the aforesaid Kafirs were hanged, some parties of Matabele approached the town very closely at nights, and on the night of 6th April one of them succeeded in capturing a herd of cattle within a mile and a half of the hospital, at the same time murdering some Zambesi Kafirs who were sleeping outside the cattle kraal. As at this time there was a herd of cattle which was penned every night in a kraal near Dr. Sauer's house, some two miles away on the other side of the town, I was asked to take some of my men and lie in wait for any Matabele who might attempt to capture them on the following night.

I went down and reconnoitred the position during the day, and after dark rode down with fifteen good men. We first off-saddled our horses, and tied them up within the paling round Dr. Sauer's house, and then took up our positions along two walls of the square stone cattle kraal. During the night, the weather, which had been fine and warm, suddenly changed; a cold wind sprang up, and masses of cloud spread over the sky from the south-east. It looked as if it was going to rain every minute, but luckily the wind kept it off. However, it was bitterly cold, and we were all of us very glad when day at last dawned and our weary vigil was over, for no Kafirs came near us; and when I examined the cattle I did not think it likely they would, as the rinderpest was rife amongst them, two lying dead in the kraal, whilst many others, the herd boy told us, lay rotting about the veld all round.

About this time the authorities determined to carry out a scheme for keeping open communications with the south by means of forts which were to be built along the road between Bulawayo and Mangwe. As a commencement in this direction, Captain Molyneux left Bulawayo, on Saturday, 11th April, with sixty men to establish a fort at Fig Tree, distant thirty miles down the road, whilst at the same time Captain Luck was ordered up from Mangwe with fifty men to build a second fort some fifteen miles from that place, in the centre of the hilly country through which the coach road passes.

Two days later I was sent down the road to establish further forts between Fig Tree and Mangwe, and to take command of all garrisons on the road, the force with which I left town consisting of sixty men of H troop of the Bulawayo Field Force (my own), forty men of E troop under Captain Halsted, and twenty of the Africander Corps under Lieutenant Webb.

We left Bulawayo on the evening of Monday, 13th April, and slept that night at Wilson's farm, reaching Mabukitwani the following evening. From information I received there concerning the movements of the Matabele, I became convinced that the dangerous part of the road was that portion of it lying between Bulawayo and Fig Tree, and not the hill passes farther on, as the inhabitants of the latter are all Makalakas, the rebel Matabele who had been living amongst them having all come up nearer to Bulawayo, and joined their compatriots on the Khami river.

According to the plan which I had been asked to carry out, the thirty miles of road between Bulawayo and Fig Tree would have been left entirely undefended, which did not appear to me to be at all advisable in view of the fact that there was a large impi under the Induna Maiyaisa encamped on the Khami, only twelve miles below the ford on the main coach road. I therefore took it upon myself to send Lieutenant Webb with his twenty men back to the Khami river, to commence a fort there, at the same time despatching a

91

messenger to Bulawayo requesting Colonel Napier to reinforce him with another twenty or thirty men. At the same time I gave it as my opinion that a fort ought also to be established at Mabukitwani.

On Wednesday afternoon we reached Fig Tree, where we found that Captain Molyneux had already nearly completed an almost impregnable fort, which had been built on a small isolated kopje, itself a natural stronghold, about 200 yards from the mule stables, hotel, and telegraph office at Fig Tree. The natural strength of this kopje had been most cunningly taken advantage of and increased by blasting a rock out here and there, and fortifying the weak places with sand-bags. Good water was obtainable in the bed of a stream at the very foot of the kopje, whilst a recess amongst the rocks near its base had been cleared in such a way as to form a stable within which some twenty horses could be completely sheltered from the bullets of any attacking force. Altogether, Fort Molyneux was a perfect little place of its kind, and did every credit to the very capable officer by whom it was built.

On the following day we went on to Shashani neck, some five and a half miles beyond Fort Molyneux. Here the road descends for a distance of three miles into the Shashani valley, winding continually in and out amongst thickly-wooded granite hills. Had the Kafirs, at the commencement of the insurrection, put a force of 1000 men armed with rifles, backed by another 1000 with assegais, into this pass, it is my opinion that they would have completely cut off all communication between Bulawayo and the south until a body of troops at least 1000 strong had been sent up from Mafeking to open the road. However, luckily they missed this opportunity, as they have missed every other chance they have had of striking a really effective blow at the white men. In fact, they have shown a general want of intelligence that stamps them as an altogether inferior people, in brain capacity at least, to the European.

About one-third of the way down the pass Captain Halsted and I found a kopje close to water, which commanded the road, and at the same time could be rendered absolutely impregnable to such enemies as the Matabele with a comparatively small amount of labour. Here I left Captain Halsted with the men of E troop to build a fort, and on Friday morning, 17th April, went on with my own troop to the Matoli river where Captain Luck had already almost completed a strong fort of earthworks and palisades in the centre of a large open space amongst the hills, by none of which, however, was it commanded. Here I met Major Armstrong from Mangwe, and as all I heard from him regarding the state of affairs in his district only confirmed me in the opinion that it would be a waste of time and men to build another fort between Matoli and Mangwe, as I had been instructed to do, whilst on the other hand I felt that it was of vital importance to establish forts without delay between Fig Tree and Bulawayo, I determined to return to town and lay my views before the administrator personally before proceeding farther southwards.

Major Armstrong having also official business to transact in Bulawayo, we arranged to ride in together forthwith. On passing Captain Halsted late in the afternoon we found that he had already made wonderful progress with the stronghold which is now known to fame as Fort Halsted. Just at dusk we reached Fort Molyneux, where we got an excellent dinner and were made comfortable for the night. Here I received a telegram from Colonel Napier, telling me that at the present moment he could not possibly spare any men from Bulawayo to reinforce Lieutenant Webb at the Khami river, as the Kafirs were massing round the town; and that as twenty men was too small a number to leave alone without reinforcements, he had ordered him to fall back on Fig Tree, or join Captain Halsted for the present.

At daylight Lieutenant Webb turned up, and as Captain Molyneux had over fifty men at Fig Tree, and Captain Halsted only forty, I sent him on to the latter. Major Armstrong and I then saddled up, and reached Bulawayo about two o'clock on Saturday, 18th April, having passed the down coach accompanied by a strong escort at the Khami river. The situation in Matabeleland was now a sufficiently curious one. In Bulawayo were some 1500 white men, women, and children, all of whom, although they were able to visit their houses in different parts of the town by day, had to seek safety within the laager at nights, and were not allowed to leave it before seven o'clock in the morning. At this time the whole of Matabeleland, with the exception of Bulawayo, and the laagers of Gwelo and Belingwe, was absolutely in the hands of the Kafirs, although, apparently by the orders of the Umlimo, the main road to the south had not been closed. A large impi lay at Mr. Crewe's farm, Redbank, on the Khami river, about twelve miles to the west of the town, besides which some thousands of rebels, amongst whom it was said was Lo Bengula's eldest son, Inyamanda, were camped all along the Umguza, considerable numbers of them being actually within three miles of Bulawayo, whilst other two large impis had taken up their quarters amongst the Elibaini Hills, and in the neighbourhood of Intaba Induna, there being altogether not less than 10,000 hostile natives spread out in a semicircle from the west to the north-east of the town. Had these different impis only combined and acted in concert under one leader they might have accomplished something; but each impi appears to have been acting

93

independently of the others, and my own belief is that they kept hanging round the town without any general plan of action, in the expectation of some supernatural interference by the deity on their behalf. At least this is what we hear from themselves, and I think it is the truth. Besides the impis to the north and west, there were others encamped within the edge of the Matopo Hills. These latter, however, although they blocked the Tuli road and destroyed the mission station at Hope Fountain, which had been established for over twenty-five years, never approached Bulawayo.

CHAPTER XVIII

Matabele advance on Bulawayo—Small force sent out to reconnoitre—Skirmish with the Matabele—I receive instructions to build a fort between Bulawayo and Fig Tree—The question of provisioning the forts—Three men of the Africander Corps killed—Attack by Matabele on Colonel Napier's farm—Captain Macfarlane sent with relief party—I ride out to see what was going on—I join relief party—Overtake Matabele near Colenbrander's farm—Fighting commences—I take command of a few Africanders—Our skirmish—Maxim jams at a critical time—Bad shooting of the Matabele—Their want of combination.

It was, I think, on Thursday, 16th April, that it was first realised that the Matabele had really advanced to within a short distance of the town. On that day, information having been received that there was an impi on the Umguza just below Government House, a small force was got together to go out and ascertain the truth of the report. This force consisted of twenty-one Scouts under Captain Grey and twenty-two of the Africander Corps under Captain Van Niekerk, Captains Nicholson and Howard Brown accompanying them, so that there were only forty-five men and officers all told.

Leaving town before daylight on the Friday morning, this little force crossed the stream on this side of Government House just as the sun was rising. It then, after emerging on to the high ground, turned to the right towards the Umguza. Soon numbers of Kafirs were seen moving about in the bush on the farther side of the river, who, when they saw the white men advancing at once opened fire

94

on them, at a distance at first of about 800 yards. This fire was not answered, but as soon as the Scouts and Africanders could be thrown out in skirmishing order, they were ordered to advance towards the river at a canter. On reaching it they at once crossed at two different places, the Africanders being on the right and Grey's Scouts on the left. When the top of the farther bank was reached the white men found themselves within 150 yards of a number of Matabele advancing rapidly towards them in skirmishing order through the bush. These latter at once fired a volley, all their bullets going high, and then turned and ran as the horsemen came galloping towards them. As Grey's Scouts got amongst them it was seen that the line of skirmishers was supported by a large body of men some distance in their rear, from which two flanking parties had been thrown out on either side. Van Niekerk charged with his men right on to the head of the left-hand flanking party and drove it back, but Captain Grey with his Scouts, whilst driving in the skirmishers on the main body, passed the right-hand flanking party, which then attempted to cut off his retreat to the river.

At once recognising that the natives were in force, and that the number of men at his command was altogether too small to cope with them, he gave the word to retire, and then both the Scouts and Africanders got back across the river again as quickly as possible, closely followed by the Kafirs. On reaching a rise some few hundred yards on the near side of the river, the white men halted, and dismounting kept the Kafirs in check for a while, but it was soon seen that their numbers were such that they would have been completely surrounded, so, one man and three horses having already been wounded, it was deemed advisable to retire and leave the field for the time being in possession of the Matabele. The wounded man was Mr. Harker, who was shot through the leg, but eventually recovered without losing the limb. The three horses that were wounded all died subsequently.

Upon reaching Bulawayo I at once had interviews with Mr. Duncan and Colonel Napier, and convinced them both that it was more necessary to establish a fort on the road between Bulawayo and Fig Tree than to add one more to the two already existing between Fig Tree and Mangwe, and I then and there received instructions to bring my own troop back again from Matoli, in order to build a fort at Mabukitwani. I should have left the same evening, to rejoin my men and carry out these orders, but the question arose as to the best means of provisioning the garrisons of the various forts, amounting altogether to 180 men. It was most inadvisable that any more food-stuff should be sent out of Bulawayo at this juncture than was absolutely necessary, so as there were three Government mule waggons at different forts along the road, I suggested that these should be sent down to Tati, where I understood that there was a good deal of food-stuff stored, to bring up full loads of the most necessary kinds of provisions, the balance of which, when the garrisons of the forts had been supplied with a month's rations, could be brought on to Bulawayo. Colonel Napier at once telegraphed to Mr. Vigers, who was in charge at Tati, to ascertain what food supplies he had on hand, and requested me not to leave Bulawayo until an answer had been received. I therefore spent Saturday night in bed, instead of on horseback riding down the Mangwe road. About eight o'clock on the following morning, Sunday, 19th April, a horse came galloping into town riderless, and with its saddle and bridle covered with blood. This horse was soon identified as having belonged to one of three men of the Africander Corps, who had left Bulawayo on picket duty in the neighbourhood of Government House on the preceding evening. It was subsequently discovered that these poor fellows had been surprised and killed by the Matabele early in the morning, two of their horses being also killed or captured, whilst the third made good its escape and galloped back into Bulawayo with a bullet-wound through its neck. The names of the unfortunate men were Heinemann, Van Zyl, and Montgomerie.

The excitement caused by this incident had scarcely subsided when news was received that Colonel Napier's homestead at Maatjiumschlopay, only about three miles to the south of the town, was being attacked by a large force of Matabele. At this homestead there were a large number of friendly natives, mostly armed with assegais, and also sixteen white men who occupied a small fort which had been built on the top of a small kopje overlooking the farm.

The first news received was that the Matabele had carried off a lot of cattle, killed a large number of the Friendlies, and were now besieging the white men in their fort. A small force of mounted men was therefore hastily got together and sent out to their assistance under Captain Macfarlane. This force consisted of a troop of the Africander Corps under Captain Pittendrigh, a few of Grey's Scouts, and some men of K troop under Captain Reid; about sixty troopers all told, with a Maxim gun in charge of Lieutenant Biscoe. It left town at about ten o'clock, taking the Tuli road.

At this time I had an appointment with Colonel Napier at his office, to get the answer expected to the telegram sent the day before to Mr. Vigers at Tati. However, on inquiry at the office, I found that

96

Colonel Napier was out, and that no reply had yet been received from Tati. On asking where Colonel Napier was, I was told that he had accompanied Captain Macfarlane. Now I had been requested not to leave Bulawayo until Colonel Napier had communicated to me the contents of the telegraphic message he was expecting from Tati, and therefore, believing that he had gone out with Captain Macfarlane's patrol, and that I would not be able to make a start for Matoli until he returned, I thought that I might as well take a ride out and see what was going on too.

Major Armstrong very kindly lent me the pony which he had ridden from Mangwe, which I knew was a very steady animal, trained for shooting. It did not take me long to saddle up, and I was soon riding hard on the tracks of Captain Macfarlane's troopers. I came up with them on the race-course, not far beyond the suburban stands, and learned from the officer in command that the attack on Maatjiumschlopay had been repulsed by the Friendlies, with the assistance of the white men in garrison there. The Matabele had not been in any force, and had evidently intended to sweep off a herd of cattle which was kept on the farm, and which the sixteen white men were there to protect.

No doubt the rebels were ignorant of the presence of these latter, for they cleared off when they were fired upon, hotly pursued by the Friendlies, who overtook and killed six of their number with clubs and assegais.

As these marauders had had ample time to reach the thick bush bordering the Umguza, where they would have been able to scatter and hide, Captain Macfarlane determined to waste no time in pursuing them, but to make a reconnaissance down the Umguza towards Government House, in the hope of coming across a larger body of rebels who would be likely to make a stand.

We therefore crossed the Salisbury road and followed down the bank of a stream which runs into the Umguza some two and a half miles from Bulawayo, just beyond a deserted farmhouse belonging to Mr. Colenbrander. The farmhouse stands on a rising piece of ground, in the angle formed by the two streams, but is about 400 yards distant from the Umguza, though close to its tributary.

When we got near the farmhouse, being still on the near side of the stream we had been following, some Colonial Boys, who proved to be scouts sent out by Mr. Colenbrander, came up and informed Captain Macfarlane that there were a lot of Matabele along the river, and that a number of them had only just left the farmhouse opposite.

The right-hand flanking party, under Lieutenant Hook, had now crossed the stream, so I galloped after them to get a look round from the high ground. Standing near the house, we could see large numbers of Kafirs spread out in skirmishing order amongst the scrubby bush on the farther side of the Umguza. As soon as they saw us, they at once commenced their usual tactics, throwing out flanking parties on either side, no doubt with the idea of surrounding us, whilst at the same time skirmishers were sent forward from the centre, evidently to take up a position in the bed of the river.

At this moment a messenger arrived recalling Lieutenant Hook to the other side of the stream, and upon riding through with him Captain Macfarlane informed me that, having just heard that another impi was approaching from the direction of Government House, he intended to take up his position on a fairly open piece of ground, near the junction of the smaller stream with the Umguza, and let the Kafirs attack him there, his force being altogether too small to risk crossing to the other side.

As we advanced the Kafirs opened fire on us, and a skirmishing fight soon commenced. I was asked to take a few of the Africanders across the smaller stream, so as to keep the Kafirs from taking possession of it, which I at once proceeded to do, but as I thus became separated from the main body I can only give an account of our own little skirmish.

As we rode up the rising ground beyond the stream, some Kafirs sent a few bullets whizzing amongst us from the shelter of the river, and then as we still advanced they very foolishly abandoned a good position and ran up the farther bank, and then along the river in a line, and in such a manner that if the one aimed at was missed, the next was very likely to be hit. The men I had with me were all good shots, and I saw several natives drop to our fire before they got round a bend of the river. Keeping a sharp look-out on ahead, I noticed a lot more coming down from the scrubby bush beyond it and crossing to our side, and rightly divining that their object was to advance up the valley behind the next ridge and then close in on us, I called to the few men with me to gallop at once to the top of the rise to prevent being taken by surprise and fired on from above.

Just at this moment we were joined by Lieutenant Hook and a few more men, and spreading out in skirmishing order, we rode to the top of the rise. We were just in time to meet a number of Kafirs—I daresay fifty or sixty altogether—making for the same position from the opposite side. They were right in the open, the nearest being within 150 yards of us. Some were armed with guns and rifles, but many of them had nothing but assegais and shields.

As soon as we appeared on the rise in front of them they all stopped, and those with rifles fired on us, their bullets nearly all going high, but on two of their number falling they commenced to retreat towards a strip of thickish bush which ran from near the bank of the Umguza river right up behind Colenbrander's farmhouse. This bush was about 400 yards from the top of the ridge from which the men with me were firing, and from its shelter a number of Kafirs were answering us and covering the retreat of their men across the valley. However, as the horses were quickly taken behind the ridge, and the men showed as little of themselves as possible, their fire did us no harm. On the other hand, several of the Kafirs fell to our shots before they reached the cover of the bush. They made no attempt to run fast, but went off crouching down at a slow trot. I myself was sitting down with my back against a stone, and shooting as carefully as possible, when a bullet struck a small stone close to my left foot and ricochetted with a loud buzzing noise close past poor Pat Whelan, a brave son of Erin, who had been with me on the first patrol to the Matopos, and who, having come out from Bulawayo on this day for the fun of the thing, thought it his duty to keep near me. "That was a fair buzzer," said Pat.

The Kafirs were now calling to one another, or some one was giving them orders in the bush, and we could see that they were all making up within its shelter towards the farmhouse. Thinking that their idea was to get behind it, and then fire on the position taken up by the Maxim, I gave the word to the men with me to mount and take possession of it first. This we promptly did, just getting there as the foremost of the enemy were about half-way between the bush and the house. They stopped and fired at us as before, and then retired to the bush again, from which they kept up a fusillade on the house, which, however, unless they had made a heavy rush, we could have held against them if necessary; but just then Lieutenant Moffat came up with a message from Captain Macfarlane, requesting me to retire on his position and endeavour to draw the Kafirs on to the Maxim.

As we withdrew from the house they at once came on out of the bush, and when we got down to the stream they were already firing at us from behind it, and, their advance not being opposed, some of them came right down into the bed of the stream.

At this time there was a really good chance for the Maxim to do some execution, for although the Kafirs were nowhere in masses, there was a straggling line of a couple of hundred of them right out in the open, and not more than 400 yards from the gun. But when the word was given to fire it most unfortunately jammed at the sixth shot, and the Kafirs had to be driven back by rifle fire. The cause of the mishap was that a cartridge-case had broken off at the rim in the barrel of the Maxim, rendering it for the time being useless. The natives now again commenced to try and get round us on both sides, and it being reported that the other impi was advancing from the direction of Government House, Captain Macfarlane gave the word to retire.

At this time I was with Captain Reid and the men of his troop, helping to keep the Kafirs from crossing the Umguza at a point where they were trying to do so a few hundred yards below us, and it was here that a man named Boyes, of the Africander Corps, was killed. He, with another man, seems to have gone down close to where the smaller stream joined the river, and was shot from the cover of the bank right through the chest, his horse being shot at the same time I think. He fell dead at once, and his companion galloped back to the main body.

Captain Macfarlane was already retiring, and the order had come to Captain Reid to do the same, acting as flanking party to the right of the main body. Unfortunately, the death of Boyes was not reported to the commanding officer until the patrol was half-way to Bulawayo, so that the poor fellow's corpse fell into the hands of the Kafirs. The only other casualty was one man badly wounded in the knee. Considering the number of bullets that pass pretty near to every one engaged in a small skirmish such as I have described, it is wonderful how few men get actually hit. The fact seems to be that in a running fight, when they are flurried and hustled, Kafirs cannot get the time they require to take good aim, and if you are near them they always shoot over you. The golden rule is to scatter out, each man firing independently in the Boer fashion.

But although Kafirs shoot very badly if hurried and kept moving, many of them are very fair shots if they can get all the time they require for aiming, as they can in hilly country, where they can take up positions behind rocks, from which they can fire at their enemy at their leisure and without exposing themselves.

On the day of which I have been speaking, some of them with whom my little advanced party was engaged were firing at us with some very peculiar bullets, which I think had probably been made by first putting a stone into the mould, and then pouring lead on to it, forming a very rough irregular projectile. At any rate you could hear these bullets coming on with a loud buzzing noise, which increased in intensity until they passed with a peculiar whizzing sound. The trouble was one did not know which way to dodge, for as you could hear them approaching but could not see them, it would have been as easy to dodge into one as out of its way.

As our small force retired the bush became more and more

100

open, so the Kafirs made no attempt to follow us. I do not think that they realised that the Maxim was out of order, and if not they probably thought that the retreat was a ruse to draw them into more open ground. What their losses were it is difficult to say, but I think that the small advance party to which I had attached myself could not have killed less than twenty; indeed, I think I saw quite that number fall. My friend Pat Whelan had fired away almost all his cartridges, and on examining my belt I found that I had nineteen less than I came out with.

However, the Kafirs again retained their position, and it was evident that their numbers were so great—we having only engaged their advanced skirmishing line—that it would not be safe to cross the Umguza and attack them on their own ground without a considerable force, both of foot and horsemen; the latter to work in the more open ground, and the former to drive them out of patches of bush.

Before returning to Bulawayo, Captain Macfarlane took a sweep round across the open ground in the direction of Dr. Sauer's house, and we there came in sight of the impi which had been reported early in the day. The main body was standing in a dense black mass on the top of a ridge just below Government House, their skirmishing lines being thrown out on either side, and in advance of the centre. Now the fact that this impi had stood idly by, not exactly watching, but at any rate listening to the firing that had been going on during the skirmish between their compatriots and the white men, shows, I think, the extraordinary want of combination amongst them, of which I have before spoken, and which has been one of the features of this campaign.

CHAPTER XIX

A force under command of Colonel Napier sent against the rebels at the Umguza—Force retire without fighting—I obtain leave to join a patrol sent out to the Umguza under Captain Bisset—Matabele dispute our advance—I attack Kafirs' centre with Colonial Boys—Matabele centre driven back—John Grootboom's escape—Matabele in flight—A good chance lost—I receive orders to retire—I dismount to get a shot—My horse bolts and leaves me—Nearly caught by Matabele—Windley comes to my rescue—Windley's horse refuses to carry double—Reach the Colonial Boys and am saved by Captain Windley's courage and self-denial—Baxter's gallant action—Gallantry and devotion to one another of Captain Grey's officers and men—Patrol retires to Bulawayo.

On the way back to Bulawayo we were met by Colonel Napier and Captain Nicholson, and it was arranged that as strong a force as could be spared from the town should be sent out again to the Umguza on the morrow, under the command of the former gentleman. Accordingly, at about eleven o'clock on Monday, 20th April, a force of two hundred and thirty white men and one hundred colonial natives, all told, left Bulawayo for the scene of the previous day's skirmish. With the force were a seven-pounder, a Hotchkiss, and a Maxim. Captain Macfarlane had command of the right flank, and Captain Van Niekerk of the left; whilst I was in charge of a detachment of men on foot, drawn from various corps, and a body of Colenbrander's natives were under the command of Captain Cardigan.

This was a most disappointing day for all those who wanted a little excitement, as the Matabele and the officers commanding our column were at cross purposes; the former wanting the white men to cross the river and fight them in the bush, and the latter being in favour of the Kafirs coming through to their side, and attacking a position defended with artillery. The result was that there was no fight.

The decision not to cross the Umguza may have been a wise one, but it was not popular with the men, who marched back to town in a very dejected frame of mind; so strong was the feeling, indeed, that it was decided to send out another patrol to the Umguza on the following Wednesday, and as I was anxious to see a good blow struck at them, I asked Mr. Duncan and Colonel Napier to give me another day's leave of absence from my work of superintending the building of forts and patrolling along the Mangwe road, in order that I might take part in the engagement. At the same time I sent a wire to Captain Molyneux at Fig Tree, requesting him to forward instructions to Lieutenant Grenfell at Matoli to march back with the men of my troop to Mabukitwani, where it had been decided that we were to build a fort, and where I undertook to meet him, unless anything unforeseen should happen, on Thursday evening.

Thus on Wednesday morning, 22nd April, for the fourth time a small force marched out of Bulawayo, in order to try and dislodge the Kafirs from their position on the Umguza, in the immediate vicinity of the town. This patrol was put under the command of

Captain Bisset, a gentleman who had had some previous experience of native warfare in Basutoland and Zululand.

The patrol consisted of twenty Scouts under Captain Grey; forty men under Captain Van Niekerk; twenty under Captain Meikle, and twenty under Captain Brand, making, with some twenty others unattached, about one hundred and twenty mounted men, with a Hotchkiss and a Maxim under Lieutenant Walsh. Besides these mounted troops, there were a detachment of one hundred colonial Kafirs and Zulus recruited by Mr. Colenbrander, and some friendly Kafirs who, however, were only armed with assegais, and who took no part in the fight. I was asked to take command of the Colonial Boys, which I could hardly do, as they had their own trusted officers with them, but I accompanied these gentlemen, and undertook to assist them in leading their men to the attack. Dr. Vigne went in charge of the ambulance waggon which accompanied the patrol.

After much valuable time had been lost in looking for the impi which was said to be behind the brickfields, but which as a matter of fact had never been there, we turned towards the Umguza, passing at the back of Government House. Here an accident occurred to the Hotchkiss limber carriage, which delayed us for more than an hour, and although the broken shaft was temporarily tied up with a chain, so that the gun could be drawn along, it was rendered useless for action until the damage done could be properly repaired.

On proceeding we changed our direction and made straight for the Umguza, and it was soon evident that the Kafirs intended to dispute our advance, as they commenced to fire on us from the low ridges covered with scrubby bush which here border the river on both sides. Captain Van Niekerk and his Africanders were soon hotly engaged on the left flank, and as the Kafirs were in possession of some ridges just in front of us as well, I was asked to advance with the Colonial Boys from the centre, and endeavour to chase them across the river. My instructions were to attack and, if possible, drive them before me, but to retire on the guns if I found them too strong.

The boys came on capitally, led by their officers, who were all mounted, and we soon drove all the Matabele in this part of the field through the Umguza, and following them up at once, pursued them for about a mile over some stony ridges covered with scrubby bush.

Up to this time I had not fired a shot, as I had been principally engaged in encouraging the Colonial Boys to come on quickly and give our enemies no breathing time. But by this time we had got right up amongst them, and I began to use my rifle.

A number of the Matabele had built little fortifications of

103

loose stones near the bank of the river, from behind the shelter of which they fired on us; but the warlike Amakosa and Zulus charged them most gallantly, and engaging them hand to hand drove them out of their shelters into the river, and killed many of them in the water. Several of the Colonial Boys were here wounded with assegais and axes, but none were killed.

It was at this time that I saw John Grootboom, a Xosa Kafir—who has distinguished himself for bravery on many occasions both during the first war and the present campaign—galloping after a Matabele just in front of me, who was armed only with assegais and shield. As the horse came upon him he ducked down, and only just escaped a blow on the head from John's rifle, which was dealt with such vigour that the rider lost his balance and fell off, and his foot catching in the stirrup, he was dragged along the road for some yards. If the Matabele had but kept his presence of mind and been quick, he might have assegaied his antagonist easily, and possibly would have done so had not Captain Fynn and myself been close to him.

We had now got the Matabele fairly on the run in our part of the field, and the only ones who were still firing at us were a party who had taken shelter in a bend of the river under cover of the bank, some three hundred yards ahead of us. I was just going with some of the Colonial Boys to dislodge them, when I saw Grey's Scouts charging down on them from the other side of the river. Finding themselves attacked from this quarter, the Matabele left their cover and ran out into the open in large numbers, exposing themselves to a heavy fire which thinned their ranks every instant.

The position was now this.—The Matabele had been driven from the banks of the river, and two or three hundred of them, panic-stricken and demoralised, were running in a crowd across some undulating ground, but scantily covered with bush, and had only Captain Meikle and Captain Brand been sent in support of the Colonial Boys and the Scouts, they might have galloped in amongst them, and could not have failed to kill a very large number of them. But no; although these officers and their men were chafing and cursing at their enforced inactivity, they were kept idly standing round the Maxim doing nothing, which was all the more inexcusable as Captain Van Niekerk with his forty Africanders had by this time silenced the enemy's fire on the left flank, and there was no farther apprehension of any heavy attack from that quarter. At any rate, one of the best chances of inflicting a heavy loss on the rebels which has occurred during the campaign was not taken advantage of.

At this time, that is just when Grey's Scouts were driving the

Matabele out of the river, some one told me that an order had come recalling the Colonial Boys, so I galloped along the line of those that were farthest in advance, and told them that the order had been given to retire. Then I thought that before going back myself I would gallop forwards and try and get a shot or two at some of the Kafirs armed with guns, who were retreating from the fire of Grey's Scouts.

In front of me lay a piece of perfectly open ground extending along the Umguza, some 200 yards broad, whilst from the edge of the open to the left the country was undulating and very scantily covered with low bush. The pony I was riding was the same that had been lent to me on the previous Sunday, and he had proved himself so absolutely steady, with rifles going off all round him, and bullets pinging and buzzing past him, that the last thing I thought of was that he might now play me false and run away. However this is what happened. I had dismounted and was sitting down to get a steady shot when some one said close behind me, "Look out, they're coming down on us from the left." I did not know that any one was near me, but on getting up and looking round, saw one of the officers of the Colonial Boys—now Captain, then Lieutenant Windley—close behind me. At the same time I saw Grey's Scouts retreating on the other side of the river, and recognised that Windley and I were a long way ahead of John Grootboom and five or six other Xosa Kafirs, who were the only members of the corps I could see, and who were also retiring; whilst I also saw that some of the Matabele we had been chasing had rallied, and seeing two white men alone, were coming down on us as hard as they could, with the evident intention of cutting off our retreat. However, they were still some 250 yards from us, and could I but have mounted my pony, we could have galloped away from them and rejoined the Colonial Boys easily enough.

A few bullets were again beginning to ping past us, so I did not want to lose any time, but before I could take my pony by the bridle he suddenly threw up his head, and spinning round trotted off, luckily running in the direction from which we had come. Being so very steady a pony, I imagine that a bullet must have grazed him and startled him into playing me this sorry trick at such a very inconvenient moment. "Come on as hard as you can, and I'll catch your horse and bring him back to you," said Windley, and started off after the faithless steed. But the brute would not allow himself to be caught, and when his pursuer approached him, broke from a trot into a gallop, and finally showed a clean pair of heels.

When my pony went off with Windley after him, leaving me, comparatively speaking, *planté là*, the Kafirs thought they had got me, and commenced to shout out encouragingly to one another and also to make a kind of hissing noise, like the word "jee" long drawn out. All this time I was running as hard as I could after Windley and my runaway horse. As I ran carrying my rifle at the trail, I felt in my bandoleer with my left hand to see how many cartridges were still at my disposal, and found that I had fired away all but two of the thirty I had come out with, one being left in the belt and the other in my rifle. Glancing round, I saw that the foremost Kafirs were gaining on me fast, though had this incident occurred in 1876 instead of 1896, with the start I had got I would have run away from any of them.

Windley, after galloping some distance, realised that it was useless wasting any more time trying to catch my horse, and like a good fellow came back to help me; and had he not done so, let me here say that the present history would never have been written, for nothing could possibly have saved me from being overtaken, surrounded, and killed. When Windley came up to me he said "Get up behind me; there's no time to lose," and pulled his foot out of the left stirrup for me to mount. Without any unnecessary loss of time, I caught hold of the pommel of the saddle, and got my foot into the iron, but it seemed to me that my weight might pull Windley and the saddle right round, so, as a glance over my shoulder showed me that the foremost Kafirs were now within 100 yards of us, I hastily pulled my foot out of the stirrup again, and shifting my rifle to my left hand caught hold of the thong round the horse's neck with my right, and told Windley to let him go. He was a big strong animal, and as, by keeping my arm well bent, I held my body close up to him, he got me along at a good pace, and we began to gain on the Kafirs. They now commenced to shoot, but being more or less blown by hard running, they shot very badly, though they put the bullets all about us. Two struck just by my foot, and one knocked the heel of Windley's boot off. If they could only have hit the horse, they would have got both of us.

After having gained a little on our pursuers, Windley, thinking I must have been getting done up, asked me to try again to mount behind him: no very easy matter when you have a big horse to get on to and are holding a rifle in your right hand. However, with a desperate effort I got up behind him; but the horse, being unaccustomed to such a proceeding, immediately commenced to buck, and in spite of spurring would not go forwards, and the Kafirs, seeing our predicament, raised a yell and came on again with renewed ardour.

Seeing that if I stuck on the horse behind Windley we should both of us very soon lose our lives, I flung myself off in the middle of a buck, and landed right on the back of my neck and shoulders. Luckily I was not stunned or in any way hurt, and was on my legs and ready to run again with my hand on the thong round the horse's neck in a very creditably short space of time. My hat had fallen off, but I never left go of my rifle, and as I didn't think it quite the best time to be looking for a hat, I left it, all adorned with the colours of my troop as it was, to be picked up by the enemy, by whom it has no doubt been preserved as a souvenir of my presence amongst them.

And now another spurt brought us almost up to John Grootboom and the five or six Colonial Boys who were with him, and I called to John to halt the men and check the Matabele who were pursuing us, by firing a volley past us at them. This they did, and it at once had the desired effect, the Kafirs who were nearest to us hanging back and waiting for those behind to join them. In the meantime Windley and I joined John Grootboom's party, and old John at once gave me his horse, which, as I was very much exhausted and out of breath, I was very glad to get. Indeed I was so tired by the hardest run I had ever had since my old elephant-hunting days, that it was quite an effort to mount. I was now safe, except that a few bullets were buzzing about, for soon after getting up to John Grootboom we joined the main body of the Colonial Boys, and then, keeping the Matabele at bay, retired slowly towards the position defended by the Maxim. Our enemies, who had been so narrowly baulked of their expected prey, followed us to the top of a rise, well within range of the gun, but disappeared immediately a few sighting shots were fired at them.

Thus ended a very disagreeable little experience, which but for the cool courage of Captain Windley would undoubtedly have ended fatally to myself. Like many brave men, Captain Windley is so modest that I should probably offend him were I to say very much about him; but at any rate I shall never forget the service he did me at the risk of his own life that day on the Umguza, whilst the personal gallantry he has always shown throughout the present campaign as a leader of our native allies has earned for him such respect and admiration that they have nicknamed him "Inkunzi," the Bull, the symbol of strength and courage. But Captain Windley was not the only man who performed a brave and self-denying deed on this somewhat eventful day, as I shall now proceed to relate.

When the Scouts were recalled, and commenced to retire from the Umguza, after having driven a body of natives from its shelter, as I have already related, they were suddenly fired on by a party of Matabele who had taken up a position amongst some bush to the left of their line of retreat. The foremost amongst the Scouts galloped past this ambush, but Captain Grey with a few of those in the rear halted and returned the enemy's fire. Trooper Wise was the first man hit, and seems to have received his wound from behind

107

just as he was mounting his horse, as the bullet struck him high in the back, and travelling up the shoulder-blade, came out near the collar-bone. At this instant Wise's horse stumbled, and then, recovering himself, broke away from its rider, galloping straight back to town, and leaving the wounded man on the ground. A brave fellow named Baxter at once dismounted and put Wise on his own horse, thus saving the latter's life, but, as it proved, thereby sacrificing his own. Captain Grey and Lieutenant Hook at once went to Baxter's assistance, and they got him along as fast as they could, but the Kafirs had now closed on them, and were firing out of the bush at very close quarters. Lieutenant Hook was shot from behind, the bullet entering the right buttock and coming out near the groin, but most luckily, though severing the sciatic nerve, just missing both the thigh-bone and the femoral artery. Nearly at the same time, too, a bullet just grazed Captain Grey's forehead, half-stunning him for an instant. "Texas" Long, a well-known member of the Scouts, then went to Baxter's assistance, and was helping him along, when a bullet struck the dismounted man in the side, and he at once let go of Long's stirrup leather and fell to the ground. No further assistance was then possible, and poor Baxter was killed by the Kafirs immediately afterwards. Whilst these brave deeds were being performed, Lieutenant Fred Crewe, with some others of the Scouts, amongst whom I may mention Button and Radermayer, were keeping the Kafirs in check and covering the retreat of the wounded men. Just as Lieutenant Hook got near to Crewe, his horse was shot through the fetlock and buttock at the same time, and rolling over, threw Hook to the ground, causing him at the same time to drop his rifle. Hook got on his legs and was hobbling forwards when Crewe said to him, "Why don't you pick up your rifle?" "I can't," was the answer; "I'm too badly wounded." "Are you wounded, old chap?" said Crewe; "then take my horse, and I'll try and get out of it on foot." Crewe then assisted Hook to mount his horse, and fought his way back on foot, only escaping with his life by a miracle, keeping several Kafirs who were very near him, but who had no guns, at bay with his revolver, whilst he retreated backwards. So near were these men to him, that one of them, as he turned, threw a heavy knob-kerry at him, which struck him a severe blow in the back. Nothing could have saved him had not the Kafirs been constantly kept in check by the steady fire of Radermayer, Button, Jack Stuart, and others of the Scouts, and also by a cross-fire from some of the Colonial Boys, directed by Captain Fynn and Lieutenant Mullins.

The splendid gallantry and devotion to one another shown by Captain Grey and his officers and men on this day will ever be

108

remembered in Rhodesia as amongst the bravest of the brave deeds performed by the Colonists in the suppression of the present rebellion. Such acts, too, speak for themselves, and bear eloquent if silent testimony against the cruel and malicious calumnies on the character of the white settlers in Matabeleland which have so frequently disgraced the pages of a widely-read, if generally-despised, weekly journal.

As soon as Grey's Scouts and the Colonial Boys had reached the guns, these latter were limbered up and the whole patrol retired slowly on Bulawayo, the Matabele making no attempt to follow. Indeed their loss must have been severe, and had Grey's Scouts and the Colonial Boys only been supported instead of being recalled, the Matabele would never have rallied, but would have been kept on the run and killed in large numbers by the mounted men. At least this is my view, and it has been thoroughly borne out by the experience gained in subsequent fights during this campaign.

Our loss on this day was, Baxter killed and Wise and Hook wounded amongst Grey's Scouts, while five or six of the Colonial Boys were wounded, but none dangerously. Wise has long ago recovered from his wound, and Lieutenant Hook is on a fair way to do so. I have forgotten to mention that my horse must have been captured by the Matabele, as he did not return to Bulawayo, and has not since been heard of. The lucky savage into whose hands he fell became possessed at the same time of a very good saddle and bridle, and a brand new Government coat.

CHAPTER XX

Telegraph wire to Fig Tree Fort cut—Patrol sent out to escort coach—I join Captain Mainwaring's patrol—Repair telegraph wire—I rejoin my troop at Dawe's store—Two murdered white men found near Bulawayo—Fort Marquand—Lieutenant Grenfell's account of the fight at Umguza.

On our arrival in town we heard that the wire was down or had been cut by the natives between Bulawayo and Fig Tree Fort. A patrol was therefore at once organised to proceed along the telegraph line, repair the break, and then go on to Fig Tree in order to act as an escort back to town for a coach now due containing a large and valuable consignment of rifles. This patrol was under the command of Captain Mainwaring, and consisted of thirty-five men of his own troop of the Bulawayo Police Force, and twenty-two men of the Matabele Mounted Police under Inspector Southey.

Being due at Mabukitwani on Thursday evening, I left town early on the morning of that day, and joining Captain Mainwaring travelled with him down the telegraph line. We found the wire broken about three and a half miles from Bulawayo. One of the poles had been chopped down evidently with small-bladed native axes, whilst the wire itself had been cut and the insulator broken.

After the wire had been repaired we continued our journey, and reached the Khami river at about 2 P.M., where we remained till about seven o'clock. Then, both horses and men being rested and refreshed, we saddled-up and rode on to Mr. Dawe's store, which is about half a mile from the old kraal of Mabukitwani. Here I heard that Lieutenant Grenfell had arrived with my troop from Matoli the same evening, and was encamped near the mule stable on the further side of the stream; so bidding good-bye to Captain Mainwaring, who decided to camp near the store, I at once rejoined my own men.

On the following morning Captain Mainwaring proceeded to Fig Tree, where he had not to wait long for the coach which he had come to meet, as he got back to my camp with it on Saturday evening. There were 123 rifles on board from which the locks and pins had been taken—each man of the escort carrying three of each—in order that, in the event of the coach being captured by an overwhelming force of Matabele, the rifles should be useless to them. However, both coach and escort reached Bulawayo safely, no rebels having been met with.

When about four miles from town they discovered the bodies of two white men lying on the roadside about 150 yards from their waggon. They had evidently been surprised by the rebels, and had made a bolt for life towards the road. The bodies had been terribly mutilated and hacked about, and seemed to have been lying where they were found for at least forty-eight hours. They were examined by Captain Mainwaring and Inspector Southey, as was also the waggon, but nothing was discovered by which to identify the murdered men except a branding iron. It was, however, subsequently ascertained that they were two Dutch transport riders named Potgieter and Fourie.

Strangely enough, these are the only white men who have been murdered on the main road from Bulawayo to Mafeking during the present insurrection, and it is noteworthy that they were not travelling along the road, but had been living for some time in their waggon some little distance away from it. I have no doubt that they were murdered by the party of rebels by whom the telegraph wire was cut on Wednesday, 22nd April. These men probably discovered their whereabouts the same evening, and were thus able to surprise and murder them during the night, or more probably at daylight on the following morning. The murderers were followers of Babian, one of the two envoys who visited England with Mr. E. A. Maund in 1899. The second envoy, Umsheti, is dead, or he, too, would be found in the ranks of the insurgents.

On Friday morning Lieutenant Grenfell and Mr. Norton rode into Bulawayo on business, and on the following day the former gentleman took part in the memorable fight with the Matabele on the Umguza, when for the first time the rebels were driven from their position in the immediate vicinity of the town, near Government House, which they have never since reoccupied.

During Mr. Grenfell's absence, Messrs. Blöcker, Marquand, and myself chose a site for a fort on a kopje near the site of the old kraal of Mabukitwani, from the top of which a magnificent view of the surrounding country was obtainable, whilst with a certain amount of work the kopje itself could be turned into an impregnable fortress. Now that work has been accomplished, and Fort Marquand will long remain as a memento of the present struggle in Matabeleland. I christened it Fort Marquand, after my lieutenant of that name, whom, he being an architect by profession, I put in charge of the working parties, so that the fort was built entirely under his direction and superintendence, and whosoever may care to examine it will see for himself that it is a very good fort, built with great care and sagacity.

On Monday evening Lieutenant Grenfell and Mr. Norton returned to Mabukitwani, in company with a detachment of the Africander Corps which had been sent down under Commandant Barnard to meet Earl Grey, who was expected by the next coach. From Lieutenant Grenfell and Commandant Barnard and his men I heard all about the fight on the previous day at the Umguza, as they had all taken part in it. All agreed that the Kafirs had suffered very heavy loss, and been most signally discomfited, and Lieutenant Grenfell was kind enough to write for me the following account of the engagement:—

"On Friday, 24th of April, it was not difficult to discern that a determined move against the Kafirs on the Umguza was in contemplation. The situation was getting unbearable, the town being surrounded by the Matabele, and the operations against them with a view to clearing the country round Bulawayo not having

111

hitherto been at all successful. In fact, an uncomfortable feeling was prevalent that we were in process of being closed in upon every side.

"It was therefore with great satisfaction that we learnt this Friday night that Captain Macfarlane was to be given as many men as could be spared, two guns, and a free hand, and go out in the morning. Great was the scrimmaging for horses among the unattached, unexpectedly sudden the popularity of the remount officer. There is a good deal to be said in favour of fighting when the state of affairs is such that you can go out after morning coffee to a certain find, with every chance of a gallop and a kill, and return to a late breakfast at say 2 P.M. There were rumours, too, that this time we really meant business, and that the natives would be encouraged to surround us on all sides, in order to give every opportunity to the machine guns and rifle fire.

"Such were the directions actually given by Captain Macfarlane to his officers, when on the march, and the tactics proved to be sound enough. The patrol consisted of 35 Grey's Scouts under Captain Grey; 25 B troop under Captain Fynn; 15 of Captain Dawson's troop; 35 of the Africander Corps under Commandant Van Rensburg; 100 Colenbrander's Cape Boys under Captain Cardigan, and 60 to 70 Friendlies under Chief Native Commissioner Taylor; 1 Hotchkiss and 1 Maxim under Captain Rixon, and an ambulance with stretchers under Dr. Vigne; making in all some 120 whites and about 170 Colonial Boys and Friendlies all told, all under the command of Captain Macfarlane. Mr. Duncan, Colonel Spreckley, Captain Nicholson, Town Major Scott, Captain Wrey, and several other unattached officers and scouts, also accompanied the force. It is worth mentioning that Messrs. F. G. Hammond, Stewart, Anderson, Farquhar jr., and two or three more, shouldered their rifles and marched out on foot, in order to participate in the day's work.

"The patrol left Bulawayo at 7.30 in the morning of the 25th of April, and proceeded in a north-easterly direction, taking the road to the right of the scene of the recent engagements on the Umguza river. The Scouts went on ahead as usual, the Africanders opening out on the left, and Captain Dawson taking command of the right flanking party, the guns bringing up the rear with an ambulance waggon and the Friendlies. This order was kept until a small bare eminence was reached on which stood four old walls, the wreck of a small farmhouse some three miles out of Bulawayo. There was a circuit of bush in front of this position, then the Umguza river, and beyond that rocky ground with thick bush rising from the river, the lines of the native "scherms" showing up black on the heights in the distance.

112

"Up to now nothing had been seen of the enemy, only some smoke from their fires. The Scouts rode down to the river with orders to draw the enemy on, while the rest of the men took up their places round the two guns. The position was very suitable for both the Maxim and the Hotchkiss; but afforded absolutely no cover for the men. The rebels, several hundred in number, no sooner saw the Scouts than they streamed down to the river, shouting out a loud challenge to come on, which was answered by our side. The Scouts drew back slowly, bringing the Kafirs well on, but were finally driven in on our position with a rush, and the Kafirs pulled up about 200 yards off in the bush, firing very rapidly. Bullets of all sorts came whistling along, from elephant- guns, Martinis, Winchesters, and Lee-Metfords, and for about an hour things were decidedly unpleasant, though up to this time we had only one man killed and one wounded. Our firing was incessant, and the shooting, though mostly at long range, very steady, and as effective probably as our exposed position and the cover afforded our assailants by the bush would allow. After the rebels had made two determined efforts to approach the Maxim, in both of which they were foiled, their fire slackened, and they apparently sent their best marksmen to the front to see what they could do.

"At this juncture, however, Captain Macfarlane ordered the Africanders to charge those on our left, and the brilliant manner in which this was carried out will not soon be forgotten by those who witnessed it. The enemy had cover here behind some rocky ridges, but the Africanders rode them out of this ground in the cheeriest way possible—they use rather more "noise" fighting than the Britishers do—and sent them flying over the river, killing no fewer than seventy-four at the crossing, and completely breaking up that wing of the enemy's line. The Hotchkiss planted several shells very well among the flying natives; whilst on our side only one horse was lost in the charge.

"About this time the Scouts were ordered to drive off the rebels to our front, and in this they succeeded admirably, but owing to the bad ground they had three men wounded. Lovett was shot here, and subsequently died from the effects of his wound, whilst John Grootboom, a very plucky colonial native, well known in Rhodesia, was also hit in two places while trying to drive some natives out of a donga.

"Meanwhile Captain Dawson with his men on the right had been holding his own under a galling fire in open ground, unable to have a good shot at the enemy who were in the bush. They were having a very warm time of it, and had lost two men killed and one wounded, when Burnham was ordered to clear the bush with 100 of

113

the Taylor's Friendlies, wearing red capes and carrying assegais. The charge was successful, and, backed up by Captain Taylor and Colenbrander's Cape Boys armed with rifles, the Friendlies cleared the bush and relieved Dawson from the hidden enemy.

"About this time a message arrived from Captain Colenbrander that a fresh impi from the west meant to attack us, and sure enough they turned up very soon after, but seeing how the others had fared they kept fully half a mile off, sending a number of shots after the Africanders, whom they tried to cut off. The Maxim and Hotchkiss, however, kept them from coming nearer. The main body of the enemy having now partially reformed, the Africanders went to assist the Scouts, and the enemy were driven off fully two miles, one of our men and one horse being wounded in the sortie.

"Captain Macfarlane thought it was now time to get home, as the wounded would take some time to see to, and there was a chance of his having to fight his way back to town; so orders were given for the ambulance to prepare to return to Bulawayo, and the whole column marched back in good order, having had by far the most successful day since the commencement of the rebellion. Our loss was four white men killed and four wounded, two Cape Boys and one Friendly wounded, one horse and one mule killed. It is very difficult to estimate the number of natives engaged, but there were probably at least as many as 2000 in all opposed to us. How many were killed it is difficult to say, but from the bodies which were counted, and from the reports of the wounded brought in by Captain Colenbrander and his boys, who were over the ground in the afternoon, the enemy's loss must have been considerable. A vidette party of four mounted men, who were sent out to Government House in the morning, allowed themselves to be surprised and surrounded by the rebels, and one, unfortunately, got killed, namely Trooper B. Parsons of D troop, the other three just escaping with their lives.

"After the return of the column in the afternoon from the Umguza, a small patrol under Lieutenant Boggie, consisting of thirty dismounted men of C troop, fifty of Colenbrander's Cape Boys, and ten of Grey's Scouts mounted, with one Maxim gun, went out in the direction of Sauer's house, and turning to the left, past Government House and Gifford's house, picked up Trooper Parsons' body, and returned to town via the Brickfields, not having seen any of the enemy. A seven-pounder was placed in position on the rise at the back of Williams' buildings, trained ready on to the ridge at the left of Government House, in order to shell the position if necessary. After the return of the patrol the Observatory reported the appearance of a large body of the rebels, who came over the ridge to the east of Government House down as far as the spruit. Trooper Edward Appleyard, seriously wounded on the Umguza in the morning, died on Saturday night, and at 11.30 on Sunday morning his body, together with those of Troopers Whitehouse, Gordon, and Parsons, was accorded a military funeral."

CHAPTER XXI

Hand over the command of Fort Marquand to Lieutenant Grenfell—Proceed towards Bulawayo—Fort at Wilson's farm—Umguza fight the first Matabele defeat—Murder of eight coolies on the outskirts of Bulawayo—Arrival of Earl Grey at Bulawayo—Matabele threaten Fort Dawson—Captain Molyneux's farm destroyed—I am sent to Khami river to build a fort—Meet Cornelius Van Rooyen—Marzwe orders his people to come to Fort Mabukitwani for protection—Marzwe's kraal attacked, and all his people reported murdered—I start with my men to visit Marzwe's kraal—Rebels defeated by Marzwe's people, and prisoners and cattle recaptured—We return to the fort—I am ordered to collect a force, and march to Bulawayo—Changes in the command of the forts—Reach Bulawayo with my force.

Lieutenant Grenfell having brought me a despatch on Monday evening, acquainting me that my presence was again required in Bulawayo, I handed over the command of Fort Marquand to him on the following morning, and rode in to town alone, meeting Lieutenant Parkin and a second escort which had been sent down to meet Earl Grey at the Khami river.

On arriving at Matabele, Wilson's farm, six miles from Bulawayo, I found Captain Dawson with his troop and a lot of the "Friendlies" busily engaged in building a fort on a commanding position some four hundred yards away from the homestead and mule stables. With Captain Dawson, too, were my old friends, the well-known American Scouts Burnham and Ingram, and that very plucky English Scout Mr. Swinburne.

Although this detachment had only arrived here on the previous day, very considerable progress had already been made with the fort, which I was very pleased to find was being built at this

115

place, as I had long advocated it, as also that another should be established at the Khami river, about half-way between Wilson's farm and Fort Marquand.

This last link in the chain of forts between Bulawayo and Mangwe did not come into existence until some few days later, and only then could it be said that it was possible to have the road properly patrolled. Whilst resting my horse for half an hour at Dawson's Fort I heard more details from him and the Scouts concerning the fight on the Umguza on the previous Saturday, which they considered to be the greatest reverse which the Matabele had yet suffered; or perhaps it would be fairer to say the only reverse, since, although, in every encounter their losses must have been very heavy compared with those of the whites, yet this was the first time that they had deemed it expedient to retreat from their position after the fight was over.

On reaching Bulawayo, however, I found that, although the impis which for the last ten days had been encamped along the Umguza in the immediate neighbourhood of the town had now moved some miles farther down the river, yet parties of them were still hanging about ready to murder any defenceless persons that they might be able to surprise, even on the very outskirts of the town, as was sufficiently proved by the fact that on the very morning of my arrival, that is on Tuesday, 28th April, several coolies had been murdered in their vegetable gardens just beyond the native location.

The following account of this affair I have taken over from the *Matabele Times* of 2nd May, by kind permission of the editor: "On their arrival in camp on Tuesday morning after night duty in the laager, the Mounted Police found a number of terrified coolies awaiting them, who informed them that they had been attacked by a large body of Matabele at their vegetable gardens, situated about two miles beyond the Matabele Mounted Police camp, and that eight of their number had been murdered. Some twelve or fifteen of the police promptly seized their rifles and bandoleers, and proceeded—on their own accord—in skirmishing order to the scene of the massacre, which they reached after a sharp twenty minutes' walk. The enemy had disappeared from sight, but the tale of those coolies who had been fortunate enough to escape proved only too true. No less than eight coolies, including one young woman, were found lying foully murdered in different parts of the gardens, and every one, though pierced through over and over again with assegai stabs, was still warm. This proves that the enemy must have rushed down on the unprotected coolies in broad daylight.

"Shortly after the return of the police to camp, a couple of

116

unarmed mounted men rode down to the gardens. They had not been there five minutes when they were fired upon from the adjacent kopjes, and they had to retire precipitately. This goes to prove that the enemy do not intend to give up their present position unless they are driven from it, and the sooner that is effected the better." The following information was also given to the public committee. Sedan deposed: "I slept at my garden near the Butts last night with an American negro called Smith. Smith this morning before sunrise started to go to his own garden. I heard shots fired just after he left me. His Zambesi boy ran over and told me Smith had been killed. I saw about forty or fifty Kafirs. I saw one man with a gun, whilst the rest had assegais and sticks. I hid myself in a ditch, and saw the Kafirs in the gardens. I saw them kill Indians with the gun and the assegais. About half an hour later I saw a picket of four white men come to the gardens. I ran to the picket and came in to town. I was too frightened to say anything." Ahchelrising deposed: "I slept in my garden and heard a shout from a lot of Indians early this morning that the Matabele were on to us. I ran away, and saw my brother Isree shot in front of me. I came to town and reported in the laager, and then went back to my garden. I saw the bodies of Goolab, Yitian, Venclayelee and his wife, Ramsamee and Chinantoniem. Smith's Zambesi boy was also killed."

On Tuesday night, 28th April, Earl Grey, accompanied by his secretary Mr. Benson, and General Digby Willoughby—who had been down to Mafeking in order to hurry forward the food supplies and relief forces—arrived in Bulawayo. The coach which brought the administrator and his party was escorted into town by Lieutenant Parkin and his men, whom I had met on their way down to meet it. They seem to have narrowly missed, or been missed by, a portion of Babian's impi, which was reported on Wednesday morning to have crossed the road near the Khami river early on Tuesday night just after the coach had passed.

On the following morning, Wednesday, 29th April, an impi of several hundred Kafirs, in all likelihood a portion of Babian's force, suddenly appeared on the rising ground about 1000 yards away from Dawson's Fort. They were probably on their way to Wilson's homestead with the intention of destroying and burning it down, but on seeing the fort manned by a number of white men, were evidently a bit taken aback, as they halted and held a council of war. They then spread out in skirmishing order, and getting down amongst the thorn trees in the river-bed below the house, advanced towards the fort as if about to attack it. However, after approaching to within 800 yards they thought better of it and withdrew, probably imagining that the place was defended with Maxim guns.

117

After retiring from the neighbourhood of the fort, they went down to Captain Molyneux's farm, some two miles distant, and destroyed and burnt everything they could, even assegaiing the pigs, the carcasses of which animals they left untouched, as the Matabele of Zulu descent do not eat the flesh of the domestic pig, although they are very partial to that of both species of the wild swine found in Southern Africa, viz. the Wart Hog and the Bush Pig.

During my visit to Bulawayo it was at last decided to build a fort at the Khami river, and I was asked to take the work in hand forthwith. As only thirty men could be spared from Bulawayo, it was arranged that twenty more should be withdrawn from Fort Halsted, five miles beyond Fig Tree, and I requested that Lieutenant Howard, an old member of the Bechuanaland Border Police, who was at present with Captain Molyneux at Fig Tree, and who had done very good service in the first war during Major Forbes' memorable retreat along the Tchangani river, should be placed in command of the two troops combined.

On Friday, 1st May, I left Bulawayo with Lieutenant Parkin and thirty men, accompanied by a mule waggon carrying kit, tools for fort-building, and provisions. We had first to take the waggon to Fort Marquand, there off-load it, and then send it on to Fort Halsted to bring back the twenty men from that place, who on their arrival at Mabukitwani could be at once despatched, together with the thirty under Lieutenant Parkin, to the Khami river, to commence building the fort there. This was all arranged by the Sunday evening, and everything got ready to proceed to the Khami river early the following morning. That evening, my old friend Cornelius Van Rooyen, commandant of the forces at Mangwe, accompanied by three of his men, arrived at my fort on his way to see Earl Grey, by whom he had been called to Bulawayo. He was, of course, an honoured guest with us, and we did all we could to make him and his men comfortable.

At this time, Marzwe, Gambo's head Induna, was camped with many of his people round the base of the hill on which my fort stood. As he had often expressed a fear lest the remainder of his people, who were living at their kraals some eight miles to the west, should be attacked some fine morning by Maiyaisa's impi, I had repeatedly told him to bring all his women and children to the immediate vicinity of the fort, since, as I had only ten serviceable horses at my disposal, it was out of the question to attempt any attack on a large impi in a thickly-wooded country, although I should be able to protect any of his tribe who were willing to take quarters round the walls of my fort.

On my last return from Bulawayo, I found that Marzwe had

taken my advice, and had sent messengers on the Saturday morning to call all his people in to the fort. These men ought to have returned with the women and children on the following day, but owing to their dilatory ways, and their unfailing habit of "never doing to-day what can be put off till to-morrow," they did not do so.

On the following morning, Monday, 4th May, Lieutenants Parkin and Webb started off early for the Khami river, taking the mule waggon with them, Lieutenant Howard and myself intending to follow them up and choose a site for the fort immediately after breakfast. Just before discussing this meal, Marzwe came out and reported to me that one of his men had heard shots fired in the direction of his kraal. None of my sentries or horse-guards having heard these shots, I half thought there was no truth in the report. However, I sent Mr. Simms and two other good men to scout round the back of some kopjes, about two miles to the west of our position, beyond which the shots were said to have been fired.

Shortly after the scouts had left, two of the men sent on the previous Saturday to bring in the women and children turned up, saying that Marzwe's town had been attacked at daylight by a portion of Maiyaisa's impi, and some of his people killed. A little later a young girl arrived at the fort with an assegai-wound in her right side just above the hip-bone. The wound was not a dangerous one, and after it had been washed and dressed, the child was able to tell her story, which was to the effect that Marzwe's kraal had been surrounded in the night, and every man, woman, and child in it murdered just at dawn.

Although, with the few mounted men at my disposal, I knew it would be madness to engage any large number of Matabele, unless I could get them in perfectly open country where there was no chance of being surrounded, I was not inclined to let this affair pass without endeavouring to ascertain exactly what had happened. Van Rooyen at once agreed to put off his visit to Bulawayo and accompany me with his three troopers to the scene of the reported massacre, and I sent a messenger to tell Lieutenant Parkin to return immediately to Mabukitwani with ten good men mounted on his best horses. When he arrived, my three scouts had also returned, having seen nothing, and I found myself in command of about twenty-five mounted men; some of the horses, however, were in wretched condition, and altogether unfit for hard work.

When the report of the massacre of his whole family, as well as a large number of his people, was brought to Marzwe, he received it with the utmost stoicism, only saying, "They wanted me; they were looking for me; they wanted my skin." Whether he believed it

119

or not I cannot say, but he never betrayed the slightest sign of emotion.

It was already past mid-day when I was at last able to get away with my little force, travelling across country under the guidance of an elderly savage armed with a shield, and two long-bladed insinuating-looking assegais, and at the same time adorned with a chimney-pot hat, of all things in the world, thus combining in his own person the attributes of primitive savagery and the most advanced civilisation of Western Europe.

Before we were a couple of miles from camp we met a lot of women and children making for the fort, who said that they had fled from some of Marzwe's outlying villages early that morning as they had heard firing going on in the direction of the chief's kraal. Soon after passing these people we got into country where a small force such as mine might have been very easily surrounded and cut up by a hostile impi, as the ground was very broken and on every side of us were small hills and rocky ridges, the whole being covered with dense, scrubby bush, in many parts of which a Kafir would have been invisible at a distance of thirty yards. Had this sort of country continued for any great distance, I would not have risked taking my men on indefinitely over ground so very favourable to any force of hostile Matabele which might chance to be there. However, after a time we emerged into country of a more open character, where the bush was much less dense, and where one was not constantly shut in amongst kopjes and scrub-covered ridges.

Just here one of my flanking parties came on a woman carrying a large bundle of blankets and other household goods on her head. On being questioned, she told us that at daylight that morning Marzwe's kraal had been attacked and three of his men killed, as well as one girl who had endeavoured to escape with the rest of the men. The girl referred to proved afterwards to be the damsel who had been wounded in the side by an assegai, but who had managed to evade her enemies and make her way to our fort at Mabukitwani. All the rest of the women and children, together with the cattle, sheep, and goats, the woman said, had been captured by Maiyaisa's people, who, however, she thought were in no great force, being only a small raiding party detached from the main body at the Khami river.

But now comes the sequel, about which the wounded girl had known nothing. Amongst Marzwe's men who had escaped from the first onslaught on the kraal was one Obas.[10] This man had

---

[10] "Oude Baas" or "Old Master," so named after Mr. Hartley, the veteran elephant-hunter, who must have been in the country when he was born (1864 to 1870).

recognised that the attacking force was not a large one, and he at once went round to all the outlying villages and collected a very considerable number of his chief's retainers, and taking command of them, followed up the raiders, and not only rescued all the women and children who had been taken captive but also killed eleven of the enemy, and retook all the cattle, sheep, and goats they were driving off. This good news was soon confirmed by Obas himself, whom we met coming on with all the recaptured women and children and cattle. He was a well-built, active-looking Kafir of middle height, light in colour, and with good features, altogether a good specimen of the best type of Matabele. He was armed with a Martini-Henry rifle, as were some few of his followers, whilst all carried assegais. He told us much the same story as we had heard from the woman who had just passed, except that he informed us that the number of Marzwe's men who had been killed was four, instead of three.

There was now no necessity to proceed any further, so we turned back to the fort, where all Marzwe's people arrived safely the same evening.

Early the following morning I rode over to the Khami with Lieutenant Howard, and after selecting a site for the fort which was to be built there, and leaving Lieutenant Howard in charge, returned to Mabukitwani. Here I found a telegram from Colonel Napier, which had been sent on to me by Captain Molyneux from Fig Tree. It was to the effect that I was to at once collect a force of forty mounted and eighty dismounted men from all the forts along the road, including Mangwe, and march them in to Bulawayo by Friday evening, as they were required to form part of a column which was to leave for the Tchangani on the following day, Saturday, 9th May.

As the time was so short, I rode the same evening (Tuesday) to Fig Tree in order to despatch a telegram as soon as possible to Major Armstrong, asking him to send me up twenty mounted men from the garrisons of Matoli and Mangwe, and on Wednesday I made all arrangements at the other forts. As Colonel Napier particularly wished Captain Molyneux and Lieutenant Howard to accompany the column, I put Lieutenant Stewart in command at Fig Tree, whilst Lieutenant Parkin took charge of the fort at the Khami river, Lieutenant Grenfell taking over the command of my own fort.

On Thursday evening I had all the men from the lower forts mustered at Mabukitwani, and after a cold rainy night we marched to Bulawayo, picking up the other detachments on our way, and reaching town before sundown on Friday evening, 8th May.

CHAPTER XXII

Large column commanded by Colonel Napier despatched for the Tchangani to meet Salisbury relief force—Matabele impi reported near Tekwe river—Matabele reported to be at Thaba Induna—I am ordered to the front—Matabele retire—Column in laager near Graham's store—Captain Grey's patrol has a skirmish with the Kafirs—Pursuit of Kafirs—No quarter—Reflections— Several kraals burnt, coin and cattle captured—Cold weather and storms—March with provision convoy and laager at Dr. Jameson's old camp—Desolation along the line of march—Burnham reports scouting party from Salisbury contingent had been met with—We reach Pongo store—Bury the bodies of murdered white men.

Owing to various circumstances, it was found impossible to get the column off for the Tchangani on the following morning, and the start was not actually made until Monday, 11th May. This column, the largest yet sent out from Bulawayo, was despatched with the object of opening the road to the Tchangani river, where it was hoped that the relief force from Salisbury under Colonel Beal, with which was Mr. Cecil Rhodes, would be met, when the future movements of the combined columns would be determined according to circumstances.

The composition of the force was as follows: Artillery, four officers and thirty-four men under Captain Biscoe; Grey's Scouts, four officers and forty men under Captain Grey; Africander Corps, three officers and fifty-nine men under Commandant Van Rensberg and Captain Van Niekerk; A troop (Gifford's Horse) two officers and nineteen men; B troop (Gifford's Horse) two officers and twenty men—the combined troops under Captain Fynn; F troop, one officer and twenty men under Lieutenant H. Lamb; four officers and 100 dismounted men under Captain Selous, consisting of detachments from H, C, D, K, and L troops, under Captains Mainwaring and Reid, and Lieutenants Holland and Hyden; also four engineers; making altogether 312 Europeans, supported by 150 of Colenbrander's Colonial Boys under Captain Windley, and 100 Friendly Matabele under Chief Native Commissioner Taylor. Also one seven-pounder, one 2·5 gun, one Hotchkiss, one Nordenfeldt, one Maxim; fourteen mule waggons carrying provisions, kit, and ammunition, and one ambulance waggon.

Of this force Colonel Napier was in command; Colonel Spreckley, second in command; Captain Llewellyn, staff orderly officer; Captain Howard Brown, staff officer; Captain Bradley, remount officer; Captain Molyneux, adjutant; Captain Wrey, heliograph officer; Captain Purssell, quartermaster; Dr. Levy, medical officer, with Lieutenants Little, Dollar, and Burnham as gallopers; whilst Captain the Honourable C. J. White and Mr. A. Rhodes also accompanied the expedition unattached, making I believe a total force of forty-two officers and 613 men.

With the column was one of two colonial natives who had been despatched on horseback a few days previously to try and carry a message through to Gwelo. They saw no signs of the enemy until after they had passed Mr. Stewart's farm, but near the Tekwe river they rode into the middle of a Matabele impi, in the middle of the night, which was watching the road and had no fires burning. They were immediately attacked, and the boy who got back to Bulawayo had his horse killed under him almost immediately, and received an assegai-wound in the arm. However, in the darkness he managed to elude his enemies, and made his way back to town. His companion neither reached Gwelo nor ever returned to Bulawayo, but he apparently galloped through his assailants at the Tekwe, only to be again waylaid, and this time killed, at the Tchangani, where his corpse was discovered a few days later lying in the road by Colonel Beal's column.

To quote the words of the correspondent with the column representing the *Bulawayo Chronicle*: "To the martial strains of the town band, on Monday, 11th May, the column under Colonel Napier left the citadel, and boldly started forth into the country lately taken from us by the Matabele. Within two hours our men had crossed from British territory into the Matabele country—to wit, the Umguza brooklet."

Arrived at the Umguza, it was found that we could not proceed until certain stores, which had been left behind in Bulawayo, reached us; and as these did not come to hand until the following morning, we did not again make a move until shortly before noon on Tuesday. For some miles our route lay through perfectly open country, but on getting abreast of Thaba Induna we came to a strip of thorn bush through which the road passes. Here a halt was made, whilst Colonel Spreckley went forward with Grey's Scouts to see if the bush was clear of Kafirs. He soon sent a messenger back reporting that the enemy were just in front of him, so Colonel Napier asked me to go on and obtain further particulars before he advanced with the whole column.

I found Colonel Spreckley about 600 yards in advance, the bush between where he had halted his men and the main body being much less dense than I had imagined, whilst in front of him

123

the country was very open indeed. However, the grass was three or four feet high, and as some Kafirs had been seen on the rise only a few hundred yards ahead, it was impossible to tell how many of them there might be there. Colonel Spreckley therefore wanted some men on foot to be sent forward to assist the Scouts in driving the Kafirs out of the long grass.

I at once galloped back to the column, and was ordered to go forward again with two of the three troops of infantry under my command, Colonel Napier bringing on the remainder of the force behind us. As soon as my footmen reached the advance guard, we all spread out in skirmishing order and went forwards as rapidly as possible. The Kafirs, however, who had been seen in the long grass could only have been a few scouts, who, on seeing the mounted men, had retired on the main body, for until we came within a mile of the little pyramidal hill which stands by itself about a mile to the south of the low flat-topped hill known as Thaba Induna, we never saw a sign of the enemy.

Then, however, standing as we were on the crest of a rise, from which the ground sloped off into a broad valley which lay between us and the aforesaid hill, we suddenly came in sight of a considerable number of the rebels. A detachment of them was on the hill itself, whilst considerable numbers were scattered over the open ground below it. Altogether some hundreds of them must have been in sight. Between the single hill and the wooded slopes of Thaba Induna itself there is a space of perfectly open ground over a mile in breadth, and it certainly looked to the eye of an old hunter, accustomed in the pursuit of game to measure distances and take in at a glance the details of the ground before him, that, had the whole of the mounted men with the column at this juncture galloped as hard as they could go to the point of Thaba Induna, and then swept round at the back of the single hill, a large number of the rebels would have been cut off from the bush and killed in the open ground.

These tactics, however, were not adopted, and the natives got off scot free, for although a few shots were fired at them with a Maxim and seven-pounder at an unknown range, none were hit, and they all retreated into the thick bush to the north of Thaba Induna. Our column then advanced for another couple of miles, and laagered up near Graham's store on the Kotki river.

On the following day the column remained in laager, and Colonel Napier took out a patrol, consisting of some 150 mounted men of Grey's Scouts, Gifford's Horse, and the Africander Corps, to ascertain if any of the rebels were still in our vicinity, and Captain

Wrey accompanied the patrol in order to send some heliographic messages to Bulawayo.

Leaving the laager about 8 A.M., this force first returned about three miles along the road to Bulawayo, and when abreast of the single hill I have spoken of as having been occupied by the rebels on the previous day, turned to the right, and spreading out in skirmishing order advanced towards the hill, which was reached without a Kafir having been seen. Here Captain Wrey was left with his heliograph party, and a further advance was made towards the bush on the north-east corner of Thaba Induna, where were found the "scherms," or military camps of the Matabele who had been seen on the previous day. These encampments appeared to have been evacuated early that morning, their occupants having probably moved off to join the impis which had retired from the vicinity of Bulawayo a short time before and taken up their quarters on the lower Umguza.

After these scherms had been burnt, a portion of the patrol was detached to the right, consisting of Grey's Scouts, a section of the Africander Corps, and a small party of Gifford's Horse, in all about eighty men. This detachment, after having advanced for a couple of miles through undulating country more or less covered with thorn bush, which in some places was fairly thick, came suddenly upon a small impi of 200 or 300 Kafirs, which I believe was a section of the Ingubu regiment.

These men had taken up a position along the crest of a rough stony ridge covered with bush, and when the approaching horsemen were still some four hundred yards distant they opened fire on them. Captain Grey immediately ordered his men to charge, which they did in extended order.

The sight of the long line of cavalry thundering down upon them seems to have turned the hearts of the savages to water, as their saying is, for after having fired a few more shots, they turned and ran, trusting to evade their enemies in the bush. A considerable number of them no doubt succeeded in doing so, but the chase was continued for a mile and a half, and when it was at last abandoned a long line of corpses marked the track where the whirlwind of the white man's vengeance had swept along. *Vae victis!*—"woe to the conquered!"—woe indeed; for amongst the men who took part in the pursuit of the Kafirs, on this, to them, most fatal day, were many who, maddened by the loss of old chums foully slain in cold blood by the natives, were determined to use their opportunity to the utmost to inflict a heavy punishment for the crimes committed, while all were bent on exacting vengeance for the murders of the European women and children who had been hurried out of

125

existence during the first days of the rebellion. Once broken, the Kafirs never made any attempt to rally, but ran as hard as they could, accepting death when overtaken without offering the slightest resistance; some indeed, when too tired to run any farther, walked doggedly forward with arms in their hands which they never attempted to use, and did not even turn their heads to look at the white men who were about to shoot them down. No quarter was either given or asked for, nor was any more mercy shown than had been lately granted by the Kafirs to the white women and children who had fallen into their power. This realistic picture may seem very horrible to all those who believe themselves to be superior beings to the cruel colonists of Rhodesia, but let them not forget the terrible provocation. I cannot dispute the horror of the picture; but I must confess that had I been with Captain Grey that day, I should have done my utmost to kill as many Kafirs as possible, and yet I think I can claim to be as humane a man as any of my critics who may feel inclined to consider such deeds cowardly and brutal and altogether unworthy of a civilised being.

This claim to humanity, coupled with the defence of savage deeds, may seem paradoxical, but the fact is, as I have said before, that in the smooth and easy course of ordinary civilised existence it is possible for a man to live a long life without ever becoming aware that somewhere deep down below the polished surface of conventionality there exists in him an ineradicable leaven of innate ferocity, which, although it may never show itself except under the most exceptional circumstances, must and ever will be there—the cruel instinct which, given sufficient provocation, prompts the meekest nature to kill his enemy—the instinct which forms the connecting link between the nature of man and that of the beast.

The horrors of a native insurrection—the murders and mutilations of white men, women, and children by savages—are perhaps better calculated than anything else to awake this slumbering fiend—the indestructible and imperishable inheritance which, through countless generations, has been handed down to the most highly civilised races of the present day from the savage animals or beings from whom or which modern science teaches us that they have been evolved. I have been told that Mr. Labouchere often jokingly says that we are all monkeys with our tails rubbed off, but with natures still very much akin to those of our simian relatives; and however that may be, we are certainly the descendants of the fierce and savage races by whom Northern and Central Europe was peopled in prehistoric times; and I am afraid that the saying of Napoleon, that "if you scratch a Russian you will find a Tartar," may be extended to embrace the modern Briton or

126

any other civilised people of Western Europe, none of whom it will be found necessary to scratch very deeply in order to discover the savage ancestors from whom they are descended.

On Wednesday afternoon subsequent to the dispersal of the natives, several kraals were burnt and a good deal of corn taken, which proved most valuable, being urgently required to keep the horses and mules in condition. About eighty head of cattle and some sheep and goats were also captured by Captain Fynn and Lieutenant Moffat. As during the time when the Kafirs were being chased by Grey's Scouts and the Africanders, Captain Wrey had received a heliographic message from Earl Grey, requesting Colonel Napier not to proceed any farther until some waggons loaded with provisions for the Salisbury column, which had already left Bulawayo, had reached him, we spent another day in laager. The weather had now turned very cold, and on the Wednesday night heavy storms of rain had fallen all round us, though we had escaped with only a few drops; but on the following night, or rather very early on Friday morning, a soaking shower passed over us, and as we were lying out in the open, our blankets got wet through, rendering a very early start impossible; although, the convoy having reached us on Thursday night, the order had been given to have everything packed up ready to move by daylight.

However we got off by eight o'clock, and reached Lee's store, distant twenty-four miles from Bulawayo, before mid-day. This store and hotel, noted as being the most comfortable on the whole road between the capital of Matabeleland and Salisbury, had, like every other building erected by a white man in this part of the country, been burnt down and as far as possible destroyed. After our horses and transport animals had had a couple of hours' feeding, we proceeded on our way, and laagered up for the night on the site of the camp where Dr. Jameson was attacked on 1st November 1893 by the Imbezu and Ingubu regiments, during his memorable march from Mashunaland to Bulawayo.

On every side of this camp but that facing towards the west, the country consisted of open rolling downs, entirely devoid of bush for miles and miles. On the western face there was a space of open ground bounded at a distance of 500 or 600 yards by a strip of open thorn bush, and it was through this thorn bush that the Matabele warriors made their advance. Naturally, as they had to face the fire of several Maxims and other pieces of ordnance, they never got beyond the edge of the bush. It seems a marvel that they should have been foolish enough to advance as they did, but it was doubtless their ignorance of the impossibility of taking a laager by assault in the face even of a heavy rifle fire, let alone Maxim guns and other destructive toys of a similar character, which led them to expose themselves so vainly. But they learnt a lesson that day which has never been forgotten in Matabeleland, as the present campaign has shown.

The three following days were entirely without incident, as we never saw a sign of a Kafir, though every wayside hotel and store had been burnt to the ground. On Monday evening we laagered up at a spot a few miles short of the Pongo store, where it was known that some white men had been murdered. Mr. Burnham, the American scout, who had ridden on ahead in the afternoon, returned to the column at dusk from the store, with the news that a scouting party from the Salisbury contingent had been there also the same day, but had returned towards the Tchangani just before his own arrival.

On the following morning, Tuesday, 19th May, we reached the Pongo store early, having passed the coach which had been captured by the Kafirs some three miles on this side of it. As I have already stated, one wheel had been removed from the coach, and the pole had been sawn in two, whilst the contents of the mail-bags had been torn up and strewn over the ground in every direction. The sun-dried carcasses of the mules still lay all of a heap in their harness, just as they had fallen when they were assegaied some six weeks previously.

On reaching the store we found and buried the bodies of the two poor fellows (Hurlstone and Reddington) who had been murdered there just seven weeks previously, on Tuesday, 24th March. Both their skulls had been battered and chipped by heavy blows struck with knob-kerries and axes. The bodies had not been touched by any animal or Kafir since the day when the murders were committed, as their clothes and boots had not been removed, and the blankets thrown over them by the patrol party sent out from the Tchangani, two days after they were killed, were still covering them. The poor battered remains of what had so lately been two fine young Englishmen were reverently placed by their countrymen in a hastily-dug grave, and a prayer said over them by the good Catholic priest Father Barthélemy. The remains of the third white man murdered here were found at some little distance from the store.

128

CHAPTER XXIII

Meet Salisbury relief force, with Mr. Cecil Rhodes, Sir Charles Metcalfe, and others—Column under Colonel Spreckley sent to the south—Several kraals burnt—Scouting party sent out under Captain Van Niekerk—Band of cattle captured—Large body of Kafirs met with—A running fight; Burnham and Blick nearly captured—Patrol return to laager—Capture a woman—Discover a body of Matabele, and send for reinforcement of men on foot—We hear heavy firing in front—Mr. Cecil Rhodes joins us with Colonial Boys—Advance and take part in the fight—Enemy's fire silenced—We retire.

On resuming our journey, we had not proceeded a couple of miles, when on cresting a rise we came in sight of the Salisbury relief force coming out of the bush ahead of us and just entering the valley which lay between us. The two columns were soon laagered up in the open ground some 500 yards apart on either side of a small stream. With the Salisbury contingent were Mr. Cecil Rhodes, Sir Charles Metcalfe, and several gentlemen who, having left Bulawayo on a shooting trip some two months previously, had been obliged on the outbreak of the rebellion to take refuge in the Gwelo laager, where they had been cooped up ever since.

Mr. Rhodes, I thought, looked remarkably well, and yet the fast grizzling hair and a certain look in the strong face told the tale of the excessive mental strain undergone during the last few months. Amongst those who had joined the Salisbury column at Gwelo were Mr. Weston Jarvis, Mr. Farquhar, the Hon. Tatton Egerton (M.P. for Knutsford) and his son. That evening Mr. Rhodes and Colonel Napier dined with our mess, and in course of conversation after dinner it was decided that, instead of returning at once with the combined columns along the main road to Bulawayo, a flying column should be sent under Colonel Spreckley through the country to the south of the hills bordering the Insiza river, whilst Colonel Napier should travel down the valley of that river itself with the main body; the two columns to meet in the neighbourhood of the ford across the Insiza, on the road from Bulawayo to Belingwe.

Early on the morning of Thursday, 21st May, Colonel Spreckley's column of about four hundred men left us and bore away to the south; the main body to which my own troop was attached making a move very shortly afterwards. We first kept the road as far as the valley beyond the Pongo store, but there turned off to the south, outspanning at about eleven o'clock amongst a lot of kraals, all of which had evidently been hastily vacated on our approach, as they were all full of grain, and pots were found cooking on fires that had only lately been lighted. The corn-bins in these villages were one and all quite full of maize, Kafir corn, and ground-nuts, showing not only that the harvest in this part of Matabeleland had been a very plentiful one, but also that the people thought they had got rid of the white men for good and all and had no reason to fear their return.

After all the grain had been removed that we could carry, the kraals were burnt and the remainder of the corn destroyed, in order that it might not again fall into the hands of the rebels, for a good food-supply constitutes "the sinews of war" to a savage people, who are not likely to come to terms as long as such supplies hold out.

In the afternoon we moved on a few miles farther, destroying several more kraals. The huts in some of these had been newly built and plastered, and we found that ground had been freshly hoed up to lie fallow until the sowing-time came. In every village were found goods of some kind or another which had belonged to the many white people murdered in this district, and the articles of women's clothing, and especially a hat that was recognised as having belonged to a young girl of the name of Agnes Kirk, made the troopers simply mad to exact vengeance on the murderers.

About two miles distant from the spot where we laagered up for the night, the huts of some white prospectors were found, but no trace of their former owners. These huts had been made use of by the Kafirs as store-rooms, and were found to be full of every conceivable description of merchandise, taken from neighbouring farmhouses and the hotels and stores along the road. The goods were all carefully packed up, and included bags of sugar, flour, and Boer meal, as well as boxes of soap and candles, tinned provisions, blankets, and many other articles. Outside the huts stood a waggon and a coach, the latter of which was known to have been brought from the Tekwe store, some five miles distant.

As it was evident that we were now in the midst of a native population, who were not only responsible for the murders of the white men in the district, the destruction of their homes, and the looting of their property, but who also seemed so infatuated by their success that they appeared to think that the compatriots of the murdered people "would never come back no more," it was determined to make an effort to prove to them in a practical manner that there is some truth in the French proverb which says that "tout vient à qui sait attendre."

130

Therefore at 4 A.M. on the following morning, the 22nd May, Grey's Scouts and a portion of the Africander Corps under Captain Van Niekerk, in all about one hundred men, were sent out down the valley of the Insiza in order to try and discover the whereabouts of the main body of the rebels in this part of the country. The members of the patrol at first proceeded on foot, leading their horses until day broke, when the order was given to mount. Shortly afterwards smoke was seen rising from a valley amongst the hills to the left, and the horses' heads were at once turned in that direction, and presently, after the first range of hills which bounds the Insiza valley had been passed, a herd of cattle was seen amongst the broken country on ahead. These cattle were found to be in charge of a small force of Kafirs, who abandoned them to the white men without making much resistance.

It was the firing which took place during this skirmish which was heard in camp soon after sunrise, and which caused Colonel Napier to send Commandant Van Rensberg and myself with a small party to ascertain what was going on. Just after these cattle had been captured, Mr. Little and some of Gifford's Horse under Captain Fynn, forming the right-hand flanking party to Colonel Spreckley's column, which was then moving forwards some four miles to the south, rode up, having been attracted by the firing. After a few minutes' conversation, no more Kafirs being anywhere in sight, Colonel Spreckley's men went on their way, whilst the Scouts and Africanders started on their return with the captured cattle towards the laager. A little farther on a halt was made, and some of the men produced some provisions from their wallets and were proceeding to discuss the same, when Kafirs were suddenly seen on the crest of a rise in front.

At this moment Captain Grey was missing, but he turned up immediately afterwards with seven of the Scouts, who had been foraging with him, each man having a dead sheep tied behind his saddle. These, however, had to be immediately cut loose and abandoned, as large numbers of Kafirs were now seen both in front and to the right, where they had previously been hidden in a deep river-bed.

A running fight was now commenced, which was kept up for some four miles before the Kafirs were shaken off. When it was first seen that the Matabele were in force, and meant to try and cut off their enemy's retreat, Captain Grey sent the American Scout Burnham, together with a compatriot named Blick, to the top of a hill on ahead, to try and ascertain the numbers and disposition of the rebels; but Burnham and his companion were cut off from the main body, and had to gallop for their lives, and had they not both

131

been very well mounted, they would probably not have got away, as the Kafirs nearly surrounded them in a very rocky bit of ground. The cattle which had been captured had to be abandoned by the men who were driving them, and very hurriedly too, as a party of the rebels made a determined attempt to cut them off from the main body.

Early in the fight Trooper Rothman of the Africanders was shot through the stomach, and, as a comrade named Parker belonging to the same corps was assisting the wounded man to mount his horse, he was himself shot through the upper part of the body, from side to side, and died almost immediately. Poor Parker had to be left where he fell, as there was no means of carrying him.

Just as the white men were descending the last hill-slope into the level valley of the Insiza river, a young Dutchman named Frikky Greeff, the son of an old elephant-hunter long resident in Matabeleland, had his horse shot through both forelegs just above the fetlocks. On being struck the poor animal fell heavily, pinning its rider to the ground. He, however, soon extricated himself, and one of the Scouts, Trooper Button, who was riding a strong, quiet horse, took him up behind him. Up to this time poor Rothman had been able to retain his seat on his horse, but being greatly weakened by loss of blood, and in fact in a dying condition, he now fell off. Lieutenant Sinclair of the Africander Corps, on seeing this, dismounted, and with the assistance of others placed Rothman across his saddle, and, mounting behind him, carried him in this way for over three miles. By this time it was apparent to all that the man was dead, so, as the Kafirs had now given up the pursuit, the body was placed on the ground in a shady place, there to remain until it could be recovered and brought in to camp.

After getting out into the open country the horses were off-saddled for an hour on the banks of a stream which runs into the Insiza, and the patrol then returned to laager. Besides the two men who were killed, two more were wounded, though not seriously, Trooper Niemand being shot through the fleshy part of the arm, and Trooper Geldenhuis getting something more than a graze just above his ankle. Singularly enough, as all the men were mixed up together, all the casualties occurred to members of the Africander Corps.

Just at sunrise the same morning Colonel Napier asked me to take a few mounted men of the Salisbury column and proceed, together with a small detachment of the Africander Corps under Commandant Van Rensberg, to a ridge of hills on our left rear, in order to burn some kraals which could be seen with the glasses in that direction.

We were just getting ready to start, when shots were heard

132

straight ahead of us down the Insiza valley; and as the firing, though never very heavy, was kept up until our horses were all saddled up, Van Rensberg and myself asked permission to take our men in the direction of the firing, as we knew that it meant that Captains Grey and Van Niekerk were engaged with a party of Matabele, and we thought that we might be able to render them some assistance.

Colonel Napier at once granted us permission to do as we wished; so we lost no time in making a move, and before we had ridden much more than a mile heard two shots at no great distance on our left front. We immediately turned in that direction, and after having crossed a small stream, again heard two more shots which sounded quite close, in fact, only just beyond a ridge of low stony hills on our left. On hearing these shots we rode to the crest of the ridge as quickly as possible, and then saw a broad open valley beyond us, in the centre of which stood a good-sized native kraal. We however could see nothing, either of our friends or our enemies, nor did we hear any further shots. We therefore crossed the ridge, and a deep river-bed beyond it, and rode towards the kraal, with the intention of burning it. Before reaching it, however, we caught sight of a few natives running through some corn stubble, and galloping after them found them to be a young woman and three little girls. These were taken prisoners and sent back to camp, as it was thought that Colonel Napier might be able to obtain some information from them regarding the whereabouts of any impis that might be about.

Just then a man carrying a shield and assegais was seen running to our right. He was soon caught and shot by some of the Africanders, just as he threw himself under a bush, where he then lay on his face, dead. "Pull him out that I may look on the murderer's face," I said in Dutch to the men, which they did, revealing the features of a middle-aged evil-looking Kafir, whom, however, I did not remember to have ever seen before.

After killing this man we rode back towards the kraal, but before reaching it, made out a number of Matabele standing on the slope of a hill overlooking a deep river-bed, about a mile distant. On looking at these natives through the glasses, I could see that they were all men, many carrying shields, and as there were too many of them to make it possible to suppose that they all belonged to the kraal near which we were standing, I surmised that they probably belonged to the impi with which Captains Grey and Van Niekerk had been engaged.

Not knowing their numbers, and recognising the impossibility of getting at them in the hills with mounted men, Van Rensberg and myself judged it advisable to send back to the laager for a reinforcement of men on foot. A man was therefore at once despatched with a verbal message to Colonel Napier, and whilst waiting for his return we took up our position on the crest of the rise we had previously crossed, in order both to guard against a surprise and keep a watch on the enemy. These latter gradually retired round the shoulder of the hill and disappeared from view.

From where we had taken up our position we could see the laager, which was little more than a mile distant, and the reinforcement of footmen we had asked for had already left it, when a heavy fusillade broke out which sounded amongst the hills to our left front. Immediately after this heavy firing commenced, large numbers of Matabele, who up to that moment had been hidden in the river-bed below the hill on which we had seen the others standing, suddenly showed themselves, and streamed out across a corn-field with the evident intention of taking part in the fight which it seemed was going on between the Scouts and Africanders under Captains Grey and Van Niekerk and another body of Matabele. Our party consisted of only twenty-two men all told, and it was rather difficult to know what was the best course for us to pursue; but we had just decided to go on and try and reach our friends without waiting for the reinforcements, when the heavy firing ceased, being succeeded by scattered shots, which showed that the fight was moving more and more to the right. The Matabele whom we had seen leaving the shelter of the river-bed must also have recognised this fact, as they soon returned, marching in lines across the corn-field where we had first seen them, and again taking up their old position.

Shortly after this Captain Windley and Lieutenant Frost came up with thirty Colonial Boys, and Captain Taylor and Lieutenant Jackson also brought a contingent of Friendly Matabele; but as but few of these latter were armed with rifles, they could not be expected to be very useful in attacking a position, though no doubt they would have done excellent service in following up a defeated foe. Mr. Cecil Rhodes, Sir Charles Metcalfe, Mr. Weston Jarvis, and Lieutenant Howard also came up with the Colonial Boys.

On their arrival we at once proceeded as quickly as possible towards the point in the hills from which the heavy firing had seemed to come, and after having advanced for about a mile and a half through thick thorn bush we found ourselves in a valley bounded on one side by the main range of hills, and on the other by a single hill very thickly wooded at the crest. At this point several natives were seen on the hills above us to the left, and a few shots were fired at them, which they returned, whilst at the same time some shots were also fired at us from the crest of the rise to our right. I therefore ordered the Colonial Boys to charge up the hill and take it, which they at once did, led by their officers and Lieutenant Howard; the few natives who had been firing from the summit at once giving up their position, and running down into the thick bush on the farther side, several of them leaving blankets and other goods behind them, whilst in one case a handkerchief had been abandoned, which was found to contain about twenty Martini-Henry cartridges. After we had taken possession of the hill, a few odd Matabele fired a shot or two at us from the valley below and from the hills above, but their fire was soon silenced by the heavy fusillade kept up by the Colonial Boys.

From the position we had taken we commanded a good view over the country to our front and right front, but we could see nothing of the mounted men under Captains Grey and Van Niekerk, and therefore judged that they had found it necessary to retreat from the Matabele by a circuitous route to the laager; and we soon saw that it would be expedient for us to do the same, as we could see a large number of rebels on a hill about 1000 yards to our right, amongst them being a man on horseback, and knew that besides those actually in sight there were many others in the river-bed under the hill, as well as the impi which had been engaged with the Scouts and Africanders, which we afterwards discovered was lying in a deep river-bed hidden from view only a short distance ahead of the hill on which we were standing.

In the valley beyond this river-bed were two small herds of cattle in a corn-field, but this seemed such a very obvious bait to entice us onwards that Van Rensberg and myself at once saw the advisability of getting back to the more open country beyond the thick thorn bush through which we had come as quickly as possible, in order not to allow ourselves to be outflanked by the impi to our right, which had now disappeared in the bush behind the hill on which we had seen it.

Had we crossed the river-bed in front of us and endeavoured to capture the cattle, we should have been completely cut off from the laager by two separate impis, which our small force would have been altogether inadequate to cope with. By keeping well to the right, however, on our return to the open country we avoided coming in contact with the enemy in the bush, and saw nothing more of them.

135

CHAPTER XXIV

Position of laager shifted—Massacre of the Ross and Fourie families—Remains of some of the Fouries found—Advance on Matabele scherms and find them deserted—Visit the scene of yesterday's fight—Burn kraals and return to camp—Bury two men killed in yesterday's fight and the remains of the Fourie family— Find the remains of the Ross family—March down the Insiza valley—Burn a large number of kraals—Colonel Spreckley's column captures cattle and donkeys—Remains of several murdered Europeans found—The murder of Dr. and Mrs. Langford—Column sent to the Filibusi district—Return to Bulawayo—I visit Essexvale—A scene of desolation.

On reaching the laager, Van Rensberg and myself, backed by Mr. Cecil Rhodes, were very anxious to have the base camp moved at once to the kraal near to which we had captured the woman in the early morning, and then at once attack the impis we had seen that same afternoon with as large a force as could be spared from the laager. However, as Captains Grey and Van Niekerk had then not yet returned, Colonel Napier thought it would be better to move the laager round the hills to the vicinity of the Insiza river and attack the rebels from that side on the following day.

This plan was at once acted upon, and the Scouts and Africanders turning up just as we had inspanned, we moved round the broken country in which the Matabele had taken up their positions, and camped in open ground beyond it, on a small stream running into the Insiza river.

Early the following morning we moved to the bank of the river itself, just opposite the spot where a Dutchman named Fourie had been building a house for a Mr. Ross, whose temporary residence whilst the house was being built could be seen still standing on a rise some mile and a half farther down the river.

At the latter end of March Mr. Fourie had been living here with his wife and six children, whilst Mr. and Mrs. Ross with an adopted daughter named Agnes Kirk were occupying temporary dwellings some little distance away from them. These eleven people—two men and nine women and children—were all murdered on the outbreak of the rebellion, Miss Johanna Ross being the only survivor of her family, and owing her escape to the fact that at the time the murders were committed she was on a visit to friends living near the main road, who, having received warning of the rising, took

136

her with them to Mr. Stewart's store at the Tekwe river, where they were relieved by Captain Grey and his men on Thursday, 26th March.

With others I went down to the scene of the massacre of the Fourie family early in the morning and found the remains of four people—a woman and three children, the body of Mr. Fourie and those of three of the children being missing. The murders had evidently been committed with knob-kerries and axes, as the skulls of all these poor people had been very much shattered. The remains had been much pulled about by dogs or jackals, but the long fair hair of the young Dutch girls was still intact, and it is needless to say that these blood-stained tresses awoke the most bitter wrath in the hearts of all who looked upon them, Englishmen and Dutchmen alike vowing a pitiless vengeance against the whole Matabele race.

At about ten o'clock a force of about 300 men under Captain Grey was despatched to the scene of yesterday's fighting, Colonel Napier and staff taking up a position with a seven-pounder gun on the top of a hill which commanded the valley in which we had seen the two small herds of cattle on the preceding day. I was placed in charge of the infantry division, which, spread out in skirmishing order, formed the centre of the line of attack.

After what had been seen that morning of the ghastly remains of the Fourie family, every one was most eager to come to close quarters with the Kafirs, but we were not able to do so, as, although we found the scherms where they had slept, with the fires still burning in them, the impis had left apparently at daylight in the morning, and it was impossible to tell in which direction they had gone, as their camp was surrounded by rough stony hills, on which their footsteps had left no trace. As the number of their scherms showed that the rebels must have been at least a thousand strong, I don't quite know why they did not wait for us and have another day's fighting, the more especially as they had been successful in repulsing about one hundred mounted men of the Scouts and Africanders on the previous day. I am half inclined to think that several rocket signals sent up from our laager during the early part of the preceding night, to notify our whereabouts to Colonel Spreckley, may have had something to do with their unexpected retreat, or possibly a peep at our laager at daylight may have given them an exaggerated idea of our numbers. At any rate they were gone, and the blow which might have been struck at them on the afternoon of the day before was now not struck at all.

On the site of the engagement of the previous morning between Grey's Scouts and the Africanders and the one section of the Matabele, we found the body of Parker, absolutely stripped of

137

clothing, even to the socks, and riddled with assegai stabs inflicted after death. The corpse was carried back to camp, together with that of Rothman, which latter, as it had been carried to some distance from the scene of the fight, had not been found and mutilated by the Kafirs. The Matabele must have removed their dead, as none were lying on the hill-side below Parker's corpse, where many had been seen to fall. However, in a small kraal situated just under the hills and within a mile of the scene of the fight, we found a Kafir lying stretched out on his back close to the door of a hut, who could not long have been dead, as his body was still warm, and his limbs quite limp. He had evidently been wounded during the fight, the bullet having passed through both thighs, and broken the right femur. Then I suppose he had been carried or had crawled to the village where we found him lying, and a cord tightly twisted round his neck showed that he had been strangled shortly before our arrival on the scene. Whether he had thus compassed his own death on hearing or being informed of our approach, or whether he had been strangled by a friend to prevent his falling into the hands of the white men, I cannot say, but as, besides having been strangled, he had a fresh assegai-wound in the right side, I fancy that he had been killed by his friends, who had fled at our approach and were unable to carry the wounded man with them.

Besides this man, another was found in a dying condition—a young fellow of two or three and twenty who must have been some one of importance, as his friends had made a stretcher of oxhide lashed to poles, on which to carry him. They seem to have been surprised in the act of carrying him away, as the stretcher was first found, and then the wounded man was seen crawling away at a little distance, but he was nearly spent, having been shot right through the chest, and died soon afterwards. His shield and assegais, and many little personal belongings, were found tied on to the stretcher.

After having burnt a few kraals and picked up a flock of sheep and goats and a stray cow or two, we returned to laager very much disappointed that we had had a ten-mile walk for nothing, so far as meeting with the rebels was concerned. The Hon. Tatton Egerton (M.P. for Knutsford) accompanied us on this outing, walking and shouldering a rifle with the rest of us, and unless I am very much mistaken no one was more eager to let off his piece at a Kafir than was he. In the afternoon a military funeral was accorded to the bodies of Parker and Rothman, and also to the poor scattered remains of the Fourie family, which having been carefully collected were all buried in one grave dug close alongside that in which the two dead troopers had been placed. The funeral service was read by the Rev. Douglas Pelly, who was attached to the Salisbury contingent.

After the service was over I took a few men of the Africander Corps, and some friendly Matabele with a stretcher, and went off to collect the remains of the Ross family. These we found had been scattered and dragged about in every direction by dogs or wild animals. We could find no trace of Mr. Ross, and it is quite possible that he had been murdered at some distance from his homestead. The broken skull of a young woman which we found close to the door of one of the huts must have been that of Miss Agnes Kirk, but of old Mrs. Ross all we found by which to identify her was a mass of long grey hair, the skull having disappeared. Besides these sad relics we also found the remains of three children, the one a boy by his clothes, and the other two, little girls, their fair hair being still plaited into several short plaits in the Boer style. These three poor children must have been members of the Fourie family who had probably been visiting the Rosses on the day when the murders were committed.

Thus, of the eleven people murdered here some remains of all were found, except of Mr. Fourie and Mr. Ross, and these being the only men were very likely led away on some pretext, such as looking at cattle, and murdered at a distance from their dwellings where there was no chance of their getting hold of rifles or revolvers. Then, the men being disposed of, the noble savages came down fearlessly to the homesteads and smashed in the heads of the women and children comfortably and at their leisure.

On Sunday, 24th May—the Queen's Birthday—we continued our march down the Insiza valley, burning a large number of kraals as we advanced. All these kraals had only just been deserted by their owners, and they were all full of grain, while, in addition, in every one were found articles of some kind or another which had been taken from the homesteads of white men. All the grain that could not be carried with us was destroyed as far as possible. In many of the kraals were found large accumulations of dried meat, and many dried skins of bullocks, cows and calves, proving that the rinderpest had been brought into this district by the natives since the outbreak of the rebellion, and had been playing havoc amongst their cattle.

As we advanced, burning kraal after kraal, on the northern slope of the range which runs to the south of and parallel to the course of the Insiza river, column after column of smoke continually ascending into the clear sky from the southern side of the hills let us know that Colonel Spreckley's column was devastating the murderers' country on his line of march as effectually as we were doing on ours.

139

On the following day we still pursued our way unopposed down the Insiza valley, burning kraal after kraal, but never seeing a sign of the native inhabitants, who had evidently received timely notice of our approach and fled into the hills. On the morning of Wednesday, 27th May, we reached the Belingwe road at about nine o'clock, and were soon joined by Colonel Spreckley's column which had been waiting for us a little farther down the road. Colonel Spreckley's force had had no general engagement with the enemy, but his scouts had captured about seven hundred head of cattle and twenty-three donkeys. They had also found the remains of several murdered Europeans, amongst whom the bodies of a miner named Gracey and those of Dr. and Mrs. Langford and a Mr. Lemon were recognised. Mr. Gracey's body lay just outside his hut, but he had evidently been killed when lying on his bed inside, as a blanket still lying there was soaked through and through with blood.

The case of Dr. and Mrs. Langford is one of the saddest of the many sad episodes of the late native insurrection in Matabeleland. They had been married but a short time, and had only left the old country three months before the rebellion broke out. Unfortunately fate ordained that they should reach Bulawayo, and leave it in order to take up their residence in the Insiza district, just before the outbreak. Thus they were suddenly surprised by a party of murderous savages when travelling in their waggon. Mr. Lemon was with them, and his body was found lying close to that of Dr. Langford; but poor Mrs. Langford's corpse was discovered some two miles away under the bank of a stream flowing a few hundred yards below Mr. Rixon's farmstead. It looked as if when first attacked the two men had held the murderers at bay, and given Mrs. Langford time to run on to Mr. Rixon's house in the hope of obtaining assistance. But when she reached the homestead she found it unoccupied, Mr. Rixon having left the day before. The poor woman then probably waited at the house for the husband and friend that never came, and then knowing that they must have been killed took refuge under the bank of the river which ran below the house. Here she seems to have lain hidden for some days at least, as she had made a sort of bed of dry grass to lie on under the bank, and as a pie-dish was found beside her body, she probably visited the house at nights to get food of some sort. The agony of mind this poor young woman must have suffered, one shudders to think of. But at last the Kafirs found her, and then, poor soul, her troubles were nearly at an end, for they lost no time in killing her. They appear to have stoned her to death, as her skull was terribly shattered and some large round stones taken from the river-bed were lying beside her corpse. None of her clothes had been removed, and two rings

140

were still on her finger, on the inner side of one of which were engraved the words "Sunny Curls, Mizpah."

On the afternoon of the day on which the columns rejoined, the Insiza river was recrossed by the ford on the main road leading from Belingwe to Bulawayo, and on the following day, 27th May, the Salisbury contingent, reinforced by sixty men of Gifford's Horse, left the Bulawayo column, and went off southwards with the intention of visiting the Filibusi district, where it was thought that an impi might be met with, and thence making their way to Bulawayo by the road which passes Edkins' store, where it may be remembered a number of white men were murdered at the first outbreak of the insurrection. As soon as the flying column under Colonel Beal had left us, Colonel Napier gave the word to inspan, and an hour later the remainder of the troops under his command were on their way back to the capital of Matabeleland, which was finally reached after an uneventful journey on Sunday, 31st May.

As on the road home the column passed near the northern boundary of my Company's property of Essexvale, I asked and obtained leave from Colonel Napier to pay a visit in company with Mr. Blöcker to the homestead where I had been living in the midst of an apparently happy and contented native population at the outbreak of the insurrection. Leaving the camp at daylight, just as the mules were being inspanned for the morning's trek, we reached the scene of our agricultural labours after a two hours' ride, only to find that the house was absolutely gone, literally burnt to ashes, there being nothing left to mark the spot on which our pretty cottage had once stood but the stone pillars and solid iron shoes on which it had rested. The roof of the stable had been burnt too, as well as all the outhouses, and a waggon, under which last wood must have been piled in order to set it alight. The only building which had not been destroyed was the kitchen, which, having been built very solidly of stone with an iron roof, was practically fireproof. The mowing machine and rake had not been touched, nor had the ploughs been interfered with. In the vegetable garden we found any amount of cabbages, cauliflowers, onions, carrots, parsnips, beetroot, tomatoes, etc., which had ripened since the natives had left, and we loaded up our horses with as much as they could carry. The potatoes had all been dug up by some animals, probably porcupines. We visited some of the native villages close round the homestead, but found them entirely empty, having been probably deserted since the time when the Matabele burnt my house down. After having off-saddled our horses for a short time, we rode back with our load of vegetables to the column, which we found laagered up some six miles farther along the road than where we had left it in the morning.

141

CHAPTER XXV

Sir Frederick Carrington takes over the command of all forces in Matabeleland—Account of Colonel Plumer'a successful engagement—General Carrington sends out three patrols to clear the country of rebels to the west, north, and north-east—No enemy met with, but much grain taken and destroyed—A large impi reported camped on the Umguza—Force under Colonel Spreckley proceeds to attack it—Kafirs charged by mounted men and bolt— Heavy Matabele losses—How this impi was deceived by a witch-doctor—Incorrect statements in Truth.

Shortly after the return of Colonel Napier's column from the Insiza district, Major-General Sir Frederick Carrington reached Bulawayo with his very able and carefully-chosen staff, and at once took over the command of all the forces in Matabeleland. And here I ought perhaps to close my narrative, which I only intend to be a history of the efforts made by the colonists themselves to suppress the native insurrection, before the arrival in Matabeleland of the relief forces sent up to their assistance. However, at the risk of wearying my readers, I will ask them to have patience yet a little longer until I bring my story up to the date of the disbandment of the Bulawayo Field Force. Some time before the return of Colonel Napier's column, the force raised by Colonel Plumer (of the York and Lancaster Regiment) for the relief of the colonists in Matabeleland had reached Bulawayo, and had already had a successful engagement with the rebels, whom he had dislodged from the positions they had taken up on the Umguza, some twelve miles from Bulawayo, to which they had retired after having been driven from the immediate vicinity of the town by the sortie under Captain Macfarlane on 25th April.

As a detachment of the Bulawayo Field Force and some of Colenbrander's colonial natives took part in this expedition, I will, before proceeding further, give a short account of what took place. Acting under instructions from headquarters, Captain Knapp of the Bulawayo Field Force left Bulawayo at 10 P.M. on the night of 24th May in command of a detachment of forty men of Gifford's Horse, with orders to report himself to Major Watts at Government House. On his arrival there the latter officer was found to be in readiness to move with the men under his command, and at about 11.30 P.M. the whole force marched in a north-westerly direction, holding a course across country between the Umguza and Khami rivers, whilst at the

142

same time Colonel Plumer moved out of Bulawayo with another column, taking a line parallel to the course followed by Major Watts. During this night march Captain Knapp was in command of the advance, himself leading the one detachment of Gifford's Horse on the right front of the column, whilst Lieutenant Warwick led the other half on the left. Colenbrander's boys under Lieutenant Mullins were placed in the centre of the advanced line.

At about 2.30 A.M. Captain Knapp came suddenly in contact with the enemy's outposts, who immediately opened fire on his party in the darkness. Captain Knapp at once dismounted his men and kept the rebels from charging by pouring volleys into the thickets where they were concealed. He was soon joined by Lieutenant Warwick and the Colonial Boys under Lieutenant Mullins, but it was not until Major Watts had come up with the main body and the Maxim had been brought into action that the enemy's fire was completely silenced.

When the firing commenced, Colonel Plumer and his men were not very far off on the left flank, and their course was at once directed towards the spot where the engagement appeared to be proceeding. Thus the two columns joined forces soon after the enemy had retired, when a square was formed, and a good watch kept during the remaining hours of darkness. However, no further attack was made.

During the first attack, Mr. Hamilton, who was acting as galloper to Captain Knapp, was shot through both legs, whilst one of the Colonial Boys was badly wounded and several horses killed.

At daylight the following morning Captain Knapp and Captain Coope were sent out to look for the enemy, and the latter officer coming across a small party of them, he at once attacked with the force under his command, consisting of twenty white men and some of Radikladi's Bamangwato natives, and drove the rebels back on their main body, which was found to be in a strong position amongst some thickly-wooded ridges about two miles to the west of Colonel Plumer's camp.

At about half-past seven or eight o'clock the whole column was moved forwards to attack them, Captain Coope's Scouts being in advance on the right, whilst Captain Knapp with the troopers of Gifford's Horse occupied a similar position on the left. These two officers, after galloping to the foot of the first ridge occupied by the rebels, there dismounted their men, and then in the face of a heavy fire, led them on foot most gallantly against the hidden enemy, whom they succeeded in driving from their most advanced position.

In this attack two of Captain Knapp's men were severely wounded, Sergeant Peacock being shot in the stomach, whilst

Trooper Slowey had his right leg so badly shattered that amputation of the limb was found necessary.

The enemy's first line of defence having been taken in this brilliant manner by the advance guard, the whole column under Colonel Plumer then came into action, and the rebels were driven from three densely-wooded ridges successively into the open valley of the Umguza, and were then pursued for a distance of three miles. When the pursuit was over, the horses were off-saddled on the bank of the Umguza and allowed to rest until 2 P.M., at which hour a start was made for Mr. Crewe's farm of Redbank on the Khami river, some sixteen miles from Bulawayo, where it was believed that a large impi was camped in a very strong position. Captain Knapp now took charge of the right-hand section of the advance guard, and Captain Coope with his Scouts was placed on the left.

After having proceeded for about two hours, the latter officer sent a messenger to Captain Knapp to inform him that the enemy were in force on his left. They then joined forces and attacked the Kafirs, who were in a strong position on a wooded hill, to reach which two deep gullies had to be crossed under a very heavy fire. Here one of Coope's Scouts was shot dead (Trooper Hays), whilst Mr. Gordon Forbes, who had accompanied the expedition as a volunteer, had a very narrow escape. He had crossed a dry gully with four of Captain Coope's Scouts, when Kafirs showed themselves on either side at a distance of only thirty yards and fired on the white men. Mr. Gordon Forbes' horse was shot in two places, and, falling with him, pinned him to the ground, the men who were with him retreating under the heavy fire, and had not some more of Coope's Scouts come up and pulled him out he would undoubtedly have been killed. At this time, too, one of Radikladi's boys was wounded in the face and another horse killed. The main column then coming up, the enemy were driven from their position and pursued through the bush till dusk, Colonel Plumer taking up his quarters for the night in the camp on the top of the hill from which the rebels had been driven.

On the following day scouts were sent out to endeavour to discover the position of the enemy, but no trace of them could be found, so, as the horses were very much knocked up, a return to Bulawayo was decided upon. During these skirmishes Captain Knapp lost five horses, in addition to the two men of his troop who were badly wounded, whilst Captain Coope also had several horses killed. These two officers and their men, being always in advance of the main column, naturally got the lion's share of the fighting. They were both thanked for the gallant way in which they had led their men by their commanding officer, Colonel Plumer, who also complimented Mr. Maurice Gifford on the excellent service rendered by the troop of horse which bore his name.

During the first week in June, General Carrington determined to send out three patrols simultaneously with the object of thoroughly clearing the country of rebels to the west, north, and north-east of Bulawayo, before making an attack with the combined forces on the impis of Babian, Umlugulu, and Sikombo, who, it was known, had taken up strong positions in the Matopo Hills, from which they could only be driven with great difficulty and at the expense of a heavy loss of life on the side of the attacking party. Thus, towards the end of the week Colonel Plumer proceeded with a force of some 600 men to the Khami river, the course of which stream it was his intention to follow to its junction with the Gwai, whilst on Friday, 5th June, Captain Macfarlane got off with 300 mounted white men and 100 Colonial Boys for the Umguza, which he was determined to thoroughly clear of rebels along its whole course. Mr. Cecil Rhodes, Sir Charles Metcalfe, and Mr. Weston Jarvis accompanied the latter force.

Both these patrols were unsuccessful in coming up with any large body of the rebels, who dispersed and fled as the white men advanced. Thus, although some kraals were burnt and a good deal of grain taken and destroyed, no decisive engagement took place, and no heavy blow could be dealt at the ever-vanishing foe. Colonel Plumer's column got back to their quarters on the Khami river on Wednesday, 24th June, whilst Captain Macfarlane's men did not return to Bulawayo until Friday, 3rd July.

Before these patrols left, Colonel Beal, who it may be remembered had parted company with Colonel Napier at the Insiza river, reached Bulawayo and formed a laager about two miles out of town to the right of the main road to Salisbury. It had been arranged that on the morning after Captain Macfarlane got away with his men to the lower Umguza, another patrol was to leave town under the command of Colonel Spreckley for the purpose of establishing forts at Shiloh and Inyati, and to this patrol I had been attached with a few of my men, the majority of my troop being stationed at Fort Marquand.

Every preparation had been made for an early start on the Saturday morning, when late on Friday evening a report came in that there was a large impi camped on the Umguza, at the ford on the main road to Salisbury. It appeared that Sir Charles Metcalfe and the American Scout Burnham, who had been riding out to Colonel Beal's camp, having missed their way in the dark, had ridden down the main road to the Umguza, and had there seen a line of camp-fires, extending over half a mile of ground, along the wooded ridge beyond the river, which could betoken nothing else but that a Matabele impi had taken up its position there. This news that a large impi was within six miles of the town having been confirmed by scouts sent out later on during the Friday night, Colonel Spreckley received orders to make an attack upon it on the following morning with all the mounted men he could muster in town, supplemented by the contingent under Colonel Beal. By nine o'clock a force of some 200 mounted men with three guns was ready, and forthwith set out for the Umguza. This force was composed of the Scouts under Captain Grey, a large contingent of Africanders under Captain Van Niekerk, thirty men under Captain Brand, and fifteen of my own troop which was all for which horses could be found.

On reaching the rising ground about a mile on this side of the Umguza, we found the Salisbury men drawn up all ready waiting for us, and they informed us that they had been watching the Matabele for some time past, and had seen them leave the camps in which they had slept in a very leisurely way and take up their positions in the open bush behind, where they were waiting for us.

They had not to wait long. The Africanders under Captain Van Niekerk were ordered to cross the river about half a mile below the ford, which they did at the same time that the remainder of Colonel Spreckley's force and the mounted men of the Salisbury contingent crossed by the main road, the latter then deploying to the left.

At this time we were hidden from the Kafirs by the slope of rising ground behind which they had retreated, but when this was crested they were seen in the bush little more than a hundred yards in front of the foremost horsemen. The order was at once given to charge, on which a whirlwind of horsemen bore down on them, Grey's Scouts and Brand's men being in the centre, the Africanders on the left, and the Salisbury men on the right.

On this occasion the Kafirs must have been quite 1000 strong, spread out in skirmishing order through the open bush in face of the long line of advancing horsemen, yet they never stood for a moment, but were seized with a panic just as the smaller number of their compatriots had been when charged at Thaba Induna, as I have already related. In the same way as these latter, they fired a hurried ill-aimed volley and then turned and ran. In the chase which followed, a large number of them were shot down, and the pursuit was only abandoned when the fleetest-footed amongst them had gained the shelter of the belt of thick bush which runs down from the western side of Thaba Induna towards the Umguza.

I am of opinion myself that the Matabele lost more heavily on this occasion than at any other fight during the campaign, for the very reason that it was not a fight but only a pursuit in which the natives were killed as fast as they were overtaken. Just as on the day at Thaba Induna, so on this occasion the panic-stricken savages accepted death when the horsemen came up with them without making any attempt at resistance, except in a few instances. One man turned on Trooper Davey of Grey's Scouts and shot him through the thigh with an old musket at close quarters, the large bullet smashing the thigh-bone and necessitating the amputation of the limb; whilst another, leaping out of a bush, rushed on to Trooper Hamilton of the Salisbury contingent and stabbed him in the right side, the assegai entering his liver. Hamilton wrenched the assegai out of his assailant's hand and then shot him. My old friend, Mr. F. C. Farley of Grey's Scouts and a well-known figure in the Bulawayo of to-day, as he was also in the native kraal of Lo Bengula many years ago, had too a very narrow escape. He had dismounted to shoot a Kafir running a short distance in front of him, when the latter turned and rushed at him shaking his shield in front of him. Farley luckily carried a double-barrelled rifle, for he missed the Kafir with the first shot, and only brought him down with the second barrel when his assailant was so near him that his assegai struck the ground close to his feet. Two other men were slightly wounded, but these were the only casualties on our side, whilst the loss sustained by the Matabele was very heavy, not only in number, but in the rank of the men who were killed, for it was naturally the young and nimble who were able to make good their escape, whilst the greater part of the older men were overtaken and slain. Some of the latter, however, outlived this fatal day by hiding themselves in the midst of thick bushes.

That this impi should have dared to come close up to Bulawayo and take up its quarters at a point on the Umguza where the bush was not nearly so thick as it is farther down the river, at the point where several large impis had already tried conclusions and failed to hold their own against the white men, certainly took everyone by surprise; but since then several hundred men of this impi have surrendered to Mr. W. Fynn, and we now know that when they approached Bulawayo they did so under the superstitious belief that their enemies would be delivered into their hands by the Umlimo, and that they would be able to kill them all without any loss to themselves.

The story is as follows: Since the outbreak of the rebellion there has appeared amongst that section of the insurgents to which the defeated impi belonged a man who professes himself to be the prophet and mouthpiece of the "Umlimo" or invisible spirit. This man, it is said, possesses the power of throwing himself into an

147

ecstatic condition, under the influence of which he swallows stones, rolls on the ground, dances on hot ashes, puts burning coals into his mouth, and goes through many other strange performances. He is known to the Matabele by the name of "Si ginya amachi," "He who swallows stones," and his utterances have come to be implicitly believed in, insomuch that when he called for an impi to go and destroy all the white men in Bulawayo, he had no difficulty in getting a number of picked men from seven different regiments to obey his behests. His orders were that the men composing this impi should take up their quarters where we found them on the Salisbury road, and there wait for the white men to attack them. They were on no account to endeavour to prevent their enemies from crossing the Umguza, but were to offer them every encouragement to do so, "for," said the stone-swallower, "once they have crossed to the east of the river the Umlimo will strike them all blind, and you will then be able to kill them without trouble, and then go on and murder all the women and children in Bulawayo." As the white men were not struck blind, whilst on the other hand a large number of the prophet's dupes lost their lives through their superstitious belief in his supernatural gifts, it would be interesting to know how "Si ginya amachi" has accounted to the survivors for his most dismal failure; for the fact that he has not yet been put to death seems to show that he has been able to offer some excuse which has saved his life up to the present time.

It is this episode of the killing of a large number of Matabele at the Umguza by the colonists *whom they had come to kill*, of which Mr. Labouchere has made so much capital lately, and which has enabled him to indulge in so many sneers against the white settlers in Rhodesia; his stock phrase being "that the natives are being shot down like game at a battue, with apparently as little danger to the shooters as to those killing hares and rabbits." Now no one knows better than Mr. Labouchere himself the utter recklessness of such a statement if applied to the whole campaign, since it is evident that he is ever on the watch for every scrap of news emanating from Rhodesia, in the charitable hope of picking up something discreditable to the settlers or to the government of the Chartered Company, and he must therefore be well aware that the number of white men who have been killed and wounded in the various engagements and skirmishes that have lately taken place in Matabeleland is very considerable. But should any one who does me the honour to read my story be either a constant or a fitful reader of the pages of *Truth*, and be inclined to believe that the editor of that journal is correct in his oft-repeated assertion that the white men in Matabeleland have suffered an insignificant loss in their encounters

148

with the natives during the present rebellion, I would ask such an one to turn to the Appendix at the end of this book, and look over the lists which I have there given both of the settlers who were murdered on the first outbreak of the rebellion, and also of those who have since been killed and wounded in battle. These lists, if compared with Mr. Labouchere's statements, will, I think, prove to the most prejudiced that Truth—the everlasting Truth which we are told is great and will prevail—is one thing, whilst Mr. Labouchere's *Truth*, sold at all the bookstalls at 6d. a copy, is quite another.

CHAPTER XXVI

I proceed with the column under Colonel Spreckley's command for Shiloh—A bad time for the horses—I find the bodies of three Zambesi boys at Stuart's mining camp—Account of the murders—A fort built on the site of the old police camp—March for the Queen's Mine—Part of the column sent on to Inyati—Bodies of six murdered men found—Narrow escape of Mr. Rees and his family—Church and mission houses at Inyati burnt down by the Matabele—Column move to Fynn's farm—Patrol fall in with a large body of Kafirs—Council of war decides to endeavour to drive rebels from their position—Kafirs decamp during the night—A faithful servant—Kafirs disheartened but afraid to surrender—Large amount of grain captured—Return to Bulawayo—News of the rising in Mashunaland—A force sent to Eastern Rhodesia—The prophetess "Salugazana"—Umlimos responsible for the outbreak in Mashunaland—Loot the object of the Mashunas—Captain Laing arrives at Bulawayo—His successful engagements with the rebels—Matibi's valuable assistance—Loyalty of Chibi and Chilimanzi—The Bulawayo Field Force disbanded—Lord Grey's address to the members of the Bulawayo Field Force.

Owing to the delay caused by the attack on and pursuit of the impi from the Umguza, as I have just narrated, Colonel Spreckley's patrol did not leave Bulawayo for Shiloh until the afternoon of the following day, Sunday, 7th June. This patrol comprised about 330 white men, about half of whom were mounted, 100 Colonial Boys, and 100 Friendly Matabele—over 500 men altogether.

As we did not proceed along the main road, but first took a

149

branch track to the old Imbezu kraal, and then followed the course of the Kotki river until we struck the main road, we did not reach the site of the old police camp near Shiloh mission station until Thursday, 11th June. Up to this time we had not seen a single native, whilst all the kraals we passed had been long deserted and all stores of grain removed, so that our horses and mules, having to depend entirely on the dry scanty grass for their sustenance, lost condition rapidly.

One day we outspanned close to a miner's camp, which was situated on a rise above the Kotki river, and as I was field officer for the day and had to post the videttes, I placed two of them on the site of the mining camp. Here we found the dead bodies of three natives, who proved to be Zambesi boys who had been working at the mine at the time when the rebellion broke out. On inquiry I found that this camp had belonged to an American miner named Jack Stuart— a lieutenant in Grey's Scouts—from whom I learned, that on hearing rumours towards the end of March that a native rising was imminent, he and his partner had gone in to Bulawayo to ascertain if there was any truth in the report. Six Zambesi boys were left working in the shaft, which had been sunk on a reef just alongside of the camp, and two days later one of these boys came to town and reported that on the previous evening a party of Matabele had visited the mine, and forthwith proceeded to murder all the Zambesi boys they found there. He himself, he said, had managed to escape by running, but he thought that all his companions had been killed. A few days later, however, another of these boys turned up who had been very badly wounded and left for dead by the Matabele.

It appears that, on seeing two of his friends attacked, this boy had made a bolt for it, but was overtaken and knocked down by a heavy blow on the back of the head from a knob-kerry. He fell on his face stunned, and was then stabbed in the back with an assegai, the weapon being driven clean through him, and then twice nearly but not quite withdrawn from the wound, and again driven through him, so that, although there was only one wound on his back, there were three in front, where the point of the assegai had come through, just below his breast-bone, and his right lung must have been punctured in three different places. This boy would seem to have lain a day and a night, insensible, where he fell, but on regaining consciousness had found strength enough to walk to Bulawayo, some twenty miles distant from the mining camp where he had been knocked down, assegaied, and left for dead.

On his arrival in town he was at once taken to the hospital, and, owing to the kind nursing and skilful treatment which he received there, he in a few weeks' time completely recovered, and although he still bears the scars of the wounds which he received, his general health appears to be as good as ever it was.

On Friday, 12th June, the day after our arrival on the site of the old police camp, a fort was built, and here Native Commissioner Lanning was left in charge with a garrison of about seventy white men and twenty Friendly Matabele and a stock of provisions sufficient to last for two months.

On the following morning we struck across country towards the Queen's Mine, a property belonging to Willoughby's Consolidated Company. That night we slept on the way there, and the fresh tracks of Kafirs and cattle having been seen late in the afternoon, a patrol was sent after them very early the next morning, the column shortly afterwards getting under way and arriving at the mining camp at about eight o'clock.

Here it was found that although a good deal of property had been destroyed by the Kafirs, but little damage had been done to the machinery and pumping gear, the savages probably not having recognised its value nor been sufficiently energetic to give themselves the trouble of smashing it up. Another short trek in the afternoon brought us to the ford of the Impembisi river, on the main road between Bulawayo and the mission station of Inyati. Here the patrol which had left us in the early morning under Captain Gradwell rejoined us just at dusk, having been unsuccessful in coming up with any Kafirs or cattle, all of whom seemed to have gone down the Impembisi river.

As the mules and horses were now getting into very low condition, it was determined not to take the whole column on to Inyati, but only to send on the contingent who were to remain in garrison there under the command of Lieutenant Banks-Wright, together with another 100 men who were to return to the main column as soon as the fort was in a fair way towards completion. This force was accompanied by four waggons carrying provisions and other necessaries for the garrison of the fort, and the Rev. Mr. Rees also went with it, in order to bury the remains of the six white men who had been murdered near the police camp of Inyati on 27th March.

Five of these bodies were found lying on the roadside near together, about a mile on this side of the police camp, while the sixth was discovered near the camp itself. The corpses had been partially mummified by the dryness of the atmosphere, and were all quite recognisable. Mr. Graham, the native commissioner, and his four companions had evidently been attacked by a large force of Kafirs soon after they had left the police station, and were killed whilst defending the waggon on which they were travelling to Bulawayo. In addition to their bodies the remains of two Colonial Boys were also found who had been murdered at the same time as their white masters.

That Mr. Graham and his companions had made a good fight of it, and sold their lives dearly, was evident from the number of empty cartridge-cases which were found on the ground round their dead bodies, Lieutenant Howard having picked up and counted eighty-five. As, however, the Matabele had removed their dead, it is quite impossible to say what loss they had suffered. The murdered men were all buried with military honours in the cemetery near the old mission station by Mr. Rees. This gentleman himself, with his wife and family, must have had a very narrow escape, as they only left the mission station on the 26th March, the day before Mr. Graham and his companions were attacked and killed; and they must too have only just passed through the Elibaini Hills on their way to Bulawayo before the rebels collected there. Both mission houses at Inyati were found to have been burnt down and destroyed, as well as the church, in which it was evident that large quantities of wood had been piled up in order to set light to the heavy beams supporting the roof. The natives had also taken the trouble to chop down fruit trees and ornamental shrubs growing round the mission houses, and had evidently done their best, not only to rid themselves of the presence of all white men in the country, but also to destroy as far as possible all traces of their ever having been there.

On Wednesday morning the men who had been sent to assist in building the fort at Inyati returned to the Impembisi, and in the afternoon the whole column moved some four miles up the river to Mr. Fynn's farm. On the morning of the same day Lieutenant Mullins—Mr. Colenbrander's brother-in-law—had been sent on to this point with some fifty Colonial Boys to look for grain, and had come across a considerable number of armed Kafirs in a very broken, densely-wooded piece of country, just to the east of the Impembisi river. As it was impossible for Lieutenant Mullins to tell the numbers of the rebels in the broken country, he retired with his Colonial Boys to the top of a single hill to the west of the river, and sent back to camp for reinforcements. Captain Grey was at once sent on with his Scouts, and the whole column followed more leisurely, arriving at Fynn's farm just before sundown.

Captain Grey had seen a considerable number of natives, evidently watching his men from the tops of different kopjes, but as the country they were in was altogether impracticable for horses, he was unable to attack them, and they on their side showed no disposition to come out of the hills. At a council of war that evening it was determined to endeavour to clear the hills in the morning with as large a force of footmen as could be spared from the laager; Grey's Scouts at the same time being sent round at the back of the hills in order to cut off any Kafirs who might be driven out of them into the level country beyond. The general impression in camp was that the Kafirs were in force, and that we should have all our work cut out to drive them out of their positions. And so we should have had, if they had only remained to dispute our advance. However, leaving the laager on the following morning just as day was breaking, we entered the hills at sunrise, and went right through them without seeing a sign of the rebels, who we found had decamped during the night and fled to what they considered a more secure stronghold—to wit, the "Intabas a Mambo," a sort of miniature Matopos some twenty miles farther eastward.

To this fastness it was not possible for Colonel Spreckley to follow them, so, as we met no other natives during our farther progress up the river to Mr. Arthur Rhodes' homestead, nor on our return journey from there to Bulawayo, we had absolutely no fighting during the whole trip.

Curiously enough, the temporary huts in which Mr. Fynn had been living before the outbreak of the insurrection had not been burnt, and on going up to a kraal some few miles higher up the river, where had dwelt a native to whom he had entrusted some Merino sheep, pigs, and a number of very handsome black Spanish fowls, Mr. Fynn found the fowls and pigs still there and in very good condition, and on making a closer examination observed fresh Kafir footprints, and therefore came to the conclusion that the man he had left in charge of his live stock was still looking after it, retiring into the hills by day and feeding his master's pigs and fowls by night. Mr. Fynn therefore asked Colonel Spreckley to allow him to take two friends that evening, and return to the kraal in the hope of being able to intercept his servant, and bring him down to the camp.

The plan succeeded perfectly, for just after dusk the man came along the footpath leading from the river to the kraal, and was suddenly confronted by Mr. Fynn, who had been waiting for him concealed behind a bush. The Kafir was at first very much taken aback, but when he recognised his master, he burst out laughing and said: "Why, is it you, Willy? you've caught me now." This man was a native of Delagoa Bay, and being lame had been able to escape being forced into taking part in the rebellion, and ever since the outbreak had been able to surreptitiously look after a portion of his master's property, for though the Merino sheep had been driven off

153

to the "Intabas a Mambo," the pigs and fowls had been left, and these the faithful servant had fed and watered regularly every night.

He was able to give us a great deal of useful information, and told us that the men who had been seen the day before amongst the hills on the other side of the Impembisi river were a portion of the impi which had suffered so heavily at the Umguza, on Saturday, 6th June. He informed us that they were thoroughly disheartened, and wished to surrender, but were afraid to do so, knowing that they had made the white men very angry by murdering their women and children. He gave the names of thirteen headmen of kraals who had been killed on that fatal day, all of whom had been personally known to Mr. Fynn, as they had been one and all living on Mr. Arthur Rhodes' block of farms before the rebellion broke out.

The next three days were spent in collecting grain, an immense amount being found stored in all the kraals on Mr. Arthur Rhodes' farms. In almost every kraal was found something or other which had been taken from his homestead, which had evidently been completely looted before it was burnt down. Several hundred head of cattle were also recovered which had been stolen from Mr. Rhodes, but the rinderpest was amongst them and they died by the score every day. As it was very important to get as much corn as possible to Bulawayo for the use of the horses and mules stabled there, and it could not be all carried in at once on the waggons at Colonel Spreckley's disposal, a large amount was stored in a kraal near Mr. Fynn's dwelling-house, and Captain Robinson with fifty men and some Friendly Matabele left in charge of it until it could be sent for.

When this matter had been arranged, the column moved up to Mr. Arthur Rhodes' desolated homestead, which was reached at mid-day on Sunday, 21st June, and leaving again the same evening arrived in Bulawayo two days later after an absence of seventeen days.

On our arrival in town we heard for the first time of the insurrection which had broken out in Mashunaland, and learned the sad news that many settlers had been murdered in the outlying districts of the country. Colonel Beal was at this time already on his way back to Salisbury with the entire force under his command, and two days after our return to Bulawayo sixty more mounted men of Grey's Scouts and Gifford's Horse, under the command of Captain the Hon. C. White, were despatched to the assistance of their fellow-colonists in Eastern Rhodesia.

When the secret history of the rebellion in Mashunaland comes to be known, I fancy it will be found that it was brought about by the leaders of the Matabele insurrection through the instrumentality of the Umlimos or prophets, who exist amongst all the tribes in Mashunaland, where they are known as "Mondoros," *i.e.* "Lions." In the district to the north-west of Salisbury there lives a prophetess known as "Salugazana," whose magical powers were apparently believed in by Lo Bengula, as he was in the habit of sending messengers to consult with her.

Now, we know that messages have been sent to this wise woman either by the leaders of the Matabele or the agents of one of the Umlimos or priests during the present rebellion, and I think that she was in all probability informed that the white men had all been killed in Matabeleland, including the column under Colonel Beal, and asked to disseminate this news amongst all the members of the priestly families throughout the country, bidding them at the same time to call upon the people to destroy the few surviving white men still left alive in the eastern province of Rhodesia.

As for the rising in Mashunaland proving that the natives of that country have been very cruelly treated by the whites, as Mr. Labouchere has asserted, it really demonstrates nothing of the kind; it only shows that the Mashunas imagined that they would be able to possess themselves of a vast amount of valuable loot with little danger to themselves, and no fear of punishment. The kindness or otherwise of the government of the whites would not be likely to weigh with them one way or the other, given the belief in their own power to kill the whites and take possession of their property without fear of retribution.

That is the crux of the whole question; for no one who has lived long amongst the various peoples generically known as Mashunas, whose principal characteristics are avarice, cowardice, and a complete callousness to the sufferings of others, will be inclined to doubt that were they governed by an angel from heaven, they would infallibly kill that angel, if his wing feathers were of any value to them, provided that they believed at the same time that the crime might be committed with impunity.

Towards the end of June Captain Laing arrived in Bulawayo in command of the relief forces which had been sent to him from Tuli and Victoria, Lieutenant Stoddart being left in command of the laager at Belingwe. On his way to Bulawayo, Captain Laing had had several successful engagements with the tribes in rebellion living between Belingwe and Filibusi, who are all Mashunas, with a small number of Matabele living amongst them; these latter having been the ringleaders of the rebellion in this part of the country. Captain Laing received very valuable assistance from Matibi, a Mashuna chief living near the Bubyi river, who sent several hundred of his men to accompany him on his march to Bulawayo. These men did good service and fought well when supported by white men. They accompanied the column as far as the Umzingwani river, twenty-five miles from Bulawayo, returning home from this point loaded up with loot of all kinds which they had taken from their rebel countrymen.

Besides Matibi, it is worthy of remark that Chibi and Chilimanzi, the two most important chiefs in the district between Belingwe and Victoria, have both not only held aloof from the present rebellion, but have given active assistance to the whites since the outbreak of hostilities, whilst Gutu's people—the Zinjanja—have also remained loyal to the Government.

I have now, I think, given a fairly comprehensive history of the late insurrection in Matabeleland up to the time when, relief forces having arrived in the country, it was deemed expedient to disband the volunteer troops which had been originally raised to suppress the rebellion, and I will therefore leave to abler and more accustomed pens than mine the task of describing all the subsequent incidents of a campaign which we will hope is now fast drawing to an end. I will only say that no one appreciates more than myself the excessive difficulties that have been encountered in dislodging the rebels from such fastnesses as the Intabas a Mambo and the Matopo Hills, or recognises more fully the brave work which has been done under the guidance of Major-General Sir Frederick Carrington, by Colonel Plumer, Major Baden Powell, and all the officers and men under their command.

The Bulawayo Field Force was not actually disbanded until Saturday, 4th July, upon which occasion the assembled troops were addressed by Lord Grey after they had been first inspected by Major-General Sir Frederick Carrington. The Administrator concluded his address to the members of the force in the following words:—"All of you have acquitted yourselves as brave men, and I would particularly commend the conduct of Colonel Napier, who throughout the campaign has performed his very arduous duties so satisfactorily. But mingled with our enjoyment there must be some pain in looking back upon many of the episodes of this rebellion. The Company has done its best to look after your comfort, but you have undergone notwithstanding some severe hardships, which, however, you have borne like men; and the only complaint I have heard is that you were not always able to go out against the enemy, but had to perform as well the hard and monotonous work of laager and fort duty. Many of you have a Matabele memento in the shape of a wound, the mark of which you will carry to your graves. Many too have lost friends; and possibly none of us realise the loss of life which has taken place both before and during hostilities; for our

156

losses have been heavy, and form a large percentage of the total number of people who were engaged in the exploitation of the country. I cannot refer to individual cases of bravery where all have done so well, but I would again especially mention Colonel Napier's services to the country. He has exhibited remarkable tact and judgment, and has freely given great assistance to the Government. I regret that he is to-day retiring from the service, but I hope that he will continue to give us the benefit of his experience. I do not like to mention any particular troop, as each has acted so creditably, but I would note the excellent services rendered by the Africander Corps in this war, as showing the whole world the complete brotherhood which exists between the two races of Dutchmen and Britons in Rhodesia. I trust that an Africander troop will again form part of the new force which is now being raised by the Government. Information reached this country by last mail that Her Majesty has been pleased to allow a medal to be worn for the last Matabele war, and I shall represent strongly to Her Majesty that the same honour ought to be conferred on the members of the Bulawayo Field Force. You have as much right and title to the distinction as those who fought in the first war, and I hope there will be a sufficient number struck for both those who fought in the first war and those who have fought during the present rebellion. I thank you for your assistance in the past, and I hope you will remain in the country to witness the prosperity which is certain to come."

And now, Lord Grey's speech to the members of the Bulawayo Field Force having formed the closing scene in the history of the corps, whose deeds in the cause of civilisation, and for the preservation of British supremacy in Rhodesia, it has been my endeavour to describe in the foregoing pages, it only remains for me to bid adieu to my readers, and to hope that the intrinsic interest of the scenes I have attempted to describe in very plain and homely fashion may be sufficient to atone for the deficiencies which will doubtless be only too apparent in my literary style.

SUPPLEMENTARY CHAPTER

CONTAINING A FEW THOUGHTS AND OPINIONS UPON MATTERS RHODESIAN AND SOUTH AFRICAN

No one, I think, who has carefully read the little history which I have just brought to a close, can fail to have been struck by the conspicuous part which has been played by the Dutch settlers in Matabeleland in the recent struggle for supremacy between the white invaders of that country and the native black races; and it will probably come as a surprise to many to find that the Boer element is so strong as it is in Rhodesia, for that country has always been considered more exclusively British as regards its white population than any other State in South Africa, not except Natal and the Eastern Province of the Cape Colony, both of which territories, though almost purely British in the large towns, yet possess a large Boer population in the farming districts, whose ancestors were living on the land before the arrival of the British colonists.

But, in the opening up and colonisation of Rhodesia by means of the pioneer expedition of the British South Africa Company, which took possession of Eastern Mashunaland in 1890, a new departure was made in South African history, for the British became the pioneers instead of the Dutch, and a British colony was established in the far interior of the country many hundred miles to the north of the most northerly Dutch state; and it is the fact that the occupation of Mashunaland in 1890 and the invasion and conquest of Matabeleland in 1893 were purely British enterprises, which has, I think, created the belief generally held in England that Rhodesia at the present day is a purely British colony. Yet this is not the case, for within the British state there are two Boer colonies, the one of which has been established subsequent to the Matabele war in the country to the south of Fort Charter, whilst the other has occupied the hills and valleys of Gazaland since the latter part of 1891. Besides these agricultural colonies, where a number of contiguous farms are occupied by Boers who have settled on the land with their wives and families, there are many other Boer farmers scattered throughout Rhodesia, whilst up to the time when the rinderpest destroyed all their cattle, a large number of Dutchmen were constantly present in the country, earning their living with their waggons and oxen as carriers from one district to another.

When the rebellion broke out, Commandant Van Rensberg at once formed an Africander Corps, the great majority of whose members were Boers, although it numbered in its ranks a certain proportion of colonists of British blood, and it is a matter of history that these Dutchmen under Commandant Van Rensberg and Captains Van Niekerk and Pittendrigh have done splendid service during the recent insurrection in Matabeleland, and have fought side by side with Grey's Scouts and Gifford's Horse, and all the other troops of the Bulawayo Field Force, in a way which has won for them the admiration and respect of their brothers in arms and fellow-colonists of British blood; and that the mutual esteem and good fellowship engendered between the two races during the recent time of common peril may be fostered and maintained in the coming years ought not only to be the earnest desire of all thinking men, but should be also one of the main objects constantly kept in view by the English Administrator of these territories.

Many years ago, at a time when the scheme for the colonisation of the high and healthy plateaus lying between the Limpopo and the Zambesi had not yet assumed definite shape in the fertile brain of Mr. Cecil Rhodes, I remember writing in the course of an article, published, I think, in the *Fortnightly Review*, that those territories were in my opinion the natural heritage of the British and Dutch colonists in the older states of South Africa. My forecast was true enough, for although in its first inception the colonisation of Rhodesia was a purely British enterprise, yet to-day, in less than six years from the date when the Union Jack was hoisted at Fort Salisbury and the country proclaimed to be a province of Britain, it already numbers amongst its inhabitants a very considerable number of Dutch Boers, who form an element of the population, which in all South African history has been found indispensable for the gradual conversion of vast uncultured wastes into civilised states.

Now I might, I think, have gone further, and said that the whole of temperate South Africa (in which must be included the high plateaus lying between the Limpopo and the Zambesi) was the joint possession of the British and Dutch races; for in all the states of that country, the old and the new alike, we find the two races living side by side, whilst, curiously enough, in the British province of the Cape Colony the Dutch outnumber the British, and in the Boer State of the Transvaal the British outnumber the Dutch.

Throughout South Africa the Dutch live away from the towns on their farms, and, speaking generally, form the agricultural and pastoral population of the country. They are naturally a kindly, hospitable race; but as the inevitable result of their surroundings

159

and the circumstances in which they have lived for generations, they are for the most part very poorly educated, and therefore ignorant, unprogressive and bigoted; whilst among the descendants of the "voor-trekkers," who some forty years ago abandoned their farms in the Cape Colony and fled, with their wives and their children, their flocks and their herds, into the unknown interior beyond the great Orange River, in order to escape from what they considered the injustice of British rule, there exists an ingrained hatred and distrust, not of the individual Englishman, but of the government of the country under whose flag they believe their fathers suffered wrong, and it is this sentiment which at the present moment, unfortunately, is being used as a political lever, which threatens nothing but disaster to the whole of South Africa, by the anti-British, but non-Boer adventurers, who are fighting for their own hands in Pretoria.

The recent deplorable invasion of Transvaal territory by a British force in defiance of all international law, to accomplish I still fail to understand what, has naturally exasperated the Dutch of the Transvaal, and caused them to look upon everything British with more distrust and suspicion than ever; but the history of that disastrous expedition, evoking as it did the most intense national sentiment, not only amongst the Boers of the Transvaal, but also in a somewhat milder degree perhaps, though still in a most pronounced manner, amongst their compatriots in the Orange Free State, coupled with the very notorious fact that in the exclusively Dutch districts both of the Cape Colony and Natal a very strong anti-British feeling was excited, must have convinced even the most infatuated that a conflict between Dutchmen and Englishmen, in whatever portion of South Africa it may arise, will be but the prelude to a war between the two races throughout every province from Cape Agulhas to the Zambesi—a war which would retard the general progress of the country for a generation, which would be infinitely disastrous to both races engaged in the struggle, and yet could be beneficial to neither, no matter which proved victorious.

In future let us hope that neither young military aspirants to fame, who, being ignorant of everything concerning South Africa, would yet climb their way to glory over the dead bodies of British and Dutch South Africans with the most light-hearted carelessness, just in the way of their professional business, nor cold-hearted self-seeking foreign politicians, who would use the ignorance and prejudice of the Boer to assist them in gratifying their jealous hatred of England, will be allowed to sway the councils of the statesmen, British or Boer, on whose decree the fate of South Africa really depends.

160

Not being a politician nor anything else but a wandering Englishman with a taste for natural history and sport, it may be held most presumptuous on my part to have written as I have done; but yet I have the most profound conviction that a war between the Boers and British in South Africa can only be a calamity of incalculable dimensions to both races; whilst the name of that statesman, whether Boer or Briton, who should without just cause on the one hand "cry havoc and let loose the dogs of war," or on the other compel the slipping of such dogs by fatuous obstinacy, and a cynical disregard for all the principles of enlightened government, will be assuredly held in execration by unborn generations of Boers and Britons alike. Neither race can get away from or do away with the other, and therefore both must try and rub off their mutual prejudices, and live harmoniously together.

This is not difficult in a new country like Rhodesia, where the representatives of the two peoples are in the nature of things thrown much together, and where there has always been a good understanding between them, which has of late been very much strengthened by the mutual assistance given by each to the other during the recent troublous times; and the fact that in these territories a very good understanding prevails between the Dutch and British gives one reason to hope that in time a similar state of things may be attained in the Transvaal, although unfortunately in that State there are several factors which militate against such a result being speedily arrived at.

In the first place, the great mass of the European population in the Transvaal, the greater part of which is British, resides in one great city, where it leads its own life, and does not come in contact with the Dutch farming population, of which it knows neither the language nor the history, and with whose modes of thought and manner of life it is altogether out of sympathy; whilst, on the other hand, the rough Boer, in too many cases, despises the ultra-civilised, sharp-witted, faultlessly-dressed European, and does not recognise that many amongst them are fine fellows and good sportsmen, and are capable of throwing off their coats and doing a day's work, hunting or fighting, with the roughest Boer amongst them, should occasion serve.

And yet these mutual prejudices and misunderstandings between the two peoples might easily be rubbed away if it were not for the presence of an anti-British clique of Hollanders and Germans in Pretoria, whose object it is to widen the breach between the Boers and the British; and as many of these men occupy official positions in the Government of the country, and are therefore more

161

in touch with the Boer legislators than the citizens of Johannesburg can hope to be, they have opportunities which they do not fail to use of increasing the distrust and suspicion already existing between the two races who alone have got to work out the destiny of South Africa between them, and amongst whom they are only meddlesome self-seeking interlopers.

All the various States of South Africa will no doubt be united sooner or later under one flag, but I am beginning to have my doubts as to what flag that will be. It is true that at the present time there exists in South Africa a very large British population of highly intelligent and energetic men, who have been attracted to that country by the diamond and gold fields. That population is constantly increasing, but it is not one which settles on the land. It is rather a population which has come to the country on a visit, in the endeavour to make a fortune with which to retire to the old country, and as the recent census taken in Johannesburg has shown, it is for the most part composed of young men, the greater number of whom are unmarried. Now I suppose it is conceivable that a day may come, say in fifty, eighty or a hundred years time, when all the treasures have been dug up out of the South African earth; and should such a day arrive, is it not also conceivable that the great mining populations which have built the cities of Kimberley and Johannesburg in what a few years ago was a sparsely-inhabited wilderness, may dwindle down to comparatively small proportions, leaving the Boer population, which during all that time will have been increasing at a very rapid rate, once more numerically very much in excess of the British?

It does not appear to me very probable that during the present generation at least the Boers, either of the Transvaal or the Orange Free State, are likely (except under compulsion, which presupposes a deplorable war) to enter any confederacy of South African States, on any terms whatever, under the British flag; and therefore should the large British mining population now existent in the country gradually vanish, and the Boer population at the same time very much increase, the eventful confederation may take place under some other flag than the Union Jack. After all, as the Boers hold as large a stake in land, if not in wealth, as the British in South Africa, and as they were the first comers, and can lay claim to having killed off as many natives, and generally prepared as much country for occupation by white men, as the British, I think they are entitled to some consideration in the matter of the flag which is eventually to fly over the confederated States of South Africa; and for my part I would rather see a confederation take place under a compound flag, composed of equal parts of the Union Jack and Dutch ensign, with a bit of a French flag let in, to represent the Huguenots who, on their first arrival in South Africa, formed one-sixth of the entire white population of the country, and to whom the South African Boers of to-day owe many of their most estimable qualities, than have the country plunged into war in order to enforce its acceptance of the Union Jack.

However, this flag question is a problem of the future, and in the meantime it is the duty of all South Africans who have the welfare of the country as a whole at heart to do all they can to obliterate the remembrance of events galling to the national pride either of Dutchmen or Englishmen, and to endeavour to bring about once more a feeling of mutual trust and confidence between the two races. The Dutch must forget Slagter's Nek and Boomplaats, and the English must learn to think no more of avenging the defeats of Laing's Nek and Majuba Hill than they do of avenging the battles lost by the British troops in America which culminated in the surrender of Cornwallis and the declaration of American independence.

Now there has been for some years past an association in South Africa called the African Bond, which in some quarters at least must be considered anti-British, since another association called the Loyal Colonists' League has been inaugurated to counteract its effects. This latter society, judging by some speeches which have lately been made by some of its members, is frankly anti-Dutch. Now, would it not be better, if, in place of the latter society, whose object seems to be to widen and accentuate the breach which, in the Transvaal at least, is existent between the two races, an association should be formed, which all clergymen of all denominations, including ministers of the Dutch Reformed Church, should be invited to join, whose object should be the gradual obliteration of race-hatred and race-jealousy between the Dutch and British throughout South Africa, by the promotion of knowledge amongst the ignorant and prejudiced of both peoples?—for that, after all, is what is most required in order to bring about mutual respect and mutual forbearance, and enable every member of every State in South Africa to work under equal laws for the general prosperity of the whole country, a prosperity which can never attain to full fruition until the Dutch and British have attained to a political unity throughout South Africa as complete as it is to-day in the Cape Colony.

And now, after this long digression upon matters South African, and the expression of many opinions which, should they be read at all, will possibly only excite ridicule, coupled with a rebuke upon my presumption in wandering from the fields of sport and natural history, where I may be at home, into the arena of politics, where, it will be said, I certainly am not, let me say a few words about the present position and future prospects of Rhodesia.

Should the lists I have given at the end of my book be glanced through, it will be seen that the number of the settlers who were murdered in Matabeleland alone at the outbreak of the native insurrection, added to those who have since been killed and wounded in the subsequent fighting, amounts to over 300, or more than ten per cent of the entire white population of the country at the time of the outbreak of the rebellion, a proportion, I think, which ought to be entirely gratifying to even the most determined enemies of colonial expansion in Africa, whilst it gives the lie direct to the statement which has so frequently been made, that the settlers in Matabeleland have run no greater risks in fighting with the Matabele in order to put down the rebellion than would be incurred by a sportsman engaged in shooting hares and rabbits at home.

I do not expect that the publication of these lists will call the blush of shame to the cheeks of those who have been so eager to vilify their countrymen in Rhodesia, but I do hope that it will arouse a feeling of indignation in the minds of many who have hitherto been more or less led astray by these dishonest, spiteful, and unpatriotic mentors, and at any rate they must be sad reading to all but the most prejudiced. However, the rebellion can now, I think, be considered as almost at an end. The Kafirs have entirely failed in their attempt to kill all the white men in Matabeleland, and to re-establish themselves as an independent nation. To the west, north-west, north, north-east, and east, the impis which four months ago had formed a cordon round all those faces of Bulawayo have one and all been driven from their positions, and have now broken up into hundreds of little bands, living in the forests with their wives and children. From all the information one can gather, the vast majority of these people are already suffering from want of food, as their cattle are all or nearly all dead from rinderpest, and a large proportion of their year's supply of grain has been taken possession of or destroyed by the white men. Under these conditions they cannot hold out much longer, and they would probably have already come in to surrender were it not that on the one hand, knowing the exasperation caused amongst the whites by the crimes they have committed, they are afraid to throw themselves on their mercy, and on the other they are kept from doing so by their chiefs, who having been the ringleaders of the rebellion, and fearing that in case of surrender their own lives at least would be forfeited, are still doing all they can to prevent their people from submitting.

In the Matopos, Mr. Cecil Rhodes and Mr. Johan

164

Colenbrander are at the present moment carrying on negotiations with the insurgent chiefs, which may or may not end in peace. Should no satisfactory arrangement be arrived at, and the war be continued, the natives will be driven to desperation, and it will not only require a much larger force than there is at present in the country, but the expenditure of a vast amount of money, and the loss of many valuable lives, before they can be absolutely all killed or hunted out of the almost impregnable fastnesses and hills honeycombed with caverns which exist all over the large area of country known as the Matopos.

Now I think that, in view of the enormous cost and great loss of life that would be entailed by the decision to make no terms with the natives, it would be better to accept their submission on lines consistent with the future safety of the country. The chiefs must stand their trial, but the lives of all those who have had no part in the murder of white men, women, and children, could be guaranteed. The whole nation must of course be disarmed as completely as possible, and the actual murderers of white people during the first days of the rebellion must be shot or hanged. But should these conditions be complied with, whilst at the same time a large police force is maintained in the country, and the native administration carried on in such a way that, although the natives are treated with firmness, their grievances will always be heard, and as far as possible remedied, I do not think we need fear another rebellion.

Of course there are those who say that it is a great mistake to hold any parley with them at all. Go on killing them, they say, until the remnant crawl in on their hands and knees and beg for mercy. Well, that end could only be attained, as I have already said, at a cost of much money and many lives; so I think that there are many here, who, some for the sake of expediency and others for the sake of humanity, would now wish to see this rebellion ended as soon as possible, if it can be done in such a way as to ensure the future safety of the settlers in the country. As soon as the chiefs submit and their people are again located on the lands from which they have been driven, I think there can be no doubt that the country will, for the time being, be perfectly safe for white men; for history has shown us that when a Kafir tribe submits it does so absolutely for the time being, and no murders of isolated individuals are committed until the chiefs are ready for another insurrection.

It may of course be said that the Matabele have not yet been thoroughly beaten, and that, having gained a good deal of experience during the last five months, their idea in submitting is to get in their next year's crops and then begin again, on the principle of "reculer pour mieux sauter." But is this at all probable? After the first war they were more or less surprised into submission to the white men, the greater part of them never having fought for their country at all. Then they found that the shoe of the white man's rule began to pinch, but they wore it for two years, and did not attempt to throw it off until the country appeared to them to have been left in an absolutely defenceless condition by their conquerors.

They have now had their rebellion, and it has absolutely failed, and they have lost at least twice as many men in the recent fighting as'they did in the first war. Nor is there any longer a cattle question to excite their resentment, for the cattle are all, or almost all, dead from the rinderpest. Therefore it appears to me, that if they are disarmed as far as is possible, and if a strong police force is maintained in the country for the next few years, their submission can be safely accepted, and the mass of the people be allowed to go unpunished; but justice and common sense both demand that all who are proved to have been implicated, either directly or indirectly, in any of the murders which marked the outbreak of the rebellion, shall be most summarily dealt with. They will be gradually discovered, and some, it may be, may not be brought to justice for years to come, but no mercy must be shown them whenever or wherever they may be found.

In less than two years' time the railway now being pushed on through the Bechuanaland Protectorate will have reached Bulawayo; and if the natives can be kept quiet by a firm and just rule until the advent of the iron horse in Matabeleland, there is little fear of their ever again rising in rebellion against the white man.

In the meantime the development of the country must remain at a standstill, and the country retained as a British possession, by an occupation which will be almost purely military, as not only has the cost of living been rendered almost prohibitive through the destruction of all the cattle in Matabeleland and Bechuanaland by the rinderpest, and the consequent substitution of mules and donkeys in the place of oxen for draught purposes, but farming also has been rendered very difficult, as, putting aside stock and dairy farming, no ploughing can be done without oxen, nor can agricultural produce be carried to market without the assistance of those useful animals, for salted and acclimatised horses and mules are too scarce and expensive to be reckoned on for farm work. The rinderpest, therefore, has for the present put an end to all European enterprise in the way of mining and farming in Matabeleland.

People in England can only realise the disastrous effect which this dread disease has had on the prosperity of the country by endeavouring to picture to themselves what the consequences would have been had a disease suddenly made its appearance in Great Britain in the early part of the present century, before the introduction of railways, which destroyed ninety-nine per cent of all the horses in the British Isles; yet even that would scarcely represent the extent of the calamity from the effects of which we are now suffering, when it is considered what an immense tract of barren wilderness yet lies between Matabeleland and the nearest railway station.

In the early part of this year there were over 100,000 head of cattle, all sleek and in excellent condition, in Matabeleland, but when it closes, I think it very doubtful if 500 will be still left alive in the whole country. Even this loss is small as compared with that sustained by Khama and his people, who were the largest cattle-holders in South Africa, and whose loss it has been computed, from reliable data, exceeds 800,000 head of horned cattle.

However, the rinderpest is a calamity which is not likely to occur again, but which, when it does occur, sweeps everything before it both in Europe and Africa. That Matabeleland as a whole is a country second to none in South Africa for cattle-breeding is the opinion of everyone who has lived there for any length of time and had the opportunity of studying the matter. When, therefore, the rinderpest has died out, and the railway has reached Bulawayo, the country will be gradually restocked; and then, too, mining machinery will be imported, and our mines will at last be worked with a result which will give the final death-blow to all those who have for the last six years been engaged in disseminating falsehoods concerning Rhodesia.

From the statistics supplied to me by the Compensation Board, which I have given in the form of an appendix, it will be seen that a good deal of farming work had already been done at the time of the outbreak of the rebellion, and that the population of Matabeleland were not all "gin-sellers" or "men who had gone out to Matabeleland in order to swindle the British public, by inducing them to subscribe for shares in worthless companies, whose so-called gold claims contained no gold." The fact, too, that farmers and prospectors were living all over the country in perfect health rather explodes the theory of a noxious vapour rising to some four feet from the ground which is so deadly to Europeans that all colonisation of the country is impossible; but this, if I remember aright, was the theory propounded by one of Mr. Labouchere's "reliable" correspondents—a fit contributor, forsooth, to the pages of *Truth*.

It is now known throughout South Africa that Matabeleland and Mashunaland are white men's countries, where Europeans can live and thrive and rear strong healthy children; that they are magnificent countries for stock-breeding, and that many portions of them will prove suitable for Merino sheep and Angora goats; whilst agriculture and fruit-growing can be carried on successfully almost everywhere in a small way, and in certain districts, especially in Mashunaland and Manica where there is a greater abundance of water, on a fairly extensive scale.

As for the gold, there is every reason to believe that out of the enormous number of reefs which are considered by their owners to be payable properties some small proportion at least will turn up trumps, and, should this proportion only amount to two per cent, that will be quite sufficient to ensure a big output of gold in the near future, which will in its turn ensure the prosperity of the whole country.

Once let the railway reach Bulawayo, and given intelligent legislation in the best interests of the settlers and miners in the country, Rhodesia will soon prove its value to the most sceptical; but the prosperity which I predict will, I am afraid, be very much retarded, if not completely destroyed, by the revocation at the present moment of the Charter which was granted to the British South Africa Company in 1889, and the substitution of Imperial rule for the present form of Government. For this reason:—Under the present régime the Company's administrator is always accessible to the people living in the country, and whatever local reforms may be deemed necessary by the latter are always capable of discussion, and can be acceded to by him on the spot, without despatches having first of all to be forwarded to the High Commissioner at the Cape, by whom they would be sent on to the Colonial Office, with the result that a local reform, urgently required, might be delayed for months or never granted at all.

Under the Company's government, too, the administrator himself would always be a man acquainted with the history of the territories he was governing, and would be probably one who not only had the prosperity of the country he was governing deeply at heart, but who also would have a very good idea as to how that prosperity was likely to be attained. During the next few years, too, which will be a very critical period in the history of Rhodesia, such an administrator would always have the benefit of the advice of the man through whose energy and genius the territories forming that state have been secured for the British Empire. But should this territory be converted into a Crown colony and governed from Downing Street on hard-and-fast lines, some of them not at all applicable to local requirements, with an administrator very likely ignorant of his local surroundings, and possibly out of sympathy with the settlers—Dutch and British—who have made the country their home, nothing but disaster is to be expected.

Surely the people who have stuck to Rhodesia through good and evil times, and who, under the auspices of the Chartered Company, have added a vast territory to the British Empire and laid the foundations of what will soon be a prosperous colony, which, given an intelligent and adaptable form of government, will be able to pay its way, ought to have some say in this matter, and not be transferred unwillingly to a rule which they know would be ill suited to local requirements, and under which local enterprises would surely languish for want of the fostering care which only a local administrator can provide.

The white population of Rhodesia have had many a growl at the government of the Chartered Company, but in most cases they have got what they growled for—to wit, the extension of the railways, both from the Cape Colony and the East Coast; the reduction of the Company's percentage of interest in the mines; and full and most generous compensation, where the claims were just, for cattle destroyed in the endeavour to stay the progress of the rinderpest, and for all losses sustained owing to the late native insurrection. Under Imperial rule they know that no compensation has ever been granted for losses sustained through a native rebellion, and they also know that little or no assistance could be hoped for in the construction of railways or other public works. Recognising all these things, having as an object-lesson just before their eyes the wretchedly slow progress made in Bechuanaland under the Imperial administration, and knowing, moreover, that the Transvaal war of 1880-81, if not the loss of the Transvaal itself as a British possession, was brought about solely by a Government from Downing Street, through an administrator entirely ignorant of local requirements and absolutely out of sympathy with the people he was chosen to govern, can it be wondered at that at a recent meeting of the Chamber of Commerce in this town, the people of Bulawayo expressed confidence in the government of the Chartered Company and in Mr. Cecil Rhodes, representing as they do a corporation of capitalists who hold the largest financial stake in the country, and whose aims and objects are identical with those of the people living in the country, whilst they resented the idea of being handed over to Imperial rule without having their wishes in the matter consulted, in order to please the Little Englander party at home?

One of the most noteworthy features at the meeting to which I have referred was the remarkable unanimity shown by the British and Dutch on this subject, for the Dutch up here believe in Mr. Rhodes, and have the most absolute confidence in his ability to insure the prosperity of the country. The natives, too, as has just been shown, look upon him as their father; and I believe that through his influence and the strength of his personality, a peace will soon be arranged with them, which would have been impossible at the present time but for his presence in the country.

Bulawayo, *26th August 1896.*

APPENDICES

APPENDIX A

*Headquarters, Intelligence Department,
Bulawayo, August 1896.*

Amended List of Persons murdered in Matabeleland during the recent native insurrection.

Names	District	Date (1896)	Details
Anderson, Joscelyn Hepburn	Sebakwe	End March	On way to Mafungabusi; engineer.
Anderson, Alex	Boola Boola	25th "	Reported killed by F. Evans, his mate, who escaped.
Bertlesen Family (6) (father, mother, and 4 sons)	Shangani River	End "	Farming 12 miles north of Hartley Hills Road.
Baragwanath, John Albert	Filibusi	24th May	Brother in the B.F.F.
Bentley, Arthur	"	"	A N.-C. from Queenstown district.
Barr, W. A.	Shangani	End March	Family, contractors at Bristol.

Barnard, Harry Edgar	Umvungu	25th"	Partner of West Brothers, Umvungu Store; late with Parker Wood, Johannesburg.
Bolton	Inyati	End March	Killed with Cyril West (Williams' Ex. Coy.)
Bowen, Jimmy	Mavene	30th"	Hammond's Mines; killed with S. Van Blerk.
Borgen or Vorgen	Shangani	. . .	Prospector.
Bowker, Trooper	Lower Gwelo	30th"	M.M.P. sent to warn people, Lower Gwelo.
Colas, Dionysius	Inyati	End "	A Greek trader.
Cunningham, James Samuel	Filibusi	24th"	One of Cunningham family, away carting wood.
Clark, W. E.	Mavene	End "	Body found—Gwelo patrol.
Carpenter, John Loran	Filibusi	24th"	Body found near Filibusi Store.
Cunningham Family (8) (father, mother, and 6 children)	Filibusi	24th March	Farmers near Store (brother, F. H. Cunningham, Dundee, Natal).
Classen, Henry	Makukapene	26th"	Body seen.
Case, George	Inyati	" "	M.M.P., killed with Graham, Handley, Hurford, and Corke.
Corke, Leighton Huntley	"	" "	Ex. M.M.P., do.
Comploier, P.	Gwelo	" "	Prospector; body buried by Napier's Gwelo patrol.
Cumming, Percy H.	Filibusi	25th"	Son of Mr. and Mrs. Cumming, Bulawayo; body seen near Filibusi Store.
Crawley, Alaine M.	"	" "	Working with J. Schultz.
Cato, Colin	"	" "	Body seen at edge of shaft.
Donovan, Timothy	Inyati	" "	Killed with Seward near

171

Name	Place	Date	Description
(?S. A.)			Ancients Reef; working for Mallert.
Durden, Charles	Ingwena	" "	Killed with Surveyor Fitzpatrick.
Dufra	Lower Gwelo	30th"	Killed at Shangani.
Daly, John (?James)	Filibusi	25th"	Left for Gambo's kraal.
Davies, Harold John	Bembisi	2nd April	Killed near Thaba N'Couga.
Danby, Lewis	Bulawayo	. . .	Prospector.
Daly, James M.	Bubi	25th March	Managing Glen's farms; sick at time of death.
Edwards, Norman	Inyati	" "	Surveyor (of Fletcher and Espiro).
Edkins, E. C.	Inyati	24th"	Storekeeper (brother in Johannesburg); body seen in store.
Eaglestone, Charles Percy	Makukapene	End March	Partner of Joseph Clinton.
Ehlert, Ferdinand (known as "Bill")	Filibusi	" "	Working with J. Jeffries. Family in Kimberley.
Earst, Ayerst Alfred	"	" "	Working with J. Jeffries.
Edgell, E. R.	On way from Gwelo to Hartley Hills	" "	Murdered by natives, as reported by Adjutant Taylor, Gwelo.
Fitzpatrick	Lower Gwelo	25th"	Surveyor; body seen.
Farquharson, James John Edward	Bulawayo	. . .	Storekeeper.
Forster, Wilson	Makukapene	" "	Prospector; body seen.
Fourie Family (8) (Stephanus, wife, and 6 children)	Tekwe River	2nd April	Farming; bodies buried by Napier's Gwelo patrol.
Fourie, Caspar Hendrick	Near Bulawayo	20th April	Transport rider, killed with Potgieter.
Farrar	Lower Gwelo	End March	Prospector, with companion (name unknown).

Foxkerk, Stanley	Shangani	25th"	Prospector.
Grenfell, Pascoe St. L.	Inyati	End "	Left Inyati for Bubi; Manager Company.
Gordon, John	Gwelo	" "	Miner.
Graham, A. M.	Inyati	26th"	A N.-C. Family in Glasgow.
Grant, John M'Innes	Filibusi	25th"	Mining with Robert Sharpe.
Grant, Jock M'Leod	"	" "	Killed with Jock Nimmo at Godlway's kraal; body buried by Salisbury column.
Greenhaugh, John	Hotel, Filibusi	" "	Working with Whawill and Reddan.
Gracey, Robert	Shangani	End"	Body buried by Napier's Gwelo patrol.
Hunter, H. E.	Bembisi	" "	Body seen.
Handley, Mark	Inyati	" "	Sub-Inspector M.M.P., son of Henry Handley, Natal.
Hurford, George	"	" "	Late M.M.P., killed with Graham, Handley, Case, and Corke.
Hurlstone, Frederick	Pongo River Hotel	" "	Partner of H. P. Selmes. Family in Coventry.
Harbord, H. M.	Mavene	" "	Store on Hartley Hill Road (brother, A. G. Harbord, Longton, near Nottingham).
Hammond, And. Robt.	Shangani	" "	Killed with Palmer and Johnson, engineers.
Hartley, Joseph	Ingwena Store	" "	Body found at Harbord's Store; age about forty-five, height 5 ft. 8 in.
Holstein	Shangani	. . .	Prospector.
Ivers, Colin Campbell	Filibusi	24th"	Body found Celtic Reef.
Johnson, W. H.	Shangani	30th"	Killed with Hammond and Palmer.

173

Jensen, Charles	"	" "	A Swede.
Johnston	Filibusi	25th"	
Jeffries, J.	"	" "	Working with Ehlert and Earst.
Kirk, Agnes	Tekwe River	2nd April	J. Ross's stepdaughter; body buried by Napier's patrol.
Keefe, Charles	Shangani	2nd March	Working with Webster.
Keefe, Christopher	"	" "	" "
Koch	Filibusi	25th	Killed with Jeffries, Ehlert, and Earst.
Livesay, E. R. Eustace	Filibusi	End March	Late Lieutenant 3rd Dragoon Guards.
Luckcass, Herbert	"	25th"	Killed at O'Maker's waggon; others escaped.
Lennock, George	Gwelo	End"	Body found Mavene; almost unrecognisable.
Langford (2), Dr. and Mrs.	Insiza	" "	Bodies found on Rixon's farm and buried by Napier's Gwelo patrol.
Lemon, C. J.	"	" "	Father G. D. Lemon, Raleigh, Bedeford, North Devon; money at Standard Bank; buried by Napier's Gwelo patrol.
Lewis, Arthur B.	Filibusi	25th"	
Lund, Severin H. C.	Gwaai River	End "	A Dane.
M'Heugh, Harry	Bembisi	" "	
Maddocks, Thomas	Filibusi	23rd"	
Melford, William B.	Gwelo	End "	
Matthews	Shangani	" "	With Van der Doorten; a Jew from Melbourne.
Mathey, Ernest	Filibusi	25th"	Body recognised near Store.
Marcussen, Andreas E.	Hartley Hills ...		Prospector.

Morrison, James E.	Queen's Reef	29th"	Refused to leave.
M'Cormack	Ingwena Store	End "	Working with H. B. Taylor; body not seen.
Macdonald, Colin	Filibusi	25th"	Killed with Classen.
Nimmo, Walter (known as Jock or Watty)	"	" "	Murdered with John M'Leod Grant.
Palmer, H. M.	Shangani	30th"	Killed with Hammond and Johnson.
Potgieter, Derk Rainer	Bulawayo Road	20th April	Transport rider.
Ottens, Wilhelm O.	Filibusi	24th March	Family lives near Assen, Holland.
O'Reilly, T.	Gwelo	End"	Murdered on Leechdale Co.'s property.
O'Connor, ("Jack") John	Filibusi	25th"	Brother saved; in Bulawayo.
Reddington, Reginald	Pongo River	End"	Clerk to Hurlstone.
Reddan, Valentine	Filibusi	25th"	Murdered with Greenhaugh and Whawill.
Rowe, F. R.	Shangani	30th"	Miner of St. Austell.
Richards, John Edward	Bulawayo	. . .	Prospector.
Ross (2), Joseph and wife	Tekwe River	2nd April	
Rowlands, John James	Bembisi		Miner of King William's Town.
Radford, A.	Shangani	End March	Partner of Leech.
Raw	Lower Gwelo	. . .	Prospector.
Sharpe, Robert	Filibusi	25th March	Killed with Grant.
Stanley, Frank Harrison	Sebakwe	End"	Brother, late Lieut. Royal Irish Rifles, c/o Armstrong Bros., bankers, 93 Bishopgate St., London.

Stobie, James	Mavene	25th"	Murdered with Joseph Hartley, both working for G. R. Ainnocks.
Smith	Lower Gwelo	. . .	Miner.
Seward, George E.	Filibusi	25th"	Killed with Cato, near Ancients Reef; working for Mallett.
Talman, Frank	Gwelo	End"	Near Pongo Store; body recognised by Robinson. Age 24; 5 ft. 5 in.; light.
Taylor, George	Shangani	" "	
Thomas, Jock	"	" "	
Tyass, George (of Natal)	Bembisi	" "	Sent with medicine to J. H. Daly.
Van Blerk, Sid.	Mavene	30th"	Hammond's Mines; age 30; killed with Jimmy Bowen.
Vaughan, Thomas	Pongo River	25th"	
Van Gorckim, Martinus Gerhardus	Bulawayo	. . .	Bricklayer.
Vavaseur, Robert	Stoneybrook Thabas M. Simbi	June	Reported murdered to Charter.
Van der Doorten	Shangani	30th March	From Rotterdam.
White, Robert	Inyati	End"	Left Inyati for Bubi.
West, Cyril (Willoughbys)	Inyati	End"	Killed with Bolton.
West Bros. (2)	Shangani	" "	
Wren	"	25th"	Cattle-inspector in district.
Wyllie, David	Gwelo	End"	Working for Warwick Colliers.
Wright, James	Bembisi	. . .	Storeman (of Johannesburg).
Woods, Arthur W. P.	Filibusi	25th"	Working and killed with E. Mathey.

White, Charles	Shangani	" "	
White, Edward	Filibusi	" "	Killed with Jack O'Connor.
Walsh, William	Mavene	End"	Body found Gwelo patrol; aged 40; buried Mavene patrol.
Whawill, John	Filibusi	25th"	Killed with Reddan and Greenhaugh.
Webster, R.	Shangani	End"	Killed with Keefes, a partner of Peacock's.
Weinand	"	" "	Cattle-inspector.
Zeeburg, H.	Pongo River	26th"	Trader.

List of Persons supposed to have been in Matabeleland at the time of the outbreak of the insurrection, of whom nothing has since been heard, and the greater part, if not all, of whom must therefore be numbered amongst those murdered by the natives.

Names	Details and Address	Last heard of.
Ansterhauzen	Thabas Mamba	Trading at Thabas Mamba.
Bird, Robert George	...	Left Cape Town 13th April.
Band	...	Late of Johannesburg Police.
Burch, Dr.	...	Reported to be in Matabeleland.
Bridge, Walter	...	
Batchelor, Franc D.	...	Reported to have been on some mining property near Bulawayo.
Bruce, Stewart	...	A Trooper in Dr. Jameson's force.
Bent		
Bowen, O		
Beaton, James	Johannesburg	Left Scotland in 1880 East for London, afterwards in Kimberley and

		Johannesburg, and left latter place probably for Bulawayo. Height 5 ft. 10 in.; black curly hair; well built; 42 years of age.
Cook, James P.	Bulawayo	Photographer's assistant, Bulawayo.
Cook, Thomas		
Cook, Robert	...	Late of M.M.P.
Carstens, John E. A.	Bulawayo	Formerly in Captain Selous' Troop.
Carter, James	"	Civil engineer in Bulawayo.
Dickson or Dixon	Gwelo	Gwelo district.
Douvre	"	"
Dixon, R.	...	Formerly in army.
Doveton, W. T.	Inyati	Seen in Bulawayo between 1-13 April, and not heard of since.
Evers, Harold Cecil	Bulawayo	Bulawayo district.
Greyling (5), John, wife, and 3 children	"	On road to Bulawayo.
Grant, Jimmy	"	Bulawayo.
Hill, John Shutter		
Jacobs, Charlie	...	Gwelo camp, 2nd June.
Jones, William Stevens	Bulawayo	Bulawayo at time Matabele War.
Kerr	Gwelo	Shangani district.
Kroger, Frans J.	Chemist	Delagoa Bay.
Lee, Thomas	Gwelo	Gwelo district.
Mackenzie, Thomas	Bulawayo	Bulawayo.
Morrison, Wm. Hutchinson	...	Late of B.B.P.
Matthews, Stuart	Bulawayo	Late of Dunraven mines.
Honey, Clifford Francis	...	Formerly of B.B.P.
Mitchell, Basil	...	
Magee, Joseph		

178

Nieuwenhaus	...	Bulawayo road.
Oosthuizen	Gwelo	Shangani district.
Orton, Henry Sambourne	...	Sebakwe drift.
Palmer, William R.	Johannesburg	Bulawayo, end February.
Reet, P.	Transport rider	Pietersburg.
Rothman, John	Bulawayo	Bulawayo.
Reynard, J. J.	...	Believed to be in Colonel Plumer's force.
Reed, William James	late Johannesburg	Bulawayo.
Richardson, Arthur	...	A prospector.
Stalmp, Frank J.	London	Bulawayo.
Spalteholz, Kurt	Dresden, Germany	Left Johannesburg for Bulawayo, December 1895.
Spalteholz, Kurt	Amsterdam	Last heard of, Pietersburg, 2nd Jan. 1896, when on road Bulawayo with party by ox waggon. Height 6 ft.; age 24; smooth face; light brown hair; sharp features. Papers of his have been found on Rixon's farm, and bag (possibly belonging to him) at Thabas Mamba.
Smith, Sidney Z.	Mafeking	Reported to have left Mafeking with M.R.F.
Tilbury, George	...	Mafeking, 24th April.
Taylor, Alfred West	...	Possibly passing under his step-father's name of Bent.
Wright, James	Bulawayo	Bulawayo.
Wilson, Edward E.	...	Bulawayo, June 1895.
Walsh, Frederick Byron.		
Webster, R.		
Walsh, I.	Bulawayo	Came in from Golingena at beginning of rebellion.

179

APPENDIX B

List of Officers, Non-Commissioned Officers, and Men killed in action during the Matabele rebellion.

No.	Rank.	Name.	Where killed.	Date (1896)
1	Sergeant	O'Leary, T.,	Cumming's Store	27th March
2	Corporal	Reynolds, Ernest E., R.H.V.	Gifford's patrol	6th April
3	Trooper	Mackenzie, S. Kenneth, R.H.V.	" "	"
4	"	Baker, Richard Arthur, R.H.V.	Gwanda patrol	10th April
5	"	Hayland, Edward, R.H.V.	" "	"
6	"	Packe, Christopher J., R.H.V.	" "	"
7	Corporal	Greer, Stewart George, R.H.V.	" "	"
8	Trooper	Forbes, J. M'Ainsch, R.H.V.	" "	"
9	"	Boyes, George Walter, B.F.F., Afcr. Corps	Macfarlane's patrol	19th April
10	"	Heinemann, J. J., B.F.F.	Vedette duty	"
11	"	Van Zyl, W., B.F.F.	" "	
12	"	Montgomerie, Henry, B.F.F.	" "	"
13	"	Baxter, Frank Wm., B.F.F.	Grey's Scouts, Bisset's patrol	22nd April
14	"	Whitehouse, George, B.F.F.	Ambulance, Macfarlane's patrol	25th April

180

15	"	Gordon, Charles, B.F.F.	Dawson's Scouts, Macfarlane's patrol	"
16	"	Parsons, Benj., B.F.F.	D Troop, vedette duty	"
17	"	Hay, Carrick, B.F.F.	Coope's Scouts, Plumer's patrol	25th May
18	Trooper	Parker, Arthur, B.F.F.	L Troop, Napier's Gwelo patrol	22nd May
19	"	Rothman, George, B.F.F.	L Troop, Napier's Gwelo patrol	"
20	"	Langton, Courtney, E Squad, M.R.F.	Thabas Mamba	6th July
21	"	O'Reilly, John, Brand's Troop, B.F.F.	" "	"
22	Corporal	Pringle, James F., A Squad, M.R.F.	" "	"
23	Sergeant	Warringham, Fred. Chas., A Troop, M.M.P.	Matopos, Babian's impi	20th July
24	Corporal	Hall, John, Belingwe F.F.	Inugu engagement, Matopos	"
25	Trooper	Bennett, Peter, E. Troop, M.M.P.	Inugu engagement, Matopos	"
26	"	Bush, William Henry, E. Troop, M.M.P.	Inugu engagement, Matopos	"
27	"	Matheson, R. B., Major Hurrell's Troop	Bezury Hills engagement	21st July
28	Corporal	Hayes, Dan., Major Hurrell's Troop	Sinango kopje engagement	7th July
29	Major	Kershaw, C Squad, M.R.F.	Sikombo engagement	5th August
30	Sergeant	M'Closkie, Oswald, C Squad, M.R.F.	" "	"
31	"	Gibb, William, D Squad, M.R.F.	" "	"
32	"	Innes, Kerr, Maxim	" "	"

		gun, M.R.F		
33	Battery Sergt.-Maj.	Ainslie, Alexander, M.M.P.	" "	"
34	Lieut., Dismnt. Troop.	Hervey, Herbert John Anthony, died from wounds, late Paymaster-General	" "	"

APPENDIX C

Headquarters, Intelligence Department,
Bulawayo, August 1896.

List of Officers, Non-Commissioned Officers, and Men wounded; or died in hospital from wounds received in action during the Matabele rebellion.

No.	Rank.	Name.	Details.	Date (1896).
1	Trooper	Hill, Eustace	Gifford's patrol, Insiza	27th March
2	"	Hocking, John	"	"
3	"	Luis, Wilton	"	"
4	Corporal	Strutt, M. M. P.	"	"
5	Trooper	Saunders, Charles	"	"
6		O'Connor, Joseph	Prospector, escaped from Filibusi	"
7	Trooper	Stracey, A. H.	Selous' patrol	28th March
8	"	Munzberg, Berthold	"	"
9	A. N. C.	Carter, Samuel	Shiloh patrol	29th March

10	Serg.-Maj.	Haden, Thomas	" (Afric. Corps)	"
11	Trooper	Celliers, John	Shiloh patrol (died in hospital, 16th May 1896)	"
12	"	Anderson, August	Shiloh patrol	"
13	Lieut.-Col.	Gifford, Hon. M. R.	Fonseca's Farm	6th April
14	Captain	Lumsden, J. W.	Fonseca's Farm (died in hospital, 10th April 1896)	"
15	Lieutenant	Hulbert	Fonseca's Farm	"
16	Trooper	Eatwell	"	"
17	"	Fielding	"	"
18	"	Walker	"	"
19	M. O.	Levy, Dr. J.	Gwanda patrol	10th April
20	Trooper	Harvey, F. J.	"	"
21	"	Whitlow, Chas. Ern.	"	"
22	"	Stowell, W.	"	"
23	"	Ormsby, O.	"	"
24	Trooper	Ferreira, J.	Gwanda patrol	10th April
25	"	De Villiers, Isaac James	"	"
26	"	Wilson, J.	"	"
27	"	Collins, C.	"	"
28	"	Ashley, W.	"	"
29	"	Kramer, S.	"	"
30	"	Blackwell, J.	"	"
31	"	Wallace, E. C.	"	"
32	"	Farrell, E.	"	"
33	"	Swift, Henry	Gwanda patrol (died in hospital, 14th April 1896)	"
34	"	Harker, George, B.F.F	Local patrol	17th April
35	"	Ter. Blanche Esiah Michael, Afric.	Macfarlane's patrol	19th "

		Corps.		
36	Captain	Grey, George	Bisset's patrol	22nd April
37	Lieutenant	Hook, Godfrey Blair	"	"
38	"	Crewe, F. H.	Bisset's patrol (Grey's Scouts)	"
39	Corporal	Wise, George	Bisset's patrol (Grey's Scouts)	"
40	Lieutenant	Lyons, M. H., Hosp. Corps	Macfarlane's patrol	25th April
41	T.S.M.	Botha, Joh. Christian	Macfarlane's patrol (Afric. Corps)	"
42	Trooper	Howell, Thos. Easton	Macfarlane's patrol (Grey's Scouts)	"
43	"	Price, F. H. Talbot	Macfarlane's patrol (Maxim detachment)	"
44	"	Appleyard, Edward	Macfarlane's patrol (Dawson's Scouts). Died in hospital same evening	"
45	"	Lovatt, Ronald Venables	Macfarlane's patrol (Grey's Scouts). Died in hospital, 29th April 1896	"
46	"	Beatty-Pownall, W. C.	Laing's Camp, Belingwe	2nd May
47	"	Hamilton, H. Rice	Unattached, Plumer's patrol	25th May
48	Sergeant	Peacock, Arthur W.	Plumer's patrol (B Troop)	"
49	Trooper	Slowey, W. John	Plumer's patrol (A Troop)	"
50	"	Beinedell, Pieter	Napier's Gwelo patrol (L Troop)	22nd May

51	"	Niemand, Jac. P. Joh.	Napier's Gwelo patrol (Mangwe detachment)	"
52	Trooper	Geldenhuis, Elias Jac.	Napier's Gwelo patrol (Mangwe detachment)	22nd May
53	Corporal	Combrink, Jacobus, Afric. Corps	Spreckley's patrol	6th June
54	Trooper	Davey, Cecil, B.F.F.	Spreckley's patrol. Serious gun-shot, right hip since amputated	"
55	Sergeant	Hamilton, Geo. Michael, R.V.H.	Spreckley's patrol. Assegai wound	"
56	T.S.M.	Morrison, S., 8 Troop, M.R.F.	Macfarlane's Gwaai patrol. Bullet wound on head	8th June
57	Trooper	Clark, A Troop, Gifford's Horse	Macfarlane's Gwaai patrol. Slight wound	"
58	T.S.M.	Blatherwick, S. M., M.R.F.	Macfarlane's Gwaai patrol	"
59	Trooper	Hill, John H., A Squad, M.R.F.	Thabas Mamba. Dangerously wounded; died same day	6th July
60	"	Meyer, George, A Squad, M.R.F.	Thabas Mamba	"
61	"	Cooper, David E., A Squad, M.R.F.	"	"
62	"	Dupreez, Arthur, M.R.F.	"	"
63	"	Dunn, George,	"	"
64	"	Potgieter, L., Belingwe F.F.	Belingwe patrol	26th June
65	Lieutenant	Taylor, Scouts, M.R.F.	Matopos, Babian's impi	20th July

66	Sergeant	Halkett, C. H., Belingwe F.F.	Matopos, Inugu engagement	"
67	"	Eadio, Malcolm, A Troop, M.M.P.	Matopos, Inugu engagement	"
68	Trooper	Dick, Duncan, Belingwe F.F.	Matopos, Inugu engagement	"
69	"	Judge, T., Belingwe F.F.	Matopos, Inugu engagement	"
70	"	Toulson, John George	Matopos, Inugu engagement	"
71	"	Parker Parker, F.F.	Severe bullet wound, thigh	"
72	"	Morgan, Charles Oglethorpe A., M.M.P.	Matopos, Inugu engagement (died 23rd July, buried at Usher's Farm)	"
73	"	Stewart, A. M., Belingwe F.F.	Matopos, Inugu fight	"
74	"	Sell, Charles A. T., M.M.P.	"	"
75	"	Millar, Fredk., M.M.P.	"	"
76	Trooper	Roger, Scott, Belingwe F.F.	Matopos Inugu fight	20th July
77	"	Wilson, Campbell, A Squad, M.R.F.	Hope Fountain	12th "
78	"	Cheres, Laurence, M.M.P.	Nicholson's patrol, Inugu gorge (died and buried at Usher's Camp, 27th July)	25th July
79	"	Bern, William, M.M.P.	" "	"
80	Trooper	Heathfield, Richard, Jr., M.M.P.	Nicholson's patrol, Inugu gorge	"
81	"	Bell, James, M.M.P.	Nicholson's patrol, Inugu gorge	"
82	Corporal	Porter, Joseph	Nicholson's patrol,	"

		Kirk, M.M.P.	Inugu gorge (died in Bulawayo hospital, 3rd August)	
83	Lieutenant	Norton, Frederick Cunningham, M.M.P.	Taylor's patrol, Sobisi	27th July
84	Captain	Lloyd, Chas. P., Engineer Train	Inyandi engagement	3rd Aug.
85	Trooper	Little, Edward Runnell, M.R.F.	Gun accident, Spargo's (died 3rd August)	"
86	"	Champion, William Lewis, M.R.F.	Gun accident, Spargo	"
87	"	Silberhazen, George, M.R.F.	"	"
88	"	Macdougall, Lorne Somerlea	Fort-Spargo	5th Aug.
89	Lieutenant	M'Culloch, Robert H., Royal Art.	Sikombo engagement	"
90	"	Frazer, Norman Warden, West Riding Regt.	"	"
91	Captain	Fowler, Charles H., M.R.F.	"	"
92	Staff-Sergt.-Major.	Josephs, William, M.R.F.	"	"
93	Sergt.-Maj.	Dumeresq, Rawlings, M.R.F.	"	"
94	Sergeant	Brabant, Arthur E., M.R.F	"	"
95	Corporal	Turnbull, Richard, M.R.F.	"	"
96	Trooper	Currie, William, M.R.F.	"	"
97	"	Holmes, Evelyn, M.R.F.	" (Died 9th August)	"

98	"	Gordon, Thomas, M.M.P.	Sikombo engagement "
99	Lieutenant	Howard, Hon. H.	" (Robertson's Cape Boys) "
100	Captain	Windley	Robertson's Cape Boys "

APPENDIX D

Headquarters Intelligence Department,
Salisbury, August 1896.

List of persons murdered in Mashunaland during the recent native insurrection.

Names.	District.	Date (1986)	Details.
Birkett, W.	Salisbury		Body supposed to be his recovered on 5th August.
Kentenge, Frank	"	18th June	Killed at the Gwibi River.
Wills, M.M.P.	"	"	" "
Loeford, S.	"	15th June	Killed at Beatrice Mine.
Tait, James	"	"	" "
Van Rooyen	"	16th June	Killed at Hartley Road.
Fourie, Benj. John	"	"	" "
Norton Family (3), Joseph, Mrs., and infant	"	17th June	Killed at Norton's Farm, on the Hungani River.
Fairweather, Miss	"	"	Killed at Norton's Farm, on the

188

Name	Place	Date	Particulars
			Hungani River.
Alexander, H.	"	"	Killed at Norton's Farm, on the Hungani River.
Grahener, H	"	"	Killed at Norton's Farm, on the Hungani River.
Harvey, J.L.	"		No particulars of murders; but six or seven weeks having elapsed without any news of these persons, and who were known to have been surrounded by rebels at the time of the rising, it is beyond all doubt that they are dead.
Dixon, James	"		
Briscoe	"		
Hite, W. D.	"		
Dowenbrock, R.	"		
Basson, Nicholas	"		
Joubert, J.	"		
Gray, Harry	"		
Curtis, J. H. (surveyor)	"		
Saunders	"		
Calcott	"		
Cass, J	Mazoe	18th June	Killed near Salvation Army Camp.
Faull, W.	Mazoe	18th June	Killed near Salvation Army Camp.
Dickenson, J., Mining Commissioner	"	"	Killed near Salvation Army Camp.
Routledge, J. J.	"	"	Killed near Telegraph Station (telegraphist).
Blakiston, J. J.	"	"	Killed near Telegraph Station (telegraphist).
Pollard, H. H.	"	...	Killed near Mount Hampden.
Nunesty, C.	"	...	Missing.
Fletcher, John.	"	...	"

189

Salthouse	"	...	"
Smith	"	...	"
Short, Henry	Charter	...	Killed.
Bester, Mrs.	"	...	"
Smith	"	...	"
Moore, John	"	...	Dunstan estate; killed Umtala Road; body recovered 3rd August.
Milton (transport rider)	"	...	Killed at Homestead Store; body found on 3rd August.
Graham, Harry	"	...	Killed at Homestead Store; body found on 3rd August.
Weyers Family (4), Jan, wife, and 2 children	"	...	Bodies recovered.
Bekers, C. D.	"	...	Killed at Campbell's Store.
Campbell, J. D.	"	...	" "
Phillips	"	...	Killed at Graham's Store.
Law, Horace, M.M.P.	"	20th June	Killed near Campbell's Store.
Tucker, M.M.P.	"	"	" "
Dickenson, A. J.	"	...	Killed near Law's Store.
White, James (Willoughby's consolidated)	"	7th July	Killed at Marandellas Mission Store.
Bremner, Lieut.	"	...	Killed near Marandellas.
Eyre, Herbert H., M.M.P.	Lo Magondi	21st June	Killed at Umvokwe Mountains.

Name	Place	Date	Remarks
Young, Arthur Liston, M.M.P.	"	"	Killed at Umvokwe Mountains.
Gambier, J. C.	"	22nd June	Killed at Menin River.
Boijes, W. H.	"	"	" "
Drysdale	"	"	" "
Mynhardt (native commissioner)	"	21st June	Killed at Mynhardt's Camp.
Shooter, F.	"	"	" "
Dougherty, J.	"	31st May	
Watkins, Charles H	"	"	Medical officer; killed at Hinnan's Store.
Jameson, Arthur John	Lo Magondi	...	Mining Commissioner.
M'Gowan J.	} "	...	{ Camp and have not been heard of.
Hodgson, A.			Were at Jameson's
Bent, F. L.	"	...	Missing.
Box, James	"	...	" .
Box, Duncan	"	...	"
Kerr, Carr, or Care	"	...	" United States man.
Ireland	"	...	"
Hermann, Louis	Abercorn	21st June	Killed at Macombis.
Tupnell, W.	"	"	" "
Steel, J.	"	"	" "
Austin, F.	"	"	" "
Smith, Newman H.	"	...	Missing.
Horn, J.	"	...	"
Jansen	"	...	"
Steele, W.	"	...	"
Cronchly, J.	"	...	"
North, A.	"	...	"
Hawkins	"	...	"

Name	Place	Date	Details
Hornby	"	...	"
Gibson, J. G.	"	...	"
Sagus	"	...	"
Newman	"	...	"
Hermann, Harry	"	...	"
Ruping (native commissioner)	"	28th June	Killed by his native police at Tahoskos.
Rhapiro, Renten	"	21st"	Shot at Abercorn Store.
Fletcher	"	" "	" "
Eaton, J.	"	19th"	Killed at Chipadgus.
Thurgood, A.	Hartley Hill	15th"	
Hepworth, J. C.	"	17th"	Killed at Wallace's farm.
Wallace, "Friday"	"	" "	" "
Moonie, D. E. (native commissioner)	"	15th"	Killed at Mashingontis.
Hunt, A. J.	"	" "	" "
Skell	"	" "	" "
Purser, A. L.	"	19th"	Killed near Hunyani River.
Carrick Edward (mining commissioner)	"	" "	" "
Wickslorn, A.			Killed while prospecting near Hartley.
Nelson	"	...	Killed while prospecting near Hartley.

The following were killed in action:—

Names.	District.	Date (1986).	Details.
M'Geer, C. M.	...	20th June	Mazoe patrol.
Van Staden, H. J.	...	""	" "
Jacobs	...	""	" "
Dillon	...	""	" "
Mitchell, J. Bentley ...	...		Wounded first Hartley patrol; died 27th June.
Stevens, Charles Trelawney		25th June	Killed Cheshwasha patrol.
Gwilkin, W. H.		20th July	Killed second Hartley patrol.

The following were wounded in action:—

Grey, Dr.	...	...	First Hartley patrol.
Bottemley, Trumpeter (Natal Contingent)	...	...	" "
Finucase, E.	Salisbury	...	" "
Burton, Arthur	"	...	Mazoe patrol at Jwito River.
Hendrikz, C.	"	...	" "
Neibuhr	"	...	" "
Ogilvie	"	...	" "
Berry	"	...	" "
Judson, Captain	"	...	" "
Cartwright, Trumpeter, M.M.P.	Charter	...	" "
Van de Merwe		...	At Hunyani.
Fitzpatrick		...	Beal's column on second Hartley patrol.
Arnott	Salisbury	...	
Kerr	"	...	

193

Lee	...	...	White's column in foraging patrol.
Fraser	...	...	Beal's column.
Brown	...	...	"
Millar	...	...	"

APPENDIX E

For the following statistics I am indebted to the courtesy of Colonel Heyman, the President of the Compensation Board, which up to 15th August 1896 had paid claims for the following items:—

Growing Crops Destroyed

Mealies	896	acres
Kafir corn	270	"
Oats	70½	"
Barley	17	"
Potatoes	67	"
Wheat	7	"
Various	151½	"
Total	1,479	acres

Trees Destroyed

Fruit trees	1,092
Gum trees	290
Various trees	19,957
Total	21,339

Domestic Animals Carried Off or Killed

Imported bulls	59
Kafir bulls	58
Oxen	4,440
Cows and heifers	9,592
Mixed cattle	7,394
Sheep and goats	5,114
Pigs	842
Horses	33
Mules	6
Donkeys	548
Imported fowls	4,348
Matabele	7,133
Ducks and geese	514
Turkeys	58
	——
Total	40,139
	=====
No. of homesteads destroyed	150
	===

Farming and Agricultural Implements Stolen or Destroyed

Ploughs	112	
Harrows	30	
Carts, various	15	
Waggons	85	
Scotch carts	52	
Picks and shovels	2,349	
Cream separators	5	
Churns	19	
Sundries	5,121	including mining implements
	——	

Total   7,788
                                        =====

Note.

Up to 15th August 371 claims had been adjudicated upon.
The full amount claimed in settlement of these claims amounted to
£166,829 : 19 : 9.
The amount awarded in settlement of the same being £111,439 : 10 :
11.
The total number of claims filed amounted on 15th August to 637,
the total amount of compensation claimed for which amounted to
£266,237 : 19 : 4.
Since 15th August other claims have been filed bringing the total
number up to about 800 for losses sustained in Matabeleland alone.
The total amount of compensation which will be paid by the
Chartered Company in settlement of these claims will, it is thought,
reach the sum of £230,000.

APPENDIX F

Schedule showing the number of Native Policemen in the employ of
the Government throughout Matabeleland, at the time of the
outbreak of the rebellion, and the proportion of the same which
remained loyal in the different districts.

Station.		Loyal.	Rebels.	Doubtful.
Headquarters	60	45	...	15
Bulawayo district	30	15	15	...
Bulilima "	30	28	2	...
Umzingwani "	30	11	19	...
Mangwe "	30	6	24	...

Usiza	"	30	2	28	...
Gwanda	"	30	18	...	12
Belingwe	"	30	Nil.	25	5
Gwelo	"	30	Nil.	30	...
Bubi	"	30	1	29	...
Total		330	126	172	32

These figures must be taken as only approximate, as it is known that three or four of the police were killed by the rebels, and it is doubtful whether others did not meet the same fate. It will not be known exactly what number of the police were murdered by the rebels until the war is over.

For these statistics I am indebted to Mr. H. Morrison Jackson, the native commissioner, who was living on my company's property of Essexvale.

F. C. Selous

APPENDIX G

Gold Output

Reef.	District.	Tons crushed.	Approx. output in ounces.
Alice	...	2	7
Auriga	...	41	49
African	...	150	97
Birthday	...	100	104
Beatrice	...	100	563
Bonanza	...	201	80
Cotapaxi	...	4857	2328
Congress on Hill	...	20	15½

Concession	...	4	7½
Dickens	...	1090	1084
Golden Quarry	...	23	96
Golden Horse Shoe	...	100	71
Glendarra	...	3	7¼
Hidden Secret and Rob Roy	...	120	60
Heathfield	...	2	20½
Inez	...	40	97
Just in Time	...	¾	27
Lion	...	2	5½
Matchless East	...	20	12
Matchless West	...	12	20
Natal	...	6	7
Old Chum	...	20	49
Nil Desperandum	...	2	2½
Panhalanga	...	50	50
Pioneer	...	18	10¾
Standard No. 2	...	278	222
Shepherds	...	6	10½
Salamander	...	799	439½
Shankaru	...	25	75
Vesuvius	...	40	90
	...	8131¾	5707½
Ancient Ruins	...	...	357
Alluvial	Manica	...	84½

For these statistics I am indebted to the courtesy of Mr. Arnold, Secretary of the Chamber of Mines.

F. C. Selous